C0-CCO-216

The Public Accounting Profession

Problems and Prospects

Stanley Charles Abraham

Lexington Books
D.C. Heath and Company
Lexington, Massachusetts
Toronto

039033
054039

Library of Congress Cataloging in Publication Data

Abraham, Stanley Charles.
    The public accounting profession.

    Includes bibliographical references and indexes.
    1. Accounting—Vocational guidance—United States. 2. Accounting—
Standards—United States. I. Title.
HF5629.A24   657'.023   77-78041
ISBN 0-669-01606-3

Copyright © 1978 by D.C. Heath and Company.

All rights reserved. No part of this publication may be reproduced or
transmitted in any form or by any means, electronic or mechanical,
including photocopy, recording, or any information storage or retrieval
system, without permission in writing from the publisher.

Published simultaneously in Canada.

Printed in the United States of America.

International Standard Book Number: 0-669-01606-3

Library of Congress Catalog Card Number: 77-78041

Contents

039033
0540339

List of Figures

List of Tables

Preface

This book attempts to shed light on the basic problems of the public accounting profession in order to make a useful contribution to the current debate over the profession's future and to afford insight into why its fundamental problems defy ready solution.

The book takes a broad and open-ended approach to identifying the profession's basic problems, probing the dilemmas, trade-offs, and conflicting values that make them so difficult to resolve. Accounting is shown to be subjective as well as objective, art as well as science. The business of measuring business is anything but simple. It is hoped that researchers and students of accounting will gain an enhanced appreciation of the complexity and richness of the profession's work.

For accounting practitioners, policymakers, and all users of accounting services, the book is intended to offer a timely contribution to the intensifying debate on the profession's future. The threat of new controlling legislation that surfaced with the Metcalf report was defused in later congressional hearings, but only temporarily. The profession was given one year—until July 1978—to make substantial progress toward internal reform. This book's recommendations make it clear that the necessary progress can be achieved without new legislation, though some of the required measures may appear unpalatable.

This book grew out of a doctoral dissertation submitted to the Graduate School of Management, University of California, Los Angeles (UCLA) in 1976. The core of the dissertation research was two in-depth surveys of leaders within and outside the public accounting profession undertaken to illuminate the profession's most critical problems and their relative solvability.

To all the survey respondents goes my profound gratitude; without their candid and thoughtful responses, the study could never have yielded its insights. Their names are listed in appendix E, except for those who requested anonymity. As I promised them, no response has been associated with its originator in the dissertation or in this book.

The original research was sponsored by the UCLA Graduate School of Management and the California CPA Foundation for Education and Research. My dissertation cochairmen, Dean John W. Buckley and Professor Richard O. Mason, of the UCLA Graduate School of Management, generously gave counsel and encouragement beyond the time of the study and reviewed early drafts of this book. Neville V. Abraham, Christopher D. Stone, and Douglas R. Carmichael also made helpful comments. I am particularly indebted to Christine D'Arc for her thoughtful and careful editing of the manuscript and for her many invaluable suggestions.

While many helped and supported me in this effort, I alone am responsible for any errors it may contain and for its conclusions.

Santa Monica, California   *Stanley Charles Abraham*
January 1978

Introduction

Now more than at any time in its history, the public accounting profession is being assailed by criticism from outside and conflict from within. Its public service ideals and its very autonomy are threatened. A barrage of lawsuits (many of them class-action) is eroding practitioners' resources of energy, money, and time. Yet new services are being demanded of them. Mounting criticism, most recently from Congress, has accused public accountants of careless work, of holding their own interests above the public interest, of not maintaining independence from the companies they audit, and of not moving fast enough to correct these deficiencies. The criticisms have come so thick and fast that the profession is reeling, unable to generate more than ad hoc responses. Expeditious, comprehensive solutions have been frustrated because the national organization (the AICPA) and the profession's standard-setting body (the FASB) rely on research and consensus, and both take time. Meanwhile the SEC, in the wake of the Metcalf sub-committee hearings, has given the profession until July 1978 to show real progress toward internal reform or face greater governmental control.

In charting the course of reform, the profession needs not only to decide what the fundamental problems are and how they are linked, but also to determine which are the result of inaction, oversight, or inappropriate action by the profession; which are the product of militant consumerism or unrealistic expectations by the public; and which are the unavoidable consequences of changes in the nation's political and economic life.

To aid that endeavor is a central purpose of this book. When the study for the book was begun in 1975, the profession was becoming aware of the magnitude of the problems it faced. In 1974 the AICPA had appointed the Commission on Auditors' Responsibilities to clarify auditors' position in the growing dispute with managements over their mutual rights and obligations. In another vein the Opinion Research Corporation had just completed a study for Arthur Andersen & Company that undertook "a full and objective appraisal of where the accounting profession stands." A broad survey of practitioners and persons associated with the profession, the study was "designed to explore what key constituent groups think can and should be done to resolve current disclosure and accounting policy problems" [1, p. xiii]. It revealed serious problems in the profession and made several recommendations. Though it was the most comprehensive diagnosis to date, it did not go far enough in analyzing fundamental, strategic problems. What was needed, instead of the brief problem descriptions of the Opinion Research Corporation study, were "appreciations" of problems, including detailed descriptions, assessments of their relative importance and solvability, obstacles to solution, and the likely consequences of inaction. The author sought to elicit the information in two in-depth surveys of leaders in the profession. Representing the major constituent groups, they included auditor and nonauditor CPAs, accounting educators, corporate financial executives, investment company executives, financial writers, government officials, and lawyers dealing with corporate financial affairs. The results of the surveys, which reveal much about the profession in 1975, are summarized in part I.

Part II summarizes events involving the profession in the two years since the surveys were taken. It describes the pressures exerted on the profession by the SEC, the courts, Congress, and by its own Commission on Auditors' Responsibilities. Then it recounts the profession's appraisal of its position and the steps it has taken toward reform. Synthesizing the survey findings with recent developments, it comments on the extent to which the profession's recent efforts have succeeded in bridging its "credibility gap." It ends with a number of actions that need to be taken and issues that need resolving if the public accounting profession is to preserve its autonomy and restore public confidence in auditors. To ease the reader's way, each chapter is prefaced by an introduction that highlights the main issues.

Throughout the book the term *profession* is often used to imply a single organization capable of independent, decisive action. Nothing could be further from the truth. The public accounting profession is an agglomeration of organizing and rulemaking bodies, firms, and individuals. Even some rules and precedents it must follow emanate from outside that framework, as when the SEC intervenes through its oversight function or a judge rules in a lawsuit involving accountants. In some actions the AICPA represents the profession; in others the FASB, or even the firms themselves represent it. Indeed the appropriate roles of these bodies are matters at issue in the book, so to avoid complicating them the broad yet often vague term *profession* has been retained.

A word needs to be said about the book's scope. Certified public accountants (CPAs) can be found teaching, employed by corporations (as management accountants, internal auditors, or financial executives), in government agencies (as cost accountants), or engaged in public accounting. This book focuses on the last of these.

Public accountants, or auditors, are the only people authorized by SEC and stock-exchange regulations to audit and attest to the accuracy and fairness of the financial statements of publicly held corporations. Public accountants typically confine themselves to auditing. They have the power to give a company a "clean" or unqualified certification, qualify it as clean subject to some large uncertainty such as a pending class-action lawsuit against the company or a proposed merger, or withhold certification. Companies without unqualified certifications jeopardize their ability to tap the nation's capital markets, to sustain shareholders' confidence in their operations, and to attract new shareholders. As it concentrates on auditing, this book largely ignores the other main activities of CPA firms—tax and management advisory services—except as they affect the practice of auditing.

In focusing on problems, this analysis is by no means intended to detract from the profession's considerable achievements. (The history and achievements of the public accounting profession in the United States are recounted in references 2 and 3). For every negligent audit there are hundreds of satisfactory ones; for every breach of ethics, several hundred instances of upholding them; for every case of incompetent work, many examples of technical innovation and genius appreciated only by fellow practitioners. As ever, it is the unusual case of unprofessional conduct that receives wide publicity and that damages the professional image. This book has been written in a spirit of respect for the high ideals espoused by the public accounting profession.

References

[1] Opinion Research Corporation, *Public Accounting in Transition* (Chicago: Arthur Andersen & Company, 1974).

[2] John L. Carey, *The Rise of the Accounting Profession: From Technician to Professional, 1896-1936* (New York: AICPA, 1969).

[3] John L. Carey, *The Rise of the Accounting Profession: To Responsibility and Authority, 1937-1969* (New York: AICPA, 1970).

Abbreviations

AAA	American Accounting Association
AACSB	American Assembly of Collegiate Schools of Business
AcSEC	Accounting Standards Executive Committee
AICPA	American Institute of Certified Public Accountants
APB	Accounting Principles Board
ARS	Accounting Research Statement
ASR	Accounting Series Release
AudSEC	Auditing Standards Executive Committee
CASB	Cost Accounting Standards Board
CMA	Certified Management Accountant
CPA	Certified Public Accountant
CPE	Continuing Professional Education
EDP	Electronic Data Processing
EFTS	Electronic Funds Transfer System
FAF	Financial Analysts Federation
FASB	Financial Accounting Standards Board
FEI	Financial Executives Institute
FIFO	First-In, First-Out
FPC	Federal Power Commission
FTC	Federal Trade Commission
GAAP	Generally Accepted Accounting Principles
GAAS	Generally Accepted Auditing Standards
GAO	General Accounting Office
GPP	General Purchasing Power
IASC	International Accounting Standards Committee
IRS	Internal Revenue Service
LIFO	Last-In, First-Out
MAS	Management Advisory Services
NAA	National Association of Accountants
NSPA	National Society of Public Accountants
NYSE	New York Stock Exchange

PLA	Price-Level Adjusted
PR	Public Relations
R&D	Research and Development
SAS	Statement on Auditing Standards
SEC	Securities and Exchange Commission
SIA	Securities Industry Association
UCLA	University of California at Los Angeles
VAT	Value Added Tax

**Part I
How Knowledgeable
Professionals Viewed
the Profession's
Problems in 1975**

Part I
Introduction

The thirteen chapters in part I summarize what respondents to two surveys had to say about the profession's problems, their solutions, and the consequences of inaction.

Diagnosis and Prognosis: The First Survey

The 138 professionals who completed the first survey questionnaire, from an initial list of 647, were a varied and distinguished group representing the entire spectrum of the profession—large and small CPA firms, auditors and nonauditors, accounting educators, corporate financial executives, investment company executives, financial journalists, governmental regulatory staff, and lawyers active in corporate financial affairs.

Collectively they were experienced and knowledgeable. Averaging fifty years in age, virtually all held senior positions in their organizations. When asked how critical they were of the accounting profession's activities or policies, the great majority rated themselves as moderately critical, which suggests that they were not "rubber stamps" but often held views running against the stream. By their answers to several questions designed to gauge their general knowledge of the field, respondents showed that they were well informed about accounting policies and literature (average score, 85 percent), current events in business and government (71 percent), and investing (78 percent).

The questionnaire asked the respondent to name three of the most critical problems facing the profession. It then probed his diagnosis, prognosis, and concern about each one through a line of repetitive supplementary questioning. (The first survey questionnaire is reproduced in its entirety in appendix C.) Twelve classes of problems emerged; these are presented in chapters 1 through 12 in order of frequency, the most often cited problems presented first. The summary of respondents' views within each chapter closely follows the line of questioning:

Statement of the problem and why it is suggested.

What the profession has done to solve it, and why those efforts have not been successful.

What the profession should have done about the problem when it first became aware of it and how things might be different now as a result.

What the profession should do now to resolve the problem and why such measures may not work in practice.

3

What may happen if the profession's actions turn out to be unsuccessful or if the profession takes no action at all.

The responses provide a rich commentary on the profession's problems as of 1975. All opinions in chapters 1-12 are those of respondents. In paraphrasing and condensing them for greater clarity and brevity, I have taken care to preserve their tone; often they are given verbatim. That has been done at some cost in readability. A trade-off was necessary between making the prose easy to read by extensive rewriting and retaining the flavor of the responses while summarizing them intelligibly. The intermittent repetitions, vagueness, and contradictions are the result of the trade-off. Without them, revealing nuances would have been lost. The responses show, more directly than any treatise could, that accounting is both subjective and objective, art as well as science.

Problems and Solutions in Perspective: The Second Survey

The inquiry might have ended with the candid and revealing responses to the first survey. Nagging questions remained, however. If the respondents were confronted with all the problems they identified, how would they react? Just because a problem was frequently mentioned, was it a grave and urgent one? Would others agree with individuals' criticisms of the profession? In other words, the responses needed to be verified and ranked, even though they yielded useful data in their own right.

That need prompted the second survey. About 70 percent of the respondents to the first survey agreed to participate in the second, and other professionals were chosen, making a total of 134 respondents. The questionnaire used the problems identified in the first survey as its point of departure. The aim was to elicit respondents' estimates of the relative importance and solvability of problems—both which ones could be solved sooner and more easily and, with the help of futures research methods, how the solution of one problem would affect the solution of others. It also explored obstacles, remedies, and the consequences of inaction. (The second survey questionnaire is reproduced in its entirety in appendix D.) The results are summarized in chapter 13.

Though the survey findings in part I are valid only for the respondents themselves and not necessarily for the constituencies they represent, many of the problems they identified and consequences they feared in 1975 have been borne out as real issues and real threats, as part II shows.

1

Role Problems

Role problems, defined broadly as problems of managing the profession's growth and development to match its view of the role it should play in society, were the problems most frequently cited in the first survey. Considering that the AICPA had recently established the Commission on Auditors' Responsibilities to study and advise on the auditor's role in society and the extent of his responsibilities, it is understandable that role problems were uppermost in many minds. This chapter discusses the nine major problems that emerged, in order of frequency cited.

Highlights

Low Image and Credibility. The respondents suggested many reasons for the profession's low credibility: unsuccessful attempts at communicating with outside groups and the public (including the habit of promising more than it was capable of delivering); financial reports that do not serve their intended purposes; apparently lower standards and levels of performance; the growing number of lawsuits against CPAs; failure to have adequate and accepted GAAP; wide differences of opinion over how to cope with problems; a poor record of disciplining members who violate the code of ethics; and "unprofessional" practices of firms in securing business. Such a catalog of reasons suggests that many individuals act in their own self-interest with little regard for the effects of their actions on the profession as a whole or for potential constraints.

Uncertainty about Scope and Structure. The respondents understood the dilemma regarding the services the profession provides and how it is structured to provide them. Increasing the scope and quality of accounting services exposes CPAs to greater liability and their clients to higher costs. Yet *not* expanding services leaves it vulnerable to the criticism of being unresponsive to public demands. Respondents also sensed that the task of ensuring competence in new areas of service may be beyond the profession; ensuring it in existing services is already a problem.

Public Misunderstanding. Public misunderstanding of the auditor's role and the meaning of his opinion was attributed to some deep-rooted problems and attitudes of accountants. First, their ability to communicate the profession's

5

position is clearly hampered by their own lack of consensus on what that position is; second, it could very well be that the public fully understands what is going on and perceives the profession's attempts to explain accounting anomalies as simply public relations. For example, although the public presses accountants to take responsibility for their role in certifying a company's financial statements, they still hear accountants maintain that management should bear the full brunt of that responsibility.

Strained Relations with Clients. The profession is already finding it difficult to produce a product that justifies the fees it charges clients; raising those fees without delivering more can no longer be done, especially by firms practicing "defensive auditing" to minimize their legal liability. Some respondents thought that fees are already too high for the quality of auditing companies are actually getting. The trend toward greater corporate disclosure has put pressure on accountants to take responsibility for detecting fraud and wrongdoing, a further irritant. Most respondents believed that disclosure should be up to management, who should assume full responsibility for its actions. Attesting to the effectiveness of a client's internal control system was also thought to be a source of strain and increased cost to the client. To keep audit costs down, auditors typically rely on the client's own system but do not examine it for deficiencies. Attesting to its proper functioning could reveal deficiencies reflecting poor management, which in turn could jeopardize auditors' access to the relevant data.

Deficient FASB. The FASB's task of setting standards for the profession combines problem solving with building consensus and ensuring uniformity of application. The strength of its leadership depends on which problems it chooses to address and how widely accepted its standards become. Its critics among the respondents point out its shortcomings without suggesting how it could realistically overcome them. For example, they demand that it notice and solve problems more quickly while criticizing it for not studying all aspects of those problems or taking all constituent views into account. They want it to exert greater influence on the major economic and political issues of the day while complaining that it does not solve accounting problems fast enough. They want it to be *the* standard-setting body for the profession yet take into account the recommendations of competing committees and study groups. And they call for a larger research staff and budget without realizing that more research means lengthier deliberations, not quicker solutions. They fear that if the FASB does not continue to make rules as fast as it can, the SEC will step in and make them instead; many others in the profession see the proliferation of rules (rather than fewer, simpler, and more powerful *principles*) as an unhealthy trend for the profession.

Inadequate Self-Discipline and Self-Regulation. Like other professionals, accountants are reluctant to report their colleagues for breaches of ethics or negligent acts. Since accountants themselves have largely created the rules by which they practice, their judgment of who is competent is often suspect, as is their professed resolve to discipline members equally suspect. Moreover the AICPA is just coming to grips with regulating firms as well as individuals. And though it is charged with regulating them, it lacks the power that the SEC and the state boards of accountancy possess. The problem is compounded because its solution depends on how the profession restructures itself, how it defines the auditor's role in society, whether it can improve GAAP, and to what extent it can regulate itself without sole reliance on legal precedents or on SEC rulings.

Narrow Concept of Role. Respondents criticized the profession's narrow concept of its societal role, advocating that it be extended to include (1) helping the federal government solve the nation's financial problems, (2) speaking out more strongly on issues about which accountants have expertise, and (3) exposing corporate violations of the law (such as environmental laws). Respondents were, however, aware of the basic dilemma involved. Broadening the profession's role might impair the ability to maintain competence and restrict liability exposure. Furthermore, any attempt to change the auditor's role would require the legal profession's assent, for the courts are playing a larger part in defining that role through legal precedent.

GAAP as a Straitjacket. Frequent complaints were voiced that GAAPs limit the discretion and judgment of accountants and waste their time going through a myriad of minuscule, overly specified rules. Neither did these critics think highly of the need to review and redraft such rules for every changing circumstance.

Intra- and Interprofession Conflicts. Respondents cited conflicts between the FASB and the CASB, between seasoned practitioners and younger CPAs, between the profession and the SEC over the setting of accounting standards, as well as conflicts between the accounting and legal professions, especially regarding tax and estate planning.

Low Image and Credibility

Respondents who cited the profession's public image as a problem perceived it as not only low but also eroding. One went so far as to characterize it as a "crisis in credibility," claiming that the profession is not understood or trusted by those who use accounting services and by the public at large.

Accounting has not achieved the public stature of medicine and law. Many people still do not know what a CAP is or does. They imagine him to be a bookkeeper in the stereotyped mode of the visored, shirt-sleeved clerk rather than a professional ranking with business executives. Accountants themselves feel slighted; popular references to them in novels, on television, and in political discourse are often disparaging. Surveys among accounting practitioners, according to one CPA, indicate the existence of a significant inferiority complex stemming from a lack of pride in themselves and in their work.

Some respondents believed that the low image was deserved. One declared that the profession viewed issues from a very narrow perspective and often would not change its ways unless compelled by outside pressure. Another pointed out that if accountants are judged by how well they serve the needs of investors, and if investors are forced to read between the lines or seek additional information to make sense of financial reports, then it is no wonder that accountants lack the credibility they seek.

The profession has grappled with the problem in a number of ways: by proposing model legislation to the federal and state governments, forming practice-review committees, revising the code of ethics, mounting public relations campaigns, tightening standards for certification and continuing education, attending to standard-setting problems, organizing workshops, publications, and television films for its various publics, experimenting with quality control and peer review for public accounting firms, and most recently by commissioning a panel on auditors' responsibilities. One respondent succinctly characterized the profession's past efforts as "a general wringing of hands plus efforts at the AICPA level to communicate with the public and the SEC."

The problem has persisted, according to one CPA, because it is "deeply embedded and long-term—it did not come about overnight and it will not disappear overnight." According to others, the profession has invited public criticism by its failure to establish acceptable accounting principles. To some it has been too timid; to others it has overzealously promised more than it can deliver. It has improved neither its visibility nor its political position. It communicates poorly with outsiders. Judges and juries, who are called on to decide accountants' fate in lawsuits, have difficulty understanding that accounting is an art, not a science, and that accountants are not guarantors of financial data. Aside from underfunded public relations efforts, changing the profession's image is difficult when the public has developed an unfavorable view of accountants' work over the years.

One respondent cited the slow workings of the FASB, partly because of the five-to-two majority requirement; another cited inadequate follow-through of the Trueblood report on the objectives of financial statements. Others mentioned the profession's failure to look into the problem ten years ago; the fear of some firms that peer review will give other firms an unfair advantage and hence impede an otherwise promising strategy to boost the profession's image; and the dissolution of support for the AICPA within the profession. Says a seasoned observer of the accounting scene, "The delays which accompany the simplest decision lead me to wonder what it is that CPAs are attempting to accomplish. Accounting is complex, but either it does report a situation, or it does not. When a huge write-off is reported, it's natural to wonder what the figures really mean."

Several respondents felt that the adoption of high educational standards and mandatory continuing education would ameliorate the problem. One advocated a graduate degree in accounting as a prerequisite to certification, while another pushed for establishing professional schools of accounting. The acknowledged trouble with these suggestions was that the profession as a whole has not yet reached agreement on its educational policy and that educational institutions resist change. Others favored political solutions, such as better "public-protecting" legislation coupled with strong enforcement, electing more CPAs to public office, and persuading the SEC that the profession has made substantial progress and should be allowed to pursue an independent course. Again CPAs were thought to be apathetic and indecisive about any of these solutions. A member of the financial press admonished the profession to stop equivocating. "Not long ago I attended a meeting of the press and accountants; it turned out to be more a defense of their position and an explanation of the reasons for doing things their way than an honest attempt at a dialog."

Respondents also noted the tendency for the business aspects of accounting practice to take precedence over professional principles. By this they meant the primacy of fee volume and such practices as buying into audit engagements (doing them at or below cost to gain a new client) and enticing clients from other firms. The growing competitiveness was thought to be not only unbecoming to the profession but also correlated with low performance standards and auditing failures. At the root of it all, according to one auditor, is the profession's "present and growing inability to discipline itself effectively. State professional conduct committees discipline only a few CPAs but *very, very rarely* face up to major firms which violate ethical rules." It is indeed difficult, says another CPA, to get anyone to level charges of unprofessional conduct against another individual or firm.

Suggestions for remedies ranged from having firms offer only accounting and related services, rather than performing any service the client will pay for, to enforcing more strictly the profession's rules of conduct for firms as well as individuals. Again the old problem of enforcing ethics across the board crops up. As one CPA cynically put it, "Ethics are to protect the 'haves' from the 'have-nots.'" Another auditor urged acceleration of the reporting and investigating of conduct violations. "It seems like forever before the AICPA moves on anything; I know this is often passed off by saying that any organization of volunteers is slow-moving, but I must wonder."

An academic favored extending professional membership to nonaccountants who work for CPA firms, though it would threaten the exclusivity of the CPA certificate as the only official credential for membership in the profession. Another respondent agreed: "The emphasis on higher education and college degrees as the sole requisite for becoming a CPA (eliminating the experience requirement) has brought to the surface a 'snobbish' attitude. The question is how to project accountants as dignified professionals and not stuffy, self-satisfied prudes." The solution, he thought, was for the profession "to create a paraprofessional program for people working in the ranks of CPA offices as well as those who are at a turning point in life and desirous of switching to the accounting profession. Experience, age, and motivation would be alternatives and substitutes for higher education." He admitted that many present CPAs would feel that less-educated people would downgrade the profession's status and image, but he asserted that such diamonds in the rough "who have had life experience . . . could meld those experiences to make the profession even more potent and human."

This problem, if allowed to continue, would lead to public disenchantment with the profession. Accounting would in time resemble a trade, an industry, and a business rather than a profession. It would lose its potential for social action and its attractiveness to potential entrants. The trust it had earned from clients and the government would diminish, increasing the likelihood of external regulation. Nonaccounting specialists would disassociate themselves from CPA firms and form independent consulting firms.

Respondents also variously predicted that the profession would remain "second-rate," would lose public confidence to the point of eventual takeover by the SEC or other governmental authority (and jeopardize the FASB's legitimacy), and promote fragmentation in the "weakened" profession. Firms would find it harder to justify raising their fees; and audit reports, already viewed with increasing skepticism, would eventually lose their value.

Uncertainty about Scope and Structure

Though the profession has extensively studied what services it should offer, how it should be structured, and what skills it should cultivate in its members, it has reached no clear agreement on them. The profession is being asked to assume new responsibilities in forecasting, monitoring companies' compliance with environmental regulations, evaluating the efficiency and effectiveness of programs, conducting management audits, and certifying prospectuses and public offerings of tax shelters and similar investments. Action has stalled mainly because of the reluctance of individuals and firms to expose themselves to the risk of more lawsuits; the associated financial burden may exceed what they can be reasonably expected to bear.

Forecasting provides an example of the pervading indecisiveness. The profession has delayed a decision, preferring to wait for SEC guidelines on the subject. The SEC's preliminary work, however, appears to be too demanding for companies to comply with fully, and possibly beyond the ability of some even to follow. To compound the problem, the profession does not know how strong the corporate demand for forecasting runs. Conceivably very few companies may be in favor of or willing to include forecasts in their annual reports.

Instead of the uncertain way in which the profession has tended to act in the past, it should have broadened the scope of practice, developed programs on accreditation and specialization, recommended appropriate legislation to embrace a broader range of services, and even separated the two segments *scope* and *structure* to clarify the debates. If that had been done, "the opponents of either one would not have been added to the opponents of the other, thereby making it virtually impossible to have an affirmative vote to solve either problem."

Some respondents urged adoption of the AICPA program on scope and structure recommended by its board of directors. Others urged still more study by state societies and other committees. Still others cited dilemmas that underlie the problem and impede its solution.

This is a controversial issue. If the profession advocates providing services in a new area, it may expose its members to unreasonable and unwarranted risks of legal liability. On the other hand, if it advocates refraining from performing such services, it may be accused of "copping out" in providing public services that it is better qualified to perform than any other group.

The obstacles are normal human ones. Members will not take the time to read and study the material. Couple this with the natural reluctance toward change and we have the very likely result of the final vote being that no change should be made.

Through some sort of inquiry of all its members, the profession should isolate what its real function is. For example, providing an independent review on the basis of articulated criteria that are mainly financial, and measure possibly new endeavors by this. However, CPA firms are already in activities that bear little relation to this, such as executive recruiting. For that matter, even tax work doesn't measure up by this yardstick.

Several respondents wanted the profession to expand its audit and attest functions to a company's internal control systems, to evaluation of a company's management (its general effectiveness and discharge of its responsibility to society), and to attestation of unaudited nonfinancial data, even those not susceptible to audit.

The push by the SEC and other regulatory agencies for more corporate disclosure was cited as a reason that the profession should consider moving into new areas. Such disclosures should have the benefit of independent attestation. However, it is not easy to determine which aspects of a corporation or its management might require attestation. Respondents pointed out significant disagreements over which types of information need independent review, how reporting standards and measurements can be developed, whether the attest function should be extended to areas incapable of quantification, and whether a CPA's assurances are legitimate in matters where specific guidelines or standards have not been developed. A lawyer raised a related issue: whether the profession "should take the lead in legislation or rulemaking to increase the responsibility of management itself in the disclosure process and management's liability for nondisclosure. This will result in a confrontation between management and the accounting profession over the scope of the public accountant's responsibility."

An auditor suggested defining a CPA's audit responsibilities by comparing them with current standards of practice. "The problem here is a lack of consensus, even among the various publics concerned with the audit process, as to what the profession's responsibility should be. An attempt to demonstrate the lack of feasibility of some of their requests may backfire and be pointed to as a self-serving attempt by the profession to limit its responsibilities."

Another auditor maintained that if the profession specified the degree of responsibility an auditor should accept in detecting fraud, in reporting the illegal activities of a client, in assessing management's effectiveness, or in disclosing disagreements with clients on matters of principle, it would surely expose CPAs to even greater legal and financial liability, especially from third parties.

Deciding which new services to provide is only part of the problem. An academic raises the question of whether to discontinue certain services now performed by many small firms and individual CPAs, such as write-up work or bookkeeping and internal accounting for small companies. He sees growing competition to provide such services from financial institutions, often affiliated with large data-processing bureaus, and he would like the profession to reverse the trend. Unless it is reversed, he reasons, it will be very difficult to audit the companies using such data-processing control systems. Data storage systems are not amenable to current audit techniques; establishing audit trails, for example, would be virtually impossible if electronic fund transfer systems come into widespread use. It also raises the awkward question of who would bear responsibility for the company's financial statements.

One respondent addressed the needs of the accounting firm that audits a company's operations in different countries. The profession should either develop and enforce truly mathematical auditing and disclosure standards or limit the practice of a firm to one country while allowing cooperative arrangements with firms in other countries.

If the pressure to expand services becomes too great, CPAs may be compelled to attest to certain kinds of information before the profession has had the chance to develop and adopt standards that would ensure uniform procedures and interpretations. Many CPAs would find themselves working in areas for which they have no training, leading to work of uneven quality and a subsequent loss of credibility. On the other hand, the profession could develop a reputation for being too rigid and for not keeping up with the needs of the public. Other professions would quickly step in to fill the breach, and the profession would lose an opportunity to increase its business. (In the case of management evaluation, one auditor thought that would be a good thing!)

New services would, according to a lawyer, dilute the effectiveness of the financial audit, the auditor's main endeavor. The resulting loss of public confidence might in time cause the auditing function to be transferred to a federal agency. He made specific predictions:

The scope of the audit will be expanded and public accountants will be passing on business matters not directly related to financial reports. That is, management advice now commonly given by auditors may eventually be incorporated in the audit report.

There may well be a divorce of audit functions and management services with split-up of firms. If the auditor assumes greater responsibility, the conventional separation between the accounting and legal profession may have to be revised.

Judicial pronouncements will be made in piecemeal fashion over a long period of time with adverse consequences on the profession.

Public Misunderstanding

Public expectations exceed those that auditors believe they can reasonably fulfill. As evidence of the gap, outsiders are continually raising questions about the auditor's appropriate role in society.

The auditor believes the public does not comprehend the nature of the audit process or the meaning of the auditor's opinion. Accounting is imprecise at best, and accountants are unable to give assurances of total accuracy. "Over the years," a corporate financial executive said, "the accounting profession has projected an image of verifying and certifying financial statements to an exactness that probably does not exist, and this in turn has caused the public to have an expectation for accounting performance that cannot be fulfilled." Neither has the profession clearly spelled out the auditor's relationships to corporate management, boards of directors, stockholders, and the investing community at large—as revealed by court proceedings in recent lawsuits involving CPAs.

Historically the profession sold itself to the SEC and to the financial community as a necessary independent verifier of corporate financial information. As corporate affairs have grown in size and complexity, auditors have found it more and more difficult to guarantee the accuracy of the information. Accountants have always claimed that accuracy is management's responsibility. The rash of lawsuits in recent years has burdened CPAs with an increasing share of the liability for misleading or erroneous information in a financial report and has made them even more averse to assuming responsibility for "fair presentation." The line between attesting to the reliability of figures and being responsible for them is fine indeed. One auditor predicted that the recently appointed Commission on Auditors' Responsibilities would find it difficult to identify a middle ground of expectations, "one which will increase the auditor's responsibilities in a manner acceptable to him and yet be less than the present 'blue sky' hopes of the investing public."

Some respondents were already skeptical of how much fruit the commission's labors would bear. They feared too great a lag between its appointment and its findings; that its final recommendations would be tepid; and that it would be unable to avoid examining peripheral areas of scope, which would fragment its efforts. Others regarded the commission as an improvement over the AICPA's own AudSEC, whose view of the responsibility of auditors had always been too narrow and whose recent agenda had been overloaded. An auditor pointed out that only so much can be accomplished by pronouncement when the problem is auditor performance. Even efforts by the AudSEC to make auditing and reporting procedures more uniform will not automatically improve the non-CPA's understanding of these activities or more clearly delineate the CPA's responsibilities.

Besides appointing the Commission on Auditors' Responsibilities, the profession has tried to correct public misunderstanding by educating those who write about accounting and auditing on the inherent limitations of accounting data and auditing methods. "To a limited extent the press seminars have helped," concedes an auditor, "but educating individuals with no technical background is difficult. Also, many members of the press take a *conspiracy* approach because it makes for better reading. The inherent limitations of financial statements and audits are viewed as some plot and the worst motives are assumed to exist." The profession has also produced carefully worded technical literature designed to reduce its legal risks. Auditors understand and follow it, but the investing public does not read it and would not fully understand it. The fault lies with both sides: accountants for producing texts so cautious in their meaning that they are clear only to the initiated, and the investing public for not doing their homework and studying annual reports and prospectuses. "Investors *want* to believe," says an auditor, "that inclusion of an audit report means the financial data are precisely accurate—a private dream world."

Another auditor thought the profession should long ago have "insisted ... that investors be forced to learn and accept the limitations on assurances of accuracy that may apply to an independent audit. Practicing auditors enjoyed the inflation of their egos arising from the investor's belief that the work of the auditor guaranteed accuracy. Now they suffer from a prior unwillingness to have that ego pricked. Thus the investor public would not have [been] permitted to nurse the unreasonably high expectations it now holds in error." Several auditors echoed this sentiment. One, for example, wished the profession had given much more attention to auditing than accounting, eventually claiming only auditing as its domain. Instead it has dissipated its resources on attempts to set accounting principles, to its detriment.

The profession should also have sought clear guidelines from the SEC on the accountant's role in financial reporting and should have strengthened its own code of ethics to require that a firm not accept a new client until the client has explained to its investors and creditors its reasons for leaving the previous firm. Had this been done, financial reports would be regarded as a CPA firm's own objective view about its client's operations and financial position rather than its agreement that the client has reported fairly.

Continued public misunderstanding about the work of auditors could lead to some form of government control over auditing; one respondent saw the profession relegated to being "policeman" for the SEC. Litigation against CPAs would increase; the cost of liability insurance premiums would go up; and the profession's image would suffer, to the point where it would cease to attract first-class entrants. One auditor speculated that because financial statements would no longer be considered reliable, thus making it more difficult for companies to raise or attract capital, investment activity would increasingly center in large institutional investors, which might become powerful enough to have their own auditing arms.

Strained Relations with Clients

Some respondents thought that audit fees were too low in view of the firm's potential exposure to class-action suits and the rising cost of malpractice insurance premiums. Another thought that fees were too high (or increasing too fast) given the scant increase in services or productivity. Firms were thought to lack the motivation necessary to keep costs down, believing that clients would pay whatever they were billed. Solving this particular problem, however, would not be easy for auditors. While low fees give a firm a competitive edge, they also force shortcuts that detract from a thorough audit. Just keeping costs in check could jeopardize an audit's effectiveness given that corporations generally grow or change from year to year.

High fees could be more easily justified if accounting and auditing standards had been more clearly defined in the past. Not only the scope of the work to be done should have been specified, but also the degree of detail necessary for the auditor to meet his responsibilities to third parties. Such standards, one corporate financial executive said, could have been used by the courts as a basis for ruling in favor of the accounting firm in any actions brought to trial.

Competitive bidding was viewed as the root of the profession's fee problems. Respondents claimed that some firms engaged in price cutting to keep busy, presumably preferring business "at cost" to cutting staff. Respondents also cited the practice of accepting work at substandard fees as a "loss leader," giving a firm entree to a company, after which it could generate other business at regular fees. But any moves to limit such competitive tactics were viewed as antitrust behavior, thus creating a double bind for the profession. Another double bind is the pressure to clarify the duties of the auditor and the standards of financial reporting, and such clarification would raise fees. When stricter audits are required or expected, costs rise. Yet the costs of not exercising such control may be greater in the end.

If unresolved, these fee problems would probably result in continuing substandard fees, lower than average salaries to CPAs who carry out audits, and lower incomes for principals—all injurious to the profession's image. If clients remained unwilling to pay the higher fees necessary, firms would be unable to afford the mounting costs of malpractice insurance, and regulatory agencies would force changes in audit procedures. On the other hand, as a corporate executive put it, if the profession "continues to increase, by mandate, the requirements for its service and to require a captive audience, the service will deteriorate and the costs increase. The inevitable results will be a collapse of the profession by its own weight."

Some respondents cited the problem of relying on a client's internal control system to reduce audit costs, only to discover that the system was deficient. If the auditor does not rely at all on the client's system, auditing costs would be too high; yet if auditors publicly disclose deficiencies in management operations, they might jeopardize future access to data and company personnel and even the likelihood of renewing the engagement. Respondents predicted that the combined effects of inadequate internal control systems and the tendency of firms to rely on them would lead to a loss of confidence in the results of audits and a questioning of the integrity or independence of CPAs.

Client objections to increasing audit costs have already resulted in numerous shortcuts in audit procedures and an inferior product. CPA firms should emphasize that clients get what they pay for; a thorough job demands extensive procedures and much cross-checking, and it is not cheap. "Quick and dirty" audits are eventually costly to the company—and the firm—by exposing them to malpractice lawsuits and a potential loss of public confidence in auditors' work.

The recent exposure of multinational corporation bribery and payoff scandals has implied that CPAs are expected to become the conscience of corporations and to disclose such unfavorable acts. This role of the accountant is certainly to be questioned and should be discouraged, according to a corporate executive. It is another manifestation of Congress's propensity to "want disclosure of everything, whether or not it is good for the country." He believed that corporations should be their own consciences, disclosing the actions and events that they consider appropriate. Until the extent of accountant's responsibilities within a client engagement is defined in a manner acceptable to all parties, more will be demanded of the auditor than is reasonable under the circumstances.

APB and FASB rulings on disclosure have insufficiently considered how management uses data (self-insurance, forecasts). The profession should set these standards jointly with management. "Perhaps the profession," reflected another corporate financial executive, "should consider the trade-off between disclosures based on the *right to know* with the possible interference of premature disclosure and potential loss to shareholders. The profession would face a conflict between its needs for a universal solution to every situation and the right to know with the stockholders' best interests at heart. (Premature disclosure of divestitures and tax details are two examples of this.)"

If the current trend goes unchecked, accounting would become a management tool only for external disclosure, having little value for internal management. An auditor agreed: "Accountants should act more as referees or finders-of-fact for the investing public. Unless they do, the amount of regulation over the profession's affairs by federal and state agencies will increase."

Deficient FASB

While many respondents applauded the installation of the FASB to replace the limited effectiveness of the APB, several others criticized the FASB's mode of operation and its decisions. They cited, for example, its inability to react quickly to a changing economy or to handle emergency practice problems.

The profession is reluctant to come to grips with critical accounting issues in a timely fashion. Historically it has subordinated its rulemaking prerogative, and the SEC has had to address important and often times unpopular accounting and reporting issues in the interest of providing investors with meaningful financial data. While establishing the FASB is a first step toward a remedy, the board is just beginning to emerge from the start-up phase, and it is too early to determine whether it will achieve success and become *the* rulemaking body for accounting and reporting issues. Its exposure draft on price-level accounting is a typical example. The board has not undertaken a full study of the issue, but limited itself to a price-level approach. One can only wonder why the issue of accounting for inflation was limited to this approach without pursuing other alternatives. (a government-sector respondent)

[Implying that the FASB's formation would not resolve fundamental problems] Our profession is at present one which reacts to issues rather than raising them and solving or proposing answers to them. We seem to be forever running scared when interacting with both national and local government agencies. We are the one group of professionals who deal with all forms of commerce and yet we are most often silent on major economic and even political issues when we could be of great help even if only in an informative way. (an auditor)

The FASB fails to deal in a timely fashion with emerging problems in the business world and fails to narrow the diversity of accounting practices. It seems as if we often do too little too late because the volume and complexity of business on an international scale increases even more rapidly. (a nonauditor CPA)

[The FASB's] lethargy is due to three things: lack of funding to provide an adequate staff, overkill in its too-lengthy and involved process [of] issuing exposure drafts, and fear that its pronouncements would encounter opposition from the SEC. (a corporate financial executive)

The critical respondents pointed out that forming the FASB was unnecessary, given the existing alternatives in the AICPA: (1) the AcSEC, AudSEC, and APB, already rulemaking and troubleshooting bodies for the profession; (2) the Scope and Structure committee (though it was criticized as being biased in favor of accounting practices in large firms); (3) the new Washington, D.C., office, designed to give the profession the visibility it lacked and to present its positions on important issues (but thought to lack a top-grade staff and an overall plan for bringing issues to practitioners early enough for consensus to be reached); (4) various reorganized senior committees devoted to specific emerging problems.

According to these respondents the FASB is simply another in a long list of groping attempts to identify and solve the profession's substantive problems. It still lacks widespread support and has already become mired in a slow and cumbersome procedure that prevents it from acting quickly and forcefully.

The pressure on the FASB would not be as intense (and its formation might have been avoided) had the profession established a national research group to anticipate and react to changes with time on its side. The profession might then have had a reputation of being forward-moving rather than the solver of yesterday's problems. An auditor noted, "We seem to be forever putting out fires in the profession. CPAs are very practical people and are reluctant to look ahead even five to ten years. If we had a long-range plan, adjusted periodically, we might well be listened to more by government officials."

The reason most often cited for the FASB's lack of wholehearted support was the fragmentation in the profession. Cliques are too busy supporting special interests and points of view in committees of the AICPA to unite behind the FASB. The extent of infighting was also implied in the following suggestions: to establish a planning commission whose "members will be elected to terms of four or more years and receive pledges from a majority of the firms represented, especially the large firms"; to expand greatly the AICPA's limited program of talking with practitioners in various cities; and to set up an "early warning system" to identify business practices that may produce distorted or misleading results. Each suggestion had an acknowledged obstacle, such as resistance from one constituency or another and lack of funds.

Respondents saw the government stepping into the breach of leadership, guidance, and foresight because, "believe it or not," the government can move faster than the profession. They also saw a decline in the quality of professional practice—smaller firms pulling away from the AICPA, and the profession's remaining reactive and passive.

The FASB was thought to be in a double bind. On the one hand, the profession's constituencies (corporations, investors, the SEC) demand rapid solutions to a host of difficult issues; on the other, the growing complexity of business and of regulatory demands preclude rapid solution. Difficult problems are by definition controversial, and many arguments are offered to support differing points of view. If the pronouncements are to command universal adherence, their achievement cannot be rushed. They must be based on intensive research and exposed to public hearing, all of which takes time. Often the debate that follows an exposure draft—and the time it takes—aids acceptance of a standard.

Critics saw the FASB habitually muddling through, as did the APB, and feared that it might suffer the same fate. They thought the FASB should stop proliferating rules, specify the purposes of financial statements (implementing the recommendations of the Trueblood report), and perform more basic research. Further it should involve AICPA practitioners in developing more practical solutions to accounting issues. All branches of business should provide support for the FASB's activities.

Pessimistic respondents thought that current FASB efforts would have the following consequences: that CPAs would become mere interpreters of rules and would lose the exercise of judgment that sets them apart as professionals; that accounting would become legalistic and lawyers would have to be hired to advise CPAs on purely accounting matters; that lawyers might take over the profession; and that regulatory agencies would probably become the rulemakers for the profession. An accounting educator speculated, "Auditing will become a useless government-controlled 'service.'"

Inadequate Self-Discipline and Self-Regulation

Accountants have long criticized the profession for not enforcing its ethical and competence standards on individual CPAs. The respondents extended that criticism to apply to errant firms, no doubt because of the numerous recent lawsuits against accounting firms. As one auditor put it, "Difficulty in achieving effective self-regulation has been troublesome for many years and stems no doubt from the fact that the profession is organized to regulate individuals. Yet the public recognizes and relies on the work of firms. Thus a key problem is how to regulate firms. Effective regulation would increase public confidence."

The chief difficulty is obtaining the necessary evidence. As always in a fraternity of professionals, "someone else" is incompetent or unethical. No one is willing to blow the whistle on a peer, even when violations are flagrant. For every person brave enough to do so, several provide contrary evidence; so evaluating the evidence becomes hazardous. Auditors, like members of other major professions, do not like to be accused of or admit to charges of ineffectiveness, inefficiency, or poor management. No firm, for example, would openly admit to being overstaffed or overpaid. Thus CPAs are unwilling to expose any colleague apparently performing below par.

How can regulation be effective when the standards by which CPAs are judged are themselves questioned? One corporate financial executive noted that "accountants have tried to pass themselves off as neutral, innocent bystanders who are simply there to state whether or not business follows accounting rules that someone else promulgates. In reality the rules are those that they themselves have set, and the public has always believed that an audit certification meant that the reports were right, not just in accord with GAAP."

The AICPA has begun experimenting with new means of enforcement such as peer review (but apparently not backing them with enough authority). It has appointed a special committee on self-regulation (although its members' divergent views nearly preclude consensus) and has strengthened its ties with the disciplinary bodies of the state boards. Respondents acknowledged that these strategies were too new to evaluate but found the outlook bleak. The rate of disciplinary actions would not increase significantly, according to an auditor, "unless something is done to stimulate a change of attitude among the profession's individual members."

Tightening its disciplinary and regulatory functions was thought necessary to bridge the credibility gap that forced the creation of the FASB. CPAs who do not perform to specified levels of excellence should be expelled from the profession. Federal legislation should have been sought that recognized firms and provided the mechanism for regulation. "With greater control over firms," says an auditor, "the competitive moves that have damaged the profession's image and the rapid—in some cases too rapid—expansion of the size of firms might have been slowed with better control over the quality of their performance." Moreover, one corporate financial executive says, the profession should have "set up its own policing board to review the activities of its members from the public shareholder's viewpoint and not from the CPA's. Corrective actions, up to and including revoking licenses for continuing poor performance, would have resulted. Had the profession acted responsibly in policing its own activities, it would not now be facing the many legal actions brought by investors, nor would the SEC have had the impetus to assume the role of dictator of accounting and reporting principles."

The profession was urged to accept the responsibility for reporting *all* significant violations for investigation and possible discipline. Despite the unrest it might create among individual practitioners, nonconforming members would "awake like sleeping lions." For peer reviews to be effective in improving performance and increasing public confidence in the profession, the results should be made public. Public confidence in firms could also be increased if they disclosed more information about their operations and activities in annual reports.

Finally it was suggested that the profession establish a board to review financial reports from the reader's viewpoint and not permit certification unless a report is judged complete, understandable, and appropriate to that user's needs. "The rub here," points out a corporate financial executive, "is that disputes would occur with management and engagements would be lost, both through management's electing to change audit firms and [through] audit firms' refusing to retain certain clients. Defining what is complete and right accounting and reporting would be difficult and would require reeducation of accountants to look at things from another viewpoint. Accountants would have to learn more about the operation of the firms they certify rather than just having knowledge of accounting principles and how to apply them."

If self-regulation is not tightened, respondents foresaw increasing numbers of incompetent practitioners. New classes of self-proclaimed "competent" accountants would clamor for licensing. The SEC might find it necessary to exert more disciplinary control over firms, thus cutting into the profession's autonomy. It might go on to mandate more "cookbook" rules for accounting; rules would be made by legislative action, with accounting following a rigid pattern and becoming utilitarian. After deteriorating into a group of attestors who affirm that rigid rules have been followed, the profession might become an arm of the government, and CPAs become civil service employees.

The profession was called ill-organized to cope with the demands of self-regulation. The profession needs to forecast the problems it will need to solve and restructure its institutions accordingly.

The profession should develop a set of standards for performance reviews and require them of all firms regularly performing SEC engagements. Naturally firms will object to external quality reviews, the process will be expensive, and it is not clear how the findings would be published. But unless some such action is taken, regulation by the government will continue unabated; CPA firms will suffer more lawsuits, yet lack the documentary evidence necessary for their defense.

Narrow Concept of Role

The profession was thought remiss in not carving out a broader social role for itself in society. No thought has been given to roles it could play besides the traditional services to clients and third parties. One suggestion was for greater participation in the nation's political life. The profession should encourage members to seek election to Congress and to take a more pivotal part in the central financial planning of government. It is this broad public responsibility that the profession seems reluctant to bear. One auditor deduced "from the figures that the government *needs* our expertise; [witness] the current $68.8 billion projected deficit, inflation, devaluation of the dollar, and related fiscal problems." Another auditor expressed dissatisfaction with the way governments managed their budgets, placing heavy emphasis on spending programs and giving scant attention to cost-benefit studies or recognizing that income is limited.

Respondents also deplored the uncertainty surrounding the profession's current role. A corporate financial executive pointed out how differently that role is perceived by "the external user, the laws, courts, and juries, and the profession itself." The cause may lie, he thought, in the wishful belief by other constituencies that the CPA guarantees financial statements and in the aggressiveness with which the profession built up its image as infallible. The profession has also sought to keep a low profile during times of great controversy (such as during the recent flurry of petty bribes, laundered slush funds, and violations of environmental laws) instead of rising to its larger public responsibility and exposing the offenses. That responsibility is difficult to confront, however, for often the people involved are clients or colleagues. It has apparently been easier for the profession to "hide behind its concept of materiality." Some respondents thought the profession could clarify its role by following a disclosure policy on all matters, disclosing, in the words of an accounting educator, "minor matters to the audit committee, larger matters to the SEC, and material matters to the public."

The profession has sought greater political visibility. It has encouraged its members to run for office, and AICPA representatives have testified before Congress and the Treasury Department on corporate financing and tax law. Yet respondents thought there was little to show for these efforts. CPAs are rather conservative and not salesmen, and the capable ones are in much demand within the profession. One respondent thought that Washington officials have a lower public image than CPAs, discouraging CPAs from seeking office. Another reason is the political climate. "The drafting of the tax laws," explained an auditor, "is heavily burdened with political pressures, and the tax legislation generally reflects a reconciliation of these pressures rather than being founded substantially on logical positions with adequate concern for long-term implications of the legislation."

The accounting profession might collide with the legal profession in assuming a broader social role. For example, if the extent of the auditor's role were changed from the traditional "fairly present," it would probably have to be validated in the courts. In any case the courts are defining the profession's role more precisely than accountants would ever have imagined. The legal, more than the accounting, profession probably controls that process.

Some respondents thought the profession had provided insufficient incentive for CPAs to run for public office or even to aid those in public office. Since the principal rewards in political life are recognition and accomplishment, CPAs who have found public service satisfying should be persuaded to get others involved. Other respondents were afraid CPAs would feel underutilized in such jobs and that their performance would suffer. Some doubted that the profession could find people of the tact, sensitivity, and competence to provide effective help to staffs of congressional committees.

The reluctance of accountants to act as policemen or in any way but conservatively made respondents pessimistic about the prospects for reporting on the social responsibility of corporations, giving adverse audit opinions to corporations that act immorally, or, with management, defining the CPA's role in conflict of interest and management fraud. One corporate financial executive said, "Its efforts to become more collaborative with other groups involved in the accounting process—the financial executive, the legal profession, the government—and to influence legislation and regulation of the legal process and public conception would all be blocked by the legal profession, consumer groups, and by the temper of the times." And the profession's reluctance to listen to points of view other than its own leads to polarized positions.

Thus respondents expect a long time to pass before the profession becomes more involved in government and political processes. As a consequence, accountants' profile will remain low, their skills underutilized, and their views unrecognized. The profession will lose the opportunity to gain important friends and will continue to have poor credibility with the public. Ultimately the government and the nation will lose by not making full use of the competence and integrity of the CPA.

GAAP as a Straitjacket

Respondents were dismayed at the trend toward, in the words of a nonauditor CPA, "codifying GAAP and auditing procedures in such detail that the use of professional judgment is being replaced by the ability to read and interpret reguiations." An accounting educator put it another way: "The profession has the discretion to prescribe the auditor's role as either a professional exercising judgment in interpreting principles or as a skilled practitioner enforcing a narrow set of specific legal rules." A corporate financial executive thought the auditor's role was much closer to the latter: "The multitude of APB, FASB, and SEC pronouncements, not counting exposure drafts, have made the profession a purely technical mechanism. Some of the accounting standards even are too detailed to be applied uniformly."

One reason for the proliferation of rules may be the profession's fear that the SEC will make these rules if it does not. Another was the competition between firms for clients. To justify a firm's position on an accounting issue or to limit the options another firm could take in its place, the firm needs to resort to very specific (legalistic) rules.

To have devised sensible GAAP for the vast majority of businesses, the profession should have resisted pressures from the SEC, moved away from detailed rules, and put teeth into the practice of professional accounting; that is,

039033

it should have disciplined members who violated the code of ethics and persuaded members to show more restraint in taking on new clients. The SEC would have had its own accounting releases which would have required adjustments in GAAP. There would have been no need to create the FASB, and the profession would have had a broader, more workable set of accounting principles.

The profession should now, according to the nonauditor CPA, "stop issuing pronouncements that read like regulations. It should weed out prior pronouncements whose applications are narrow and difficult to apply and, by determining the mechanics of reconciling GAAP with SEC accounting, recognize not one but two sets of accounting principles. Of course, the accountants working with the SEC would have dual burdens and would object. But don't tax practitioners also have problems in reconciling GAAP and tax returns?"

The profession should also acknowledge that certifying a financial statement as "presenting fairly" does not always mean adhering to GAAP and thus take a stand against unfair applications of GAAP. It should develop broader GAAP or ones with alternatives, moving them slowly but surely toward principles. Only because of pressure by business and accounting firms have exact rules had to be drafted in the past; the form of such rules cannot be changed without altering the corresponding roles accountants have created for themselves over the years. Yet to use more judgment in certifying financial statements and to rely less on detailed rules, accountants would need broader training in business management and the competitive free-enterprise system. The profession really needs to reevaluate its roles in independent attestation and in financial reporting and to set forth the limitations. Because relying on more rules and regulations is the easier path to follow, change is unlikely.

If the trend toward more rules continues, practitioners will find themselves spending an abnormal amount of "compliance time," which is of no benefit to the client and thus represents a service of doubtful economic value. Lawsuits against CPAs will be more successful because shades of noncompliance will be easier to pinpoint by plaintiff attorneys. Young accountants will lose the challenge to exercise their judgment; in the end they will be no better than their concept of the regulations they must interpret.

The profession would in time divide into auditors and other groups giving management advice on accounting, tax, and related matters. It would become ripe for absorption by government, since narrow interpretations of rules would be all that would be required (rather like the statutory auditors in Europe). The profession would become too specialized; financial reports would be understood only by professionals; and the accounting profession would continue to lose credibility. Finally, a corporate financial executive predicted, "The accounting profession would strangle in its own red tape, and financial reports will become less reliable than they are now even though they will have been prepared according to the 'rules.' "

Intra- and Interprofession Conflicts

FASB versus CASB. The CASB determines the cost accounting rules for companies doing business with the federal government. Its rules govern their performance only under their government contracts. When these businesses are audited, public accountants have to reconcile often conflicting regulations and procedures set down by both the FASB and the CASB. The number of such businesses is growing steadily. Unless the FASB gives more attention to cost accounting, its pronouncements—insofar as they overlap—will be undermined by the CASB.

Older versus Younger CPAs. Conflicts with younger CPAs stem from their different values and motives. They seem to favor a more responsible social contribution by the profession. To the extent that older practitioners ignore their desires, in fact or in appearance, younger members and potential entrants will experience disenchantment and disappointment and may seek careers elsewhere.

FASB versus SEC. Either the SEC seems too impatient with the profession's pace of action, or it criticizes rulings for incompleteness or insignificance when they do appear. In reaction the SEC issues its own regulations, a move that only increases the fundamental differences between itself and the profession, undermines the FASB's authority, and gives accountants the additional burden of adhering to two sets of rules.

Accounting Profession versus Legal Profession. The increasing complexity of our tax system not only requires more legal interpretation but also seems to put more pressure on accountants to take sides. Advocacy is in direct contradiction with the profession's traditional emphasis on objectivity and independence. And short-term distortions for tax purposes contradict the profession's stated aim of producing as accurate and realistic a set of financial statements as possible.

The profession's ability to serve the public interest would diminish if it played a lesser role in tax practice. As one auditor argues, "Since the profession has 'grown up' with the nation's tax system and has developed significant capabilities in working with it, the system would suffer from the loss of suggestions and comments that would follow from less involvement by CPAs in it. Since both legal and accounting capabilities are necessary for effective tax determinations, both professions would be adversely affected by a reduction in the role of either one."

2 Financial Reporting Problems

Financial reports are the accounting profession's primary tangible product. They range from unaudited interim financial statements to increasingly complex, formal attestations for clients and the wider investing public. Small wonder the respondents cited problems concerning them second most often. Financial problems have been grouped into ten types.

Highlights

Producing Realistic Financial Statements. The rapid and dramatic rise in inflation in recent years has made the historical-cost method of accounting virtually obsolete, but no replacement has been found that will reflect price-level changes and provide a fair picture of reality. Use of any new method alone (such as replacement cost or current value) would have the disadvantage of departing from convention and precluding comparison with past records. And using a new method along with historical cost would escalate the time and cost of auditing and the complexity of reports.

Solution of the problem has lagged mainly because of serious disagreement about the severity of inflation's effects and the best way to account for them, disagreement not only within the profession but also within the SEC and the business community. Objections that additional current-value accounting would only complicate a financial statement should be overcome by showing that with simple explanation such figures can clarify the economic condition of a company for stockholders and potential investors.

Unclear Objectives of Financial Statements. Despite the work of the Trueblood commission in 1973 on the objectives of financial reporting, the profession still seems unsure of what financial statements are supposed to do, what they should contain, and for whom they are intended. "What did the Trueblood report mean by *basic* objective anyway?" asked one respondent. "*All* the information useful in making economic decisions or merely that the information provided must be useful?" And who decides that question of scope? One educator phrased the problem succinctly: "Public investors want statements that tell the current worth of a company and that are good predictors of its future profitability. Accounting statements are constructed to do neither." More fundamentally, the profession has not decided what constitutes "useful" information to a particular

27

user, a definition essential to the development of any financial reporting standard. What a company should disclose and how disclosures should be presented are crucial questions the profession should resolve if it is to regain credibility among those who rely on financial statements.

Whether to Certify Unaudited Financial Statements. Proponents argue that interim statements and forecasts should be certified because many people read and act on them. Opponents object to the increased cost to clients, increased exposure to lawsuits, and the interference of such attestation in the year-end audit. Moreover the profession is not clear on the purpose or contents of interim reports. The 1973 guidelines issued by the APB were not mandatory and thus have been randomly adopted. One or two respondents held that management should issue interim statements with no involvement from accountants at all.

The SEC has urged companies to produce forecasts, but accountants feared that if actual company performance turns out to be anything less than predicted, they will be the first to be blamed, whether or not they approved the figures or the methods. They also expressed concern that accountants' involvement in preparing or attesting to company forecasts would jeopardize their traditional objectivity.

Excessively Technical Financial Reports. Financial reports are becoming more and more obscured by technical detail, rather than clearer and less complex. Technical footnotes proliferate, and to one respondent the apparent precision of financial results belies the "crude and inexact . . . foundations of accounting." What progress has been made toward simplicity and clarity has come only at the insistence of regulators and other third parties. Obvious improvements—such as expressing reported income or earnings per share as a range of figures or as alternative values depending on the accounting method chosen, or explaining why one method was chosen when a choice was available—have not been adopted. Of course, making financial reports more understandable depends on the resolution of related problems, such as developing adequate GAAP, limiting the number of alternative accounting methods, and deciding on the format and purposes of financial reports.

Accounting for Business Combinations. The profession, through lax and variable accounting standards, abetted the movement toward large conglomerates in the 1960s. Investors suffered when the conglomerates later proved unable to sustain financial performance commensurate to their size. Respondents were troubled about the accounting processes used to combine the assets, interests, and operations of two companies that merge, especially whether and how to account for goodwill.

Tax System Problems. The respondents urged the profession to follow through on its investigation of the tax effects of inflation on financial reporting, offer advice on tax policy as a matter of individual rights rather than corporate advocacy, and overhaul the nation's tax system.

Accounting for Foreign Operations. How can financial reporting be made uniform when accountants from different countries, whose training and standards vary widely, help prepare the reports of multinational corporations? How should fluctuating exchange rates be taken into account? How should foreign assets be valued, particularly when a foreign subsidiary is nationalized by the country's government? What controls should be placed on transfer pricing between a parent and its foreign affiliates or between foreign affiliates to prevent the shifting of profits to tax-haven countries?

Subjective Definition of Materiality. Materiality, the concept that governs decisions about which transactions or costs are taken into account when drawing up a company's financial reports, is not defined clearly enough to serve as an operational guide. If the profession does not clarify it, accountants and auditors may face a government- or court-imposed solution.

Meeting Demands for Increased Corporate Disclosure. The burden of advising clients on the accounting aspects of increased disclosure required by government agencies distracts accountants from their regular work. Instead of fighting the imposition of greater disclosure, as it should have done, the accounting profession has simply created more rules to cope with it.

The Hidden Problem of Pension Reserves. Accountants should be advocating greater corporate disclosure of pension reserves. So long as companies continue to avoid reporting them, their financial statements will be misleading. In some cases the amounts involved exceed the company's equity.

Producing Realistic Financial Statements

Respondents were distressed over the disparity between what is reported in a company's financial statements and the company's economic reality. The gap between reported and real profits has widened as inflation has soared. "Inflation and current values are the principal reasons why financial statements are no longer so useful," said an educator. Having read the December 1974 FASB draft, "Financial Reporting in Units of General Purchasing Power," he predicted that "the FASB will recommend supplementary nonattested price-level adjusted information in annual reports rather than both price-level adjusted and current-value statements, perhaps side by side with cost figures and both attested."

Respondents thought the profession had failed to deal aggressively enough with price-level accounting, current-cost accounting, and other alternatives to historical cost. "Financial statements do not reflect the price-level adjustments

0540339

or current value of assets," said a government-sector respondent. "Often, financial statements with supplementary data do not reflect or measure financial strength, cash, or funded debt requirements to finance replacement or acquisition of new assets." The assumption that "a dollar is a dollar is a dollar" can no longer be tolerated in financial reporting. (The problem has become very visible through the recent trend of companies changing to a LIFO basis of accounting for inventories in order to avoid reporting so-called inventory profits.)

In times of high inflation, respondents pointed out, it is illogical for the profession to persist conducting accounting on a historical-cost basis when alternatives such as price-level, replacement-cost, and fair-value methods are available. The FASB's recently issued exposure draft on price-level accounting puts needed pressure on the profession to endorse replacement-cost depreciation and delete from reported profits inventory profits due to inflation. Proper accounting rules are needed even in inflationary times.

Because accountants measure the value of depreciation in terms of replacement cost, managers and investors are not fully aware that real capital is being seriously eroded by the high rate of inflation. The FASB seems to favor a price-level approach; the SEC favors fair-value supplements to historical-cost statements.

The accounting profession has not yet taken effective action for the following reasons, among others:

It always waits until it is threatened before doing anything aside from setting up a committee to study the problem (we have studied *this* one for over twenty years!). (an auditor)

The profession thinks it is politically acceptable just to make index adjustments to cost—not a change in principles—to save face. Not having developed adequate principles yet, it thinks it alright to separate the price-level problem from the price change problem. (an educator)

The profession has perhaps failed to understand the full economic impact of current practice, and it is unfamiliar with appropriate statistical methodology involving price indexes required for the adjustment. (a government-sector respondent)

The profession lacks a clear consensus that anything should be done and disagrees as to the methods for solving this problem. (a lawyer)

Respondents also blamed the business community for opposing change of any kind. According to an auditor:

Businessmen are reluctant to have their reported profits substantially deflated, that is, to have them expressed in constant dollars. First, they are apprehensive as to how their profits (and other ratios in their financial statements) will compare with other companies. Second, they are equally apprehensive that downward restatement of profits and earnings per share will further depress the market prices and their stocks. American business over the last ten years has had to resort to debt financing, partly because of the adverse relationship between the cost of debt financing and that of equity financing. In the aggregate for American business, debt in relation to equity is climbing to dangerously high levels. We need a better climate for raising equity capital—a fair and objective statement of profits in terms of constant dollars should contribute significantly to that better understanding.

Of course, the purpose of developing accounting principles is to present economic events and business transactions as they really are. In moving toward cash accounting, the FASB is looking for simplistic answers to complex questions. In the past it was acceptable for accountants to produce for their clients one net income figure without qualifying its significance, an obviously simplistic solution. Now a qualitative analysis of financial statements is necessary.

The APB Statement 3 of June 1969 recommended that general price-level statements be presented as a supplement to historical-cost statements. An educator pointed out that since "supplementary statements weren't mandatory . . . few companies prepared them. Some objections to preparing them have been the complexity and high cost of converting the data, concern over the appropriate index number to use, and the fact that price-level effects on net income is disallowed for tax purposes." The APB spent years trying to come up with basic accounting objectives. Meanwhile pressing day-to-day accounting issues inundated its agenda, and it rendered opinions on an ad hoc, piecemeal basis, even as they are rendered today. According to a government-sector respondent, the FASB exposure draft referred extensively to APB Statement 3 but did not explore other avenues of reporting. "There is a recent indication," he said, "that the SEC may issue for comment a release on the issue proposing that companies provide some form of supplemental disclosure of the impact on operations of using replacement-cost data in computing cost of sales and depreciation charges."

Most respondents approved of the FASB exposure draft and of reporting the effect of price-level changes, though some held that the statements should not be required until there is more demand for such information by users. One government-sector respondent asserted that the FASB discussion memorandum on price-level accounting does not go far enough. "It doesn't deal with how 'value' is related to specific enterprises, nor does it accept or understand the use of 'purchasing power' as an appropriate measure."

One respondent reported that by surveying various companies, the profession had tried to gather empirical data showing what effect price-level restatements might have on financial reports. (The companies asked to participate in the surveys had apparently not been very responsive.) He also suggested that tax and other government authorities, unlikely to recognize any other "inflation" method of accounting, would resist the profession's efforts to change.

A government-sector respondent criticized the AICPA's ARS 6 for not considering "an attribute such as the purchasing power of the same number of dollars" and for not quantifying "the number of units or other measurements that can be replaced with the same number of dollars." Another respondent criticized the AICPA's guidelines on methods of presenting supplementary financial data for not reflecting the current value of assets, current replacement costs, or units that can be replaced or acquired with net working capital. Despite various research studies, asserted a lawyer, "neither fair-value accounting nor price-level accounting [has] been found to be a substitute for cost recovery in the earning process."

The profession should have recognized the problem earlier by adopting inflation accounting for business, the economy, and government, though the move might not have been popular with those whose debt would have been adjusted upward to compensate for the effects of inflation. If price-level and cost-basis statements had been shown side by side when inflation began to distort the latter, price-level statements would not have produced such disruption and would not now be considered such a radical innovation.

If the profession had required supplementary statements when inflation first accelerated, according to an educator, "statement users would have had better information for making business decisions. Many users think in terms of current prices and dollars of the most recent period and not of any past date. Failure to have shown adjusted data may mean that taxes and dividends were actually reducing invested capital. Failure to point out this distortion continually overstates profit in a period of rapidly rising prices and may stimulate business activity excessively." Basing supplemental statements on current values instead of adjusting for price-levels would have provided a good test of whether and how the use of current values is feasible. A corporate financial executive thought that price-level-adjusted supplements should have been required when inflation reached predetermined levels.

Before inflation began to climb, the profession should have issued a formal opinion or accounting procedure rather than just a statement requesting voluntary disclosure from companies. Had it acted more strongly, most companies would probably have been willing to have statements prepared on a price-level basis or some other basis recognizing inflation's effects. The public would also have been more aware that profit variations are not true dollar variations but largely the results of inflationary effects. One government-sector respondent believes that if the profession had carried out more value accounting research during major price-level movements, such as after wars or during a depression, it could have avoided the problem. "But it didn't," he says, "mainly because the decision wasn't entirely its own. Industry and regulatory agencies really discouraged change efforts."

The profession has yet to demonstrate its willingness to meet the challenge of financial reporting in a changing economic environment. The SEC would not interfere if the profession were addressing accounting disclosure and measurement problems in a meaningful way. "In some enterprises where uniform equipment is used," said a government-sector respondent, "the profession could have converted fluctuating monetary terms into stable units of measurement (equipment-tons, gallons) in order to forecast capitalization or funded debt required for replacing the same or similar units. Business organizations could then have forecast or planned their financing requirements in an orderly way, thereby avoiding panics in financial markets."

Development of a clear purpose for accounting and basic accounting standards would take care of this problem. There is still no consensus on such standards. The latest study, done in 1960, never received the debate necessary to change standards or have them accepted—perhaps because of the vested interests of corporations and honest differences among accountants.

The profession should determine acceptable ways of computing current value, such as using market value or conducting appraisals, and try them in limited areas of practice, such as the determination of real estate assets. Supplemental statements based on current values, however, would compromise accountants' objectivity; current-value figures are subjective and susceptible to manipulation. Even though inflation accounting would not be politically popular, the profession should encourage its use in accounting for all financial transactions and measurements. For example, the government could use inflation accounting in the revenue code, though Congress may object.

The difficulty with the price-level-adjusted method lies in interpreting the resulting statements to users; with the current-value method it lies in preparing the statements themselves. Either method would involve an onerous cost to clients in preparing the first set of statements. Yet if both methods were tried, accountants would become preoccupied with deciding which one was better and would not use both simultaneously. Perhaps investors should be the ones to decide which alternative to use.

The profession should require the study of alternative costing methods in accounting courses and include such problems in CPA examinations. However, the academic community would surely accuse practitioners of wanting to force-feed this topic to students and would object to the infringement on their control of accounting curricula.

Research should be extended to the complex operations common to larger companies—handling preferred stock, various reserve accounts, fixed assets—while obtaining full cooperation from the companies participating in the research. The results might help accountants explain price changes in internal as well as external financial reports.

The FASB should ask that the results of more than a hundred companies' experiments with price-level statements be made public, following the lead of Shell Oil. Investors and others need to see how such statements look and work, so long as the companies were willing to make the data public.

"The leadership ought to be sounding off more on the need for change," said a government-sector respondent. "There is no one voice in this many-faceted profession. The AICPA and state society leaders ought to be discussing more frequently the need for change and not just sitting back and waiting for the FASB and the SEC and others to carry on." The FASB should address this issue more broadly and not limit its review to price-level accounting.

The profession should issue guidelines for measuring price-level changes adjusted to current values, disclosing useful supplementary data about inventories or other assets that can be purchased with working capital. These data contain assumptions that are subject to change depending on the prevailing economic climate and the purchasing power of the dollar.

The profession should educate the public to appreciate that financial data are always open to interpretation. Measurements more precise than historical monetary cost may be useful in determining the stability, liquidity, and earning potential of corporate enterprises. Supplementary data can be misinterpreted and misleading if the reader does not know management's long-range aims and objectives. For example, the funding requirements for a going concern are different from those of a merged or dissolving one. The profession should also educate the business community about the distorting effect of inflation on financial statements. "The matter of inflation adjustments raises policy issues that are beyond the competence of most accountants," noted a government-sector respondent. "The profession needs an advisory board of economists and financial specialists; it does not recognize that accounting training and experience do not qualify an individual to speak authoritatively on national economic policy issues as they are affected by accounting practices."

Current counterproposals to price-level accounting using the GPP deflator have suggested that those who support replacement-cost accounting have no responsibility for determining such amounts. The AICPA should acknowledge the various meanings of replacement cost and rule that the idea is still too subjective for endorsement. Yet it should advise use of the GPP deflator for tax purposes.

Though it might initially confuse the investing public, and despite the considerable cost of implementation, the profession should require certain price-level data as supplementary information to financial statements. Financial statements should also be required to carry the value of investments at their market price, even though it might make tax reporting more complicated. To many companies, investments are not significant; other noncurrent assets are more important.

If the profession does not soon decide on an appropriate method of accounting for inflation, it will

cause preparers of statements to continue to overstate profits in a period of rapidly rising prices, which could then lead to the running down and depletion of productive plant capacity, and cause managements to make expensive errors in costing, budgeting, and correct pricing of products. (an educator)

make it difficult for the profession to convince government authorities to recognize the effect of general price-level changes in computing net income—especially true in the area of taxes. (an educator)

confuse investment analysts, politicians, and the general public as to the true worth of a business enterprise, especially if accountants and other interested parties don't educate themselves in price-level or methods of accounting other than historical cost. (a corporate financial executive)

If inflation remains high, pressure will mount for the accounting profession to explain financial reports; the use of archaic accounting techniques would draw wide criticism. Financial statements will become further removed from reality. The SEC might mandate the use of an alternative method, such as the subjective replacement-cost one that is now unacceptable to the profession.

Investors might come to ignore regular financial statements when making investment decisions, and analysts and other users would become increasingly suspicious of financial statements in times of inflation. Appraisers lacking professional standards may mislead users of financial statements by estimating the replacement costs of property as far from their realizable value. Inappropriate values may be used, with insufficient discrimination between liquidation value and market value, for example.

The public would become convinced that traditional financial statements are useless; the meaning of present "profits" would be a mystery; confidence in published reports would decline; and reliance on misleading data would lead to unprofitable investment decisions.

Useful data for investors would come from other sources. For example, the SEC would establish disclosure policy and measurement principles, overriding and undermining the FASB in a stroke. The NAA might take over the profession's leadership role in finding an acceptable way to account for inflation. And even appraisers, bankers, and brokers might be able to make their interpretations of company financial statements appear legitimate to the public. The place of profits in our economic system will continue to be misunderstood; balance sheets will continue to be meaningless and provide no general comparability among companies; and financial statements may become outdated by the time they are issued. A government-sector respondent pointed out that "net working capital or net earnings may appear to be adequate for a substantial dividend distribution when, quite to the contrary, they are insufficient to replace inventories or useless assets. Corporate capital budgets will not be meaningful unless acquisitions or replacements are measured in price-levels adjusted to current values of units to be purchased."

Company profits will continue to be overstated and therefore overtaxed, resulting in a diminished flow of funds for long-term investment and slowing the development of adequate productive capacity. Capital costs will become excessive. Ultimately, ventured a lawyer, "a court might hold that under certain circumstances, a historical-cost financial statement did not 'fairly present' the financial condition of the company or its results of operations, and hold the CPA liable for damages."

Unclear Objectives of Financial Statements

Although the Trueblood report attempted to define the purposes of financial reporting, it was not sufficient, and the profession has not since considered the question in depth. Rather than attacking the basic problem, the profession has devised rules for specific problems and has been caught up in "putting out brush fires." The various users of a financial report (which also have not been clearly defined) are unsure of what the report should provide.

The confusion is revealed in two comments:

What are the objectives of financial statements? Should the focus be on the balance sheet? Should the emphasis be on the historical cost or current values of the enterprise's assets and liabilities? (a corporate financial executive)

The obligations of the auditor to his client and to the public that uses the statements are not well defined. Consequently, in situations where different methods will give different results, the auditor has no firm basis for making a choice. (an investment company executive/financial press respondent)

A corporate financial executive believed the problem may have stemmed from "confusion and misdirection as to what tests to apply in setting accounting rules and standards." An educator asserted that the profession "has failed to understand the full nature of the issue and of empirical testing. There seems to be a great wariness of becoming attuned to the issue and a naïve defensive attitude when the issue is encountered."

Critics contend that the Trueblood report and the FASB's more recent deliberations did not effectively delimit the scope of financial reporting or consider alternative viewpoints, especially those disagreeing with the Trueblood commission and those of nonaccountants on what information they need.

Aspects of the problem are revealed in several comments:

There are strong differing views on all sides of the issue which preclude reaching a consensus. Various proposals will require expanded areas of expertise by reporting companies and auditors, with responsibilities in new untested areas. Value bases would move from objective measures to subjective judgment. (a financial executive)

Too many constraints continue to govern measurements of financial statement items, such as "realization" and "matching." Auditing considerations and management bias continue to overrule objectives of "usefulness" in financial statements. (an educator)

The profession has been slow to accept the Trueblood philosophy [providing users with information for predicting, comparing, and evaluating the earning power of an enterprise]. Accounting firms are necessarily in close touch with their clients, whereas their contacts with statement users and the public are peripheral. Clients pay the fees and often take the attitude that the auditor owes them "loyalty." (an investment company executive/financial press respondent)

A related problem is that accountants are constrained by having to use GAAP in preparing financial statements. The last respondent just quoted pointed out that "the APB and its successor, the FASB, have both attempted to establish rules to reduce the number of cases in which a choice of methods has to be made. Yet the gray areas in GAAP are enormous. The FASB has tried to be conscientious and as a result has proceeded only slowly. Some of its proposals have been vigorously resisted by corporate financial officers or SEC staff. And new developments, such as inflation, have created problems not covered by accepted accounting practice."

When it became aware of this problem, the profession should have persuaded the various kinds of user to reconcile their differences on what the objectives of financial statements should be. It could then have devised several types of statement tailored to different uses, such as budgeting, forecasting, investing, operations, and management. It was too much to expect that a single statement could satisfy all purposes. The profession could have avoided many of the subsequent misuses of financial statements. According to an educator, "This problem goes all the way back to basic principles founded on statements being used to report on the trusteeship of management. The profession should have either changed principles or convinced laymen that accounting couldn't do this job. If the public in turn understood the limitations of accounting statements as forecasters of future profits, the problem would be largely resolved."

The view that the responsibility for financial statements belongs with management in its stewardship capacity was shared by a company financial executive:

The profession should have decreed that the objective of financial statements is primarily to report on how management has used corporate assets. It should then have insisted that management accept the burden of producing and publishing useful balance sheets and income statements. However, it may be too late to return to the stewardship concept. Too many other interest groups, such as financial analysts, creditors, labor unions, and government, are already in the picture trying to determine what financial statements should or should not contain. Many troubling issues such as R&D expense, deferred taxes, and earnings-per-share calculations, for example, would no longer be issues were management to make its own decisions in its financial report. Given the legal liability which goes along with the responsibility for determining what to disclose, managements would be self-motivated to fairly present results.

Another corporate financial executive declared: "The issue should have been thrashed out many years ago before the APB began writing rules on an ad hoc basis, often bending to the profession's defensive and regulatory pressures to write rules to constrain business practices. As a result, financial statements written today would reflect economic reality more meaningfully, with rule-making power squarely retained within the profession."

The profession should have stated clearly that its primary obligation was to the users of financial statements and that client interests would be overridden if a conflict arose. The public would be more acutely aware of the problems of reporting the complex affairs of a big corporation and thus less inclined to blame accountants when a big corporation got into trouble.

To resolve the question of scope, the profession should critically examine the meaning of "basic objective" in the Trueblood report. It is not clear whether all information useful in making economic decisions must be provided or whether whatever information is provided must be useful. The profession should commission another body to experiment with the Trueblood recommendations. One strategy would be to develop different types of financial statement for different purposes, with standards for each type. The profession should adopt "usefulness" as the main criterion for judging financial statements and develop procedures to permit auditors to give an opinion on current-value statements. The resulting high cost of auditing and the need for more research to develop measurement methods would inhibit implementing this suggestion.

An educator said that the profession is unsure of the very nature of that problem. "It should first decide which course to follow—to change principles or to educate the public. Then it should study how to accomplish one or the other. Its greatest problem is that accountants are not themselves aware of the problem; also, the courts, Congress, and the SEC do not appear to be willing to permit accountants to abandon the 'fairness' concept. The profession should resolve the fairness question and make clear those responsibilities the auditor can accept."

The profession should insist that auditors refuse to attest statements that involve a disagreement on principles. It should also require that clients explain why they want to change auditors after an auditor makes a decision they disapprove of. Some of the best CPA firms might lose clients to more accommodating rivals; some businessmen would protest loudly, blaming the accountant for arbitrarily making them look bad. In some cases auditors may have taken an unnecessarily tough stand.

Other suggestions for remedial actions included supporting the efforts of the FASB, holding hearings and seminars, paying more attention to theory and research, and educating the users of financial statements on the limitations of financial data—spelling out what types of accounting data are useful for what purposes. If the user insists on using financial data without understanding their value and limitations, no other remedy is going to help. Unless it clarifies the purposes of financial reporting, the profession will continue to fall short of public expectations. The courts and the SEC will increasingly determine the scope of a financial statement, threatening the FASB's role.

As the usefulness of financial statements wanes, so will the profession's prestige. Government auditors may replace today's independent professionals. Statisticians and economists will step in to furnish information to investors and other users; financial reports by accountants may fall into disuse or serve only legal purposes. Lawsuits against members of the profession will proliferate.

The scope of the profession's work will expand as it tries to meet all expectations through the means of financial reports, thus raising the cost of its services—and that of malpractice insurance premiums—to intolerable levels. Both the profession and the capital markets will suffer as a result. Arbitrary and inconsistent rules will proliferate in the absence of an underlying rationale. Accounting might cease to exist as an independent profession, accountants working either for corporations or the government. An investment company executive/financial press respondent believes that "accounting would not keep up with the needs of business and investors. It would ossify, as has the railroad industry."

Whether to Certify Unaudited Financial Statements

Although the AICPA's AudSEC has set forth alternative proposals for disclosing interim financial statements, the SEC is expecting the profession to do more than that, such as certify them. Some firms have also presented counterproposals to the SEC, though perhaps with the hidden motive of looking for additional work despite the increased risk of public disappointment and misunderstanding. Even the FASB is studying the problem. All these groups have to cope with the uncertainty surrounding the auditing of interim financial statements. A certain result is that the cost to the client for this service will increase.

First, the profession needs to determine whether interim reporting serves any purpose and then to establish reporting procedures that best meet the purpose. Interim reports are important to many users. Yet failing to say why they are needed has made the profession's rulings "directionless and inconsistent." APB Opinion 28, issued in 1973, did not conclude what interim reports really should accomplish. For example, should they primarily report (1) quarterly or year-to-date cumulative data, (2) the events of the interim period separate from the annual period or integrated with it, or (3) the interim period's actual contribution to, or its pro rata share of, the annual results? FASB Statement 3, issued a year later, significantly modified the APB positions. It concentrated on procedures without clearly identifying any purpose, concept, or justification for them, thereby exposing the FASB to the criticisms that used to be leveled at the APB.

Second, the profession has never specified the minimum work necessary to prepare an unaudited financial statement (many more unaudited than audited statements are prepared in the United States). It is possible to prepare an unaudited financial statement simply by copying amounts from the client's books without further inquiry, and no doubt some CPAs do just that.

The AICPA has set up a committee to consider whether to establish separate accounting standards, principles, and procedures for clients having small businesses. Such distinctions would downgrade the profession's reputation and devalue financial statements. It has issued guidelines for preparing unaudited financial statements, but they are mandatory only for CPAs who are members of the AICPA.

Instead of all this, said an auditor, the profession should have required CPAs to make a limited review of interim financial statements, reporting only to the client's board of directors or audit committee, not to the public. Reviewing interim statements would now be standard practice. However, this probably would not have quieted the demands of regulatory bodies for accountants to associate themselves with such statements. Alternatively, accountants could have included work on interim reports as part of the annual audit without making them a separate issue.

With regard to certifying interim statements, the profession should have tried to separate principles from the procedures required to implement them. Then the procedures would not have developed into the present onerous, time-consuming, and costly practices that make it economically impractical for CPAs to serve the needs of small businesses. The profession might also have conducted research to find out how interim reports were being used and how they could be made useful at marginal extra cost. It could then have established a purpose and consistent procedures for interim reporting.

The profession should have recognized three types of statement: audited; unaudited, requiring a minimum amount of work; and statements prepared on clients' stationery or on blank paper not identifying the CPA. Courts would then have had better guidance for decisions in suits against CPAs.

The profession should now take the position that the value of any report by independent auditors is severely limited unless it is audited and that unaudited reports only confuse and disappoint their users and cause the SEC "to call the profession 'obstructionist.'" The profession should also endorse AudSEC's position, and accountants should encourage their clients to comply with it.

The public needs to understand why auditors should be associated with interim statements. However, the average investor doubts that audits are necessary in the first place. Of course, the danger in preparing any financial statement is that it may be used by unintended users for unknown purposes. Therefore, preparing information for a specific audience still does not solve the problem. And reducing rather than increasing the auditor's involvement with unaudited statements would only increase the accountant's exposure to potential liability. To cover itself the profession should develop a disclaimer for the transmittal letters accompanying financial statements that indicates precisely the extent of the service performed.

According to a corporate financial executive, "The profession should stress the complications that would arise were CPAs to audit interim reports. More specifically, costs would double and it would take people away from the regular audit, in turn requiring yet more people and higher costs. It should concentrate instead on communicating the real impact of this change on the business community, making them aware that the benefits they might derive may not justify the costs. However, the business community may construe such a warning as possibly an attack on them, thus creating further tension between industry and the profession."

Another corporate financial executive approaches the problem from a different perspective. "Accounting firms, whether individually or together, should write to their congressmen as well as to the SEC and FTC, explaining the impracticality of auditing interim statements and stressing that clients do discuss and review with them any major and important issues that occur throughout the year. They should have adequate and well-prepared replies to questions that probably will be put to them by elected representatives (they will push for doing what they think the public demands in this regard). The only problem with this approach is how to develop and disseminate such a letter." According to a nonauditor CPA, preparing unaudited statements is not an auditing function and should not be a responsibility of full-time auditors. Nor should the matter be under the direction of the AICPA's AudSEC. Of course, the audit departments of large national firms would oppose the idea.

Through the state societies and legislatures, the profession should prescribe by law the minimum amount of work to be done on unaudited statements. Of course, laymen might interpret it as yet another scheme by accountants to increase their business. The profession should recommend one or the other—reporting year-to-date or separate quarterly data—for all industries.

If the profession does not solve this problem, a regulatory agency will probably preempt the decision and require interim financial statements to be certified. The profession could limit auditor involvement to a prescribed set of procedures when publicly associating with interim financial statements. This would enhance public confidence in interim statements, though it might raise questions about the "integrity" of the annual accounting period. The profession might be railroaded into giving apparent approval to unaudited financial statements, thus confusing the public over the difference between audited and unaudited reports. Misleading interim reports will draw censure for the accountant. Management consultants, analysts, or others might join in—or take over—this work. On the other hand, requirements might escalate to the point where CPAs will in fact audit rather than simply review interim reports.

Paradoxically, an accountant can be sued and convicted of negligence in an audit when all he was doing was preparing an unaudited statement. And the public continues to rely on interim statements when present rules say that no reliance can be placed on them because they are not properly audited.

The need to review forecasts and interim statements will add to the pressures affecting auditors' objectivity in auditing the same historical periods at a later date. The threat of litigation for misconduct in reviewing forecasts and interim statements will not be strong enough to motivate accountants to raise the quality of their work, but it too will affect their objectivity. By virtue of their role as auditors, CPAs will become increasingly identified with company forecasts. The SEC favors that association and is encouraging companies to produce such statements for its stockholders. Attesting to forecasts goes beyond what is required in an audit; yet auditors are the first to be held responsible for them and hence are vulnerable to charges of fraud.

The profession should refuse to be associated with forecasts until sufficient research is completed. As an auditor put it, "Forecasts are predictions about what will happen in the future; with the very best of goodwill, ability, and knowledge, there will be differences, often substantial, between reality and the forecasts. CPAs would lose credibility as a result." The profession could instead associate itself only with the preparation of forecasts and not take responsibility for the assumptions involved. Disclosing management's assumptions behind the forecasts may expose sensitive information. The profession should solicit the opinions of investors, shareholders, and financial analysts and study the legal liabilities involved for CPAs and their clients. Forecast data should be governed by company policy only; outside auditing firms, which deal mainly with historical data, should not become involved.

If certifying interim statements and forecasts seriously impairs the auditor's objectivity, it will come to light only gradually and through the courts. A consequence would be a serious loss of investor confidence. If the profession does not resolve the problem, investment funds might be channeled away from the capital markets, to the detriment of the economy. Even if accountants were to certify them, forecasts would not be believed. As it is, forecasts prepared by companies and by independent financial analysts often differ substantially.

Excessively Technical Financial Reports

All too often, financial statements are so technical that the reader must be a CPA to make sense of them. An investment company executive/financial press respondent believes that the problem stems from the profession's "failure to instruct the public in the limitations of accounting—the imprecision in measurement, the conventional basis for its principles, and the often problematic choice among alternatives. In contrast to the apparent precision of financial results, the foundations of accounting are astonishingly crude and inexact. An awful lot of people lost an awful lot of money partly because they didn't understand what reported earnings really amounted to. The problem remains pervasive. Many people continue to put more confidence in financial statements than they should."

Laymen who sit on juries in lawsuit trials of accountants are often unable to understand the technical and professional issues involved. Recent cases indicate that even judges do not understand the difference between audited and unaudited financial statements. The profession has not faced the problem or mounted an effective effort to improve the public's understanding of the CPA's role, responsibilities, and liabilities. Certain attorneys recognize this weakness and take advantage of it.

There is no consensus among the public about the accounting profession's primary function; the public is aware only of the arbitrariness of accounting methods. The profession responds to accusations about its subjectivity by professing greater faith in its own objectivity, thus increasing the already large credibility gap that exists. To admit that accounting is subjective, warned an educator, "is to give away its birthright!"

An educator pointed out that no mechanisms or processes have been set in motion to redefine the social contract the profession needs to stabilize its environment. "The profession is almost totally insensitive to the strategic nature of its problems and is in danger of overreacting to every tactical probe or needle stuck into its hide by the set of diverse views regarding its function."

Information provided to the investing public is overly technical and not understood by the typical investor. Stockbrokers prefer to sell stock for its emotional appeal rather than to explain the financial pros and cons. Many annual reports are now more comprehensible, but most are still hard to understand. The profession's main approach, according to an investment company executive/financial press respondent, has been "to improve accounting practice by eliminating alternative treatments and by reconsidering the objectives of accounting. This latter effort, begun by the Trueblood group, urged that more emphasis be placed on cash flows, which is somewhat closer to an economic concept of income."

Other respondents counter that eliminating alternative methods is not really feasible. Even if it were, the imprecision of accounting measurement and its conventional basis would remain. In practice and in doctrine, emphasis has been placed on highlighting uncertainties through greater disclosure and qualifying opinions. That is a needed step, but it addresses only one aspect of uncertainty in financial statements—not the estimates, choices, or sampling imprecision inherent in the process.

When the problem first became apparent, the profession could have established liability limits for accountants, kept accounting principles simple and uniform while allowing fewer options and alternatives, established standard reporting requirements, and restricted footnotes to only the most crucial information not given in the body of the statement. An educator pointed out: "The profession should have resisted the temptation to hide behind the 'objective' facade of accounting. CPAs have tried to have it both ways. They have used language, as in the short-form opinion, that conveyed an aura of precision to the public, and also reinforced the public's notion of objectivity within accounting. Had they been more straightforward with the public, they would not now be in a position of appearing to abandon objectivity."

The investment company executive/financial press respondent would have preferred the profession to discourage the growth of securities analysis that focused on reported earnings: "It should have reported income or earnings per share as a range or as alternative values depending on the accounting method chosen. In certain instances where alternatives existed, it should have included a discussion of both alternatives and the impact of choosing one of them. As a result, the accounting profession would not be viewed with such skepticism today; there might be more informed use of financial statements. Also, the speculative 'go-go' period of the sixties would have evolved differently."

"Perhaps the profession should have emphasized quarterly net earnings instead of annual earnings figures," suggested an auditor. "Figures for twelve quarters could have been included in the annual report, thus putting more emphasis on changes and trends, and highlighting unusual (nonrecurring) transactions. This would yield the major advantage of spreading the audit over four quarters rather than confining it to the end of the year."

An educator asserted, "The profession needs to break out of the straitjacket thinking imposed on it by 'rationality.' Progress will be a function of the success with which society or the profession finds ways other than rational ones to deal with subjectivity. The compulsive way in which it responds tactically to strategic issues results in the fact that every action it takes simply sets in motion stronger counterforces."

Any moves to restrict the number of acceptable methods of accounting for like-business transactions and to advocate fewer footnote disclosures would be opposed by business itself, which demands sufficient latitude. Any change in accounting methods would also temporarily distort reported operating results and financial condition.

The profession should discourage reliance on quarterly results as anything but rough indicators. Quarterlies involve almost arbitrary allocations and are accurate only to 15-20 percent. However, a demand exists among investors and analysts for easily understood, timely financial reports, even if they are illusory.

Finally, an investment company executive/financial press respondent would like the profession to advocate greater use of plain language and pictures and charts and to severely restrict footnotes in annual reports.

What might happen if no improvements are made? An educator predicts a rigidity in the profession, "a 'rule mentality' which protects itself from vulnerability. Once this happens, it wouldn't make any difference whether the SEC or some other government agency takes over or not, for one bureaucratic response is roughly equivalent to another." Others feared more rule setting by the SEC and other governmental agencies, with regulators eventually assuming the attest function. Complex footnotes, incomprehensible except to a few, would proliferate. Such complexity could lead to special interpretive reporting aimed at the average small investor or general public. Investors, backed by regulatory agencies and the courts, are demanding higher standards.

Investors would continue their undue reliance on financial statements for investment decisions, slighting other information about a company. The myth that income or "health" as measured by accounting conventions can be equated with commonsense notions of earnings and wealth will continue.

Problems in Accounting for Business Combinations

How to account for mergers and acquisitions became a problem in the 1960s; by not resolving it, the profession lost much credibility. The problem remains unresolved. It is an example of how sluggishly the profession has responded to changes in economic conditions or institutional developments. The profession should appoint a committee to catalog financial and economic changes as they begin and to forecast the necessary adjustments in GAAP.

The two APB opinions separating the merger accounting question from that of "goodwill" made an artificial distinction. Rather than accomplishing better accounting, they revealed the extent of feuding among CPA firms and corporate preoccupation with earnings per share.

The profession should have established a single standard of accounting for all business combinations, recognizing neither distinctions between purchase and pooling (except for major combinations) nor goodwill on the balance sheet to be amortized, written off, or posted to a continued account to retained earnings. This would have avoided the rather artificial way of accounting for mergers and would not have penalized earnings for forty years. The FASB should do what the APB should have done ten years ago. Those who prefer some other method might be unhappy and seek an SEC, IRS, or legislative remedy. Also, some unforeseen unfair application might require interpretations, modifications, or exceptions, thereby complicating the issue and impeding the adoption of a single standard.

If the problem is not resolved soon, sophisticated investors will continue to be misled until they come to understand that goodwill must be stripped from balance sheets and income statements and that other adjustments must be made before financial statements can properly serve investment purposes. A new wave of mergers would catch the profession unawares, still without any systematic, realistic way of accounting for them and reporting their effects. Present accounting conventions could further distort earnings figures, causing a new wave of public skepticism and contributing to another go-go era on Wall Street.

Tax System Problems

The tax system is biased against the accumulation of capital necessary to replace and modernize the nation's production facilities. The system is inequitable and complex, both for businesses and individuals. The current income tax laws also deter efforts to cope with the effect of inflation on financial reporting. Inflationary pressures, the economic recession, and a resurgence of the LIFO inventory concept prompted the problem, as did the debates about new tax legislation. Like Congress, the profession has coped only with symptoms, and has "patched and scratched" the tax laws and regulations, further complicating them instead of simplifying. However, the AICPA's appointment of a task force to study the tax effects of price-level changes is a welcome step.

In offering advice on tax policy, the profession should have acted less as advocates for large clients and more in the interest of individuals. If it had, the tax laws and regulations might now be less complex in their application to individuals and small businesses, and the profession might have contributed to an overhaul of the nation's tax laws. The profession should have better communicated the urgency of the problem, describing more clearly the concepts involved and creating an intelligible and feasible plan for its resolution.

Toward that end, the profession should now separate the governmental function of raising revenue from all the subsidy, social welfare, and other programs in the tax laws. That is a staggering effort and would be resisted by many clients who benefit from present tax policies, ranging from small taxpayers such as farmers and nonprofit organizations to big oil companies and other giant corporations. Tax practitioners and tax specialists within the profession might also oppose such a scheme.

To increase the public's awareness of business's tax burden, the profession should encourage clients to disclose their total taxes, including all hidden excise and use taxes, both in financial statements and in their product pricing. It should assess the potential consequences of tax policies under various realistic circumstances, make legislative proposals, and testify before Congress on ways to improve the situation.

If the problem continues, public frustration will increase and our voluntary tax reporting and collection system will further break down; firms will get richer from their tax practices; the nation's production facilities will continue to become less efficient and competitive in the world economy; the nation's standard of living will decline; and economic and technological progress in the private sector will probably not achieve its potential, moving the nation closer to a government-managed economy.

Accounting for Foreign Operations

Americans need an accurate picture of the operations of foreign and multinational corporations—how earnings are accounted for and assets valued—especially as exchange rates are changing. Company reports of international investment activities have not uniformly followed accounting rules; nor have they disclosed adequate information on those activities. One reason could be that accountants in other countries have widely differing training.

There is probably no correct way to handle this problem. However, the profession should have specified one method of accounting for changes in the investment value of assets due to fluctuating exchange rates. It should adopt one rule for converting foreign earnings, which should also cover how and when earnings of foreign subsidiaries are shown on the books of the parent company. Foreign assets of multinational companies could thereby be valued more consistently, and a better picture would be provided of how foreign earnings contribute to a company's earnings. Earnings comparisons of multinational companies would also become easier and more realistic.

The profession should adopt firmer rules for accounting for international investments and valuing earnings, including disclosures by companies of their rationale for determining exchange rates. Companies are now so involved in international investments and operations that it may be impossible to recast their books. Even if it were possible, the reported earnings of some companies would change drastically. Unless the profession resolves this problem, the muddled way of valuing and carrying foreign assets on a company's books will persist. The consequences would be serious when a foreign country nationalized a company.

Less developed countries are becoming bolder in their criticism of the way multinational corporations account for transfer pricing between the parent and its foreign affiliates and among foreign affiliates of the same parent. The suspicion is that a special method of transfer pricing is being used to shift profits to tax-haven countries.

All the profession has done about this problem is to respond to IRS rulings on the subject, though those rulings do not affect many of the foreign-to-foreign transactions of these companies. The profession should require that intracompany transfer prices reflect all costs of production, allocated overhead, and reasonable profit margins. This might have a drastic effect on the parent corporation's tax liabilities and level of reported earnings. This problem should be tackled together with the one on how companies consolidate the earnings of foreign affiliates, particularly those not wholly owned. If the problem is not solved, each country will probably devise its own set of rules governing transfer pricing, resulting in inconsistencies in form and application.

If the real contribution of foreign operations to earnings is not known, multinational companies will continue to draw criticism for avoiding taxes. Corporations will continue to exploit their foreign subsidiaries in efforts to avoid disclosure rules at home. And to the extent that foreign operations are part of the corporate report, financial statements will mislead.

Subjective Definition of Materiality

The general belief that materiality and fairness are inherently subjective concepts has confounded the profession's attempts to define them operationally. CPAs tend to rely on their professional judgment for definitions, perhaps because all do not agree on the requisite criteria.

When the problem was first noticed, the profession should have formally recognized the need for explicit criteria, undertaken the necessary research, and developed authoritative criteria that met the needs of information users. Financial information would now be closer to what users expect it to be, and the profession would be fulfilling its social function more honestly.

The profession should now sponsor the necessary empirical and conceptual research to develop operational definitions. User needs appear to be quite diverse, however, so it may be difficult to draw meaningful generalizations on which to base the appropriate criteria. How can the profession achieve a consensus among its members? Should materiality take into consideration the size of an enterprise as well?

If the profession itself cannot define materiality, then arbitrary and poorly conceived criteria for defining it may be imposed by governmental regulatory authorities. Courts also might determine such standards after the fact. The profession would fail to uphold its public service ideal and would provide users with information not really useful to them. Losses from lawsuits would increase as accountants continued to miss immaterial but large items in audits.

Meeting Demands for Increased Corporate Disclosure

Federal agencies such as the SEC, IRS, FTC, FPC, and CASB have encroached on the accounting and financial reporting responsibilities of corporate management by increasing their demands for supplementary reports. The profession, rather than resisting the invasion, has complicated matters and overreacted by insisting on a large number of rule changes. Whether such a strategy can deflect the underlying threat of legal liability is moot; its most telling result is to expand the need for disclosure and accompanying rules.

The AICPA and individual CPA firms have taken issue separately with federal agencies on their proposals and rules. Federal agencies have ignored the profession, perhaps in part because it has not presented a united front. The FASB has not yet reacted to the issue; the AICPA will probably preempt the FASB's authority. Governmental agencies will not wait for the FASB to act.

Respondents wished that the profession had given more support to the APB, which perhaps could have influenced the government agencies. The profession's only chance now is to fully support the FASB, though individual firms are reluctant to give that support when FASB views run counter to their own. The AICPA and CPA firms should challenge any federal agency that tries to set accounting rules or principles, but the SEC would take disciplinary action against the CPA firms and force them to comply with its own thinking. Governmental agencies use their mandated power to achieve compliance. "If push came to shove," one respondent said, the profession would find that "business would not support it."

The profession should involve corporate accountants in the rulemaking process; had it done so, rules would now be in effect rather than in development by the FASB. Perhaps the profession should seek congressional assistance in sorting out the legal issues involved, though Congress is generally apathetic.

The profession should stop settling cases out of court. In court the real issues have a chance of being resolved. Such resolution would be worth the additional legal expenses incurred. In any event CPAs could ultimately pass such extra costs on to the client.

If the profession does not clearly define its own standards, the government will surely step in more aggressively to do so. There would be continued legal problems, higher legal costs, and eventual lack of confidence in the accounting profession.

The Hidden Problem of Pension Reserves

The profession has not pressed companies to quantify or disclose their pension liabilities. The commitment to provide pensions is not properly disclosed in most annual reports; neither is the commitment's impact on the future stream of corporate income assessed. Good figures are unavailable, and the effect of changing assumptions on the aggregate liability at any given date remains uncertain.

Had the profession insisted on much more disclosure when it first recognized the problem, pensions would probably have been deferred to future periods. In wage negotiations, it is often easier to give way on pension cost concessions because the impact is not felt at the time.

The profession should study the problem further, possibly together with the economics profession (the National Bureau of Economic Research is presently considering such a study). Some portion of the deferred pension costs may be considered a real liability and should be kept on the balance sheet. Although such actuarial and investment decisions should perhaps be made public, American corporations would resist any addition to their already lengthy list of disclosures. Yet the sum tied up in pension reserves is larger than the total equity of many American companies. In the end, the public, the press, and government will continue to be misinformed if these costs are not disclosed.

3 Rulemaking

Standard setting or rulemaking is crucial because it is the way the profession solves its technical and measurement problems. Once accepted, the solution to a problem (for example, how to value goodwill or inventories) becomes a standard that must be observed by accountants, implying that it should both resist obsolescence and be enforceable. The process by which a solution is sought is democratic and consensus-seeking, not autocratic. To have the force of law when no body of the profession is empowered to give it the force of law, a standard must emanate from a widely respected source.

Highlights

Too many ad hoc rules have become standards. The results are that more rules are required to cover even slightly different situations; they do not resist obsolescence; they require less judgment to interpret, demeaning the CPA; and their specificity facilitates litigation against CPAs. It takes time and deliberation for the FASB to devise a standard to solve a certain problem. But meanwhile auditors need to solve it for their clients; as a result, solutions are not uniform across the profession and each firm becomes a standard setter, if only temporarily. The confusion and duplication produced explain why government regulatory agencies have often stepped in to make rules for the profession. Such intervention threatens the stature and legitimacy of the FASB and bodes ill for the acceptability of its pronouncements. On the other hand, coherent, consistent GAAP cannot be devised in the absence of an underlying theoretical framework.

Need to Define GAAP

The current GAAP are not general enough. The profession's strategy has been to augment its body of accepted accounting principles by incremental rules in response to individual problems as they occur, rather than to define principles that could guide action on a class of problems. As a result, the demand for more rules continues to outstrip the profession's ability to make them; the specificity of the rules exposes accountants to lawsuits; and in trying to catch up by means of these incremental rules, the profession does not have the time or "distance" to draw up a set of GAAP that will apply broadly and gain wide acceptance.

51

Recent lawsuits have demonstrated that accounting principles are no longer able to delineate the role and responsibilities of CPAs. In the past forty years, according to an auditor, the profession has "continued to rehash many accounting practices without resolving any of them." New accounting practices arise without any authoritative basis, and the public becomes suspicious of the resulting financial information. Another auditor complains that GAAP are uniform neither in construct nor in application, and until the basic principles of accounting are spelled out, the FASB will continue to "reshuffle the rulemaking function" without making any real improvement.

Respondents were troubled about the range of accounting methods permitted by the current GAAP. Radically different financial answers are produced, depending on which method is used. Because the profession takes a laissez faire approach and does not specify the conditions under which accountants may use different methods, companies and accountants are free to use whatever method conveys the financial picture they desire. The result is a degrading of financial information and of the work of CPAs.

Widely differing accounting practices, even within the same industry, also distort results and prevent comparability among financial reports. Examples are LIFO versus FIFO inventory valuations, accelerated versus straight-line depreciation methods, and including versus ignoring the effects of inflation. The very diversity of these accounting practices makes it difficult to distinguish between correct and incorrect accounting. This situation compounds an existing problem: lawsuits by third parties often rely on accounting measurements.

Another reason for the inconsistency and inefficiency in standard setting is the multiplicity of standard-setting bodies. In the profession itself there are the AICPA and its own rulemaking committees, the FASB, and the larger firms. Lack of adequate action by the FASB has led to the involvement of the SEC, IASC, CASB, and AICPA. The profession verbally supports the FASB but undercuts it in practice by establishing the IASC as a potential force for standard setting in accounting and by enlarging AudSEC's role. Although the AICPA itself established the FASB in part to address this problem, it is still not clear who should be setting standards. Nor is it clear who will have the authority to enforce them, once set. The FASB has yet to prove itself in meeting these challenges.

One respondent criticized the FASB for its narrow perception of the profession's role in society today. It views accounting as little more than an extension of double-entry bookkeeping. Another pointed to its failure to establish the broad principles by which new problems could be solved. Despite the support and encouragement it has received, the FASB is hampered by its structure and its inherited backlog of problems from dealing effectively with emerging problems.

The FASB, of course, represents constituencies other than accountants. Rather than aiding effective solutions to problems, an accounting educator noted, its special interests have been an obstacle. It was no better before; giving the FASB the power to set accounting standards was an admission by the AICPA of its own failure. The FASB's job is complicated by the SEC's frequent shifts of position and its lack of support for FASB conclusions, by the FASB's own slowness and lack of objectivity, and by congressional actions (which the respondent did not specify) that are contrary to the FASB's intent. Another respondent believed that much of the FASB's work has become political. The FASB has not clearly defined its role relative to the SEC; it needs a better procedure for selecting board members; it moves too slowly on issues, despite their increasing complexity. Much of FASB's research is too esoteric, generalized, and irrelevant to the real world. Nor is it persuasive enough to force the desired consensus.

The FASB's pronouncements turn out to be ineffective because the SEC often disagrees with them; because various management groups and accounting firms, which often adopt their own solutions while waiting for a pronouncement to appear, do not always agree with them or carry them out; and because the profession has no means of enforcing uniform compliance with them.

The AICPA has explored the possibility of establishing separate GAAP for a company's external and internal reports. Practitioners objected, fearing that standards requiring less than full disclosure from the client would expose the preparer to legal liability.

Disagreement within the profession on the appropriate remedial efforts is another stumbling block. Should standards be based on the needs of the CPA, on what can be enforced, or on the needs of management? What about the interests of investors? Current remedial efforts depend on the private-sector approach of setting standards by consensus, an inherently difficult process. Consider the problem of reaching agreement on standardized practices for each industry. Each national accounting firm supports its own client's position for fear of losing the client, rather than taking a broader view that may be best for the profession. Clients, for their part, refuse to be constrained, preferring the flexibility of accounting options. The profession has not recognized that a private-sector group without enforcement power cannot do the job. The profession needs the help of a public agency able to force management compliance with the rules.

Competitiveness among large, medium, and small CPA firms has impeded attempts to solve this problem. Each group wants resources directed to the problems it perceives. Too much emphasis is thus placed on status, and the smaller firms feel that their views are neglected. Consider the difficulty the profession has had in reaching agreement on the objectives of financial reporting. Each attempt to solve the problem has been made without the necessary frame of reference. Personal preferences of the committee and of AICPA and FASB board members taint resolution of the issues and force compromises. Moreover, no sounding board is available for the profession to assess the consequences of emerging business practices that may affect financial reporting.

The AICPA's accounting procedures committee, the APB, and the AAA, have all had some success in reducing the number of accounting alternatives. But definitive resolution remains elusive. An auditor said, "if success means that each set of accounting problems shall have only one answer, then I doubt that it will be achieved. . . . [Yet] without that degree of success, I believe the FASB effort will not be effective. . . . It will take time, a lot of time." That comment well portrays the differing expectations of CPAs themselves, another pressure imposed on the FASB and its work. Tough issues are hardly ever resolved, and agreement on others is achieved only after a very long time.

When the profession became aware that GAAP were inadequate, it should have

established an independent board whose pronouncements would have been binding on all. This would have led to fewer confrontations with the SEC, fewer legal actions against CPAs, and more public confidence in the profession.

adopted the premise that different users of financial statements require different types of information and then established GAAP on that basis.

been more objective rather than self-serving. There would now be less confusion in interpreting financial statements and less intervention by the SEC and Congress in determining GAAP.

convinced the SEC to let the AICPA delineate GAAP, which the SEC would then enforce on registrants. The responsibility for GAAP should never have been delegated to the FASB; it should have been retained in a revitalized, full-time APB, its membership broadened to include representatives from the various sectors of the business community. One body, the AICPA, would then have been responsible for all GAAP, and only one body would have had to relate to the SEC.

sponsored more organized and pragmatic research, carried out more by "case-oriented analytical" researchers than by "ivory tower" ones.

perceived the need for collaboration between the academic world, the financial executives, the legal profession, and CPAs. Much present conflict might have been avoided, and solutions to problems would have been more widely accepted.

developed methods to account for the effects of inflation on financial statements, eliminated alternative accounting treatments of financial transactions, narrowed the choice of accounting principles, and created a body to enforce its principles with on-the-spot opinions and decisions. Reports for investors, managers, bankers, and creditors would now be more informative and realistic, and it might have prevented the disclosure of events after investors had already been defrauded.

One respondent admonished firms to support the FASB in striving for consensus on pronouncements by putting the profession ahead of their personal positions. The FASB for its part should speedily finish defining the objectives of financial reporting to provide a frame of reference for future deliberations. The requirement that five of the seven board members approve all decisions slows the FASB's progress and thus compromises many of its objectives. The present business environment—increased activity of the SEC and CASB, the uncertain state of the economy, and the public's distrust of accounting practices—all make the FASB's job more difficult. The time it will take to establish financial reporting objectives will leave less time to devote to other pressing problems. Yet, as another respondent pointed out, expediting the process of issuing standards may slight consideration of some aspects of a standard. Moreover, client-firm relations may become strained as a result of ill-founded changes brought about by the new standard, alienating the segments of the profession that side with those clients.

There should be a sounding body to notify the FASB of emerging practice trends and to get it to act without delay. Regrettably, the profession cannot agree on what an emerging practice is, the FASB cannot act quickly because of its overcrowded agenda and its "due process" approach, and the SEC might intervene if it did not agree with the resolution produced. The FASB ought to include an appeals court to consider controversies and dispose of them promptly. Some firms or constituencies might not recognize such a group, and CPAs might disregard the procedures or even withdraw from membership in the AICPA. The FASB should identify the problems that must be resolved, place them in priority order, set up a timetable for their resolution, and then organize itself to meet that agenda. Such a program would require the cooperation of the SEC and CASB.

The FASB should ask the ten or twelve largest national firms to submit a list of the principles on which they all agree. The FASB might then adopt them as the nucleus of a complete list of accepted GAAP. That measure would probably not succeed because corporate management, through the FEI, would object to the "attempt to put management in a straitjacket"; and CPAs not in the firms consulted would protest being neglected.

Other suggestions centered on whether the FASB should perform the standard-setting function. One idea was to press for a conference between the FASB, CASB, SEC, IASC, and AICPA to set ground rules on who would be responsible for what, apart from existing legal responsibilities. Another called for the FASB to join with the SEC, the NYSE, or even the CASB to acquire the enforcement powers it lacks. Three obstacles would have to be overcome: (1) Neither the SEC nor the NYSE wants the job and may need prodding from Congress to take it. (2) The FASB might resent the subsidiary role the scheme implies. (3) There is an ideological conflict within the profession about explicitly recognizing government as an essential part of the profession.

One respondent urged that the AICPA support the FASB in every action it takes despite disagreement by individual members; relegate AudSEC to a minor role or even eliminate it; cease its participation in IASC and instead encourage the FASB to represent American accountants in IASC. Other respondents urged the AICPA to bring the FASB back into its sphere of control. They pointed out that the Financial Accounting Foundation, for all practical purposes an arm of the AICPA, has not found an effective way of funding the FASB. Of course, business would object strenuously and would surely pressure Congress to oppose the action. The SEC, as a result, might assert itself again and assume eminent domain over the setting of GAAP. One respondent said that if the FASB fails, the profession should insist that the AICPA be allowed to try once more to solve these problems on its own.

Five other miscellaneous suggestions are worth noting:

The AICPA should form an official group to discipline departures from GAAP quickly and effectively. Such self-criticism might, however, invite others to criticize the profession; also, if members are "convicted" by their peers, it would be more difficult to mount an adequate defense against outsiders' lawsuits.

The profession needs a program of research to clean up the problems of GAAP as they apply to industry, such as historical-cost accounting, determining meaningful principles for not-for-profit programs, and how to eliminate balancing features of financial statements. CPAs traditionally trained would resist such a program; so would lay organizations that have developed fund accounting and object-of-expenditure systems without official approval from the profession.

To understand the problem of using accounting alternatives, the profession should explore the reasons for management's preference for a given accounting treatment in a specific situation and require management to explain those reasons to financial statement users. Of course, managements would be reluctant to divulge their real reasons; accountants, because of their legal vulnerability, would be reluctant to insist on such disclosure.

Solutions should not be sought collaboratively; the results might differ from those wanted by the profession and might weaken any enforcement mechanism. Collaboration with the IASC should cease; business environments and accounting practices differ so much in each country that rules drawn up to fit the international arena may be inapplicable in this country. It would needlessly complicate the profession's already difficult job.

The profession should insist that whenever a company changes auditors it must explain the reasons to its investors.

Three consequences of the profession's failure to resolve this problem soon were frequently mentioned: the government would take over the setting of GAAP and perhaps all auditing functions of the profession; the profession's prestige and public confidence would erode further; and unrealistic and inaccurate financial statements would proliferate.

The SEC might step in to set standards for the profession or regulate GAAP more closely. Congress might even legislate accounting principles or nationalize the profession, putting it under the control of the SEC or the GAO. The accounting profession would then consist of government-employed auditors. It would lose the attest function to the SEC or another government agency and cease to exist as a profession. Or, business consortiums with power and prestige might write the rules, and other professionals might fill the vacuum. Accounting might even become a branch of the law.

The profession would lose credibility with the financial community; its integrity would be questioned more frequently, its standards lowered, its professional stature degraded; and the profession would eventually fall into disrepute.

Different financial statements for different purposes would result. They would not be comparable, would reflect "muddled" work, would continue to mislead, and would lack consistency and uniformity. Capital available to private industry would be depleted because of the payment of excessive taxes on inflated profits. Investments and capital would be poorly deployed. The nation's resources would be misallocated, and the capital markets still distrusted. Users of financial statements would remain confused. Chaos would result if every accounting firm set its own standards.

The volume of litigation against accountants would cause the courts to play a stronger role in deciding accounting principles. In turn, more litigation would result, especially class-action suits, based on allegedly misleading financial statements.

The FASB will do nothing more than the APB did, namely fight the brush fires ignited by alternative accounting practices. As a result, it will become a puppet for the SEC or will die. Industry will drop its financial and moral support of the FASB.

The rate of social change would accentuate the inability of CPAs to provide needed services to an increasingly service-oriented society. The CPA's role would cease to have public utility if it came to be limited to an attest function based on outmoded GAAP and GAAS. The rising costs of complying with the ever-increasing complexities of reporting would encourage smaller businesses to turn to practitioners who are not regulated by the profession. More practitioners will fail to keep up with changing requirements and technology, and substandard work will become more common. CPAs will become more timid, afraid to make changes or to innovate. The quality of entrants to the profession, and the profession's ability to attract qualified ones, will deteriorate.

Need for an Underlying Theory or Framework
to Support GAAP

The profession needs to develop a broad conceptual framework for accounting in order to satisfy the needs of users of financial statements. No standard-setting body can issue rational accounting standards in the absence of such a framework. Accounting has developed neither a clear statement of its purposes and basic standards, nor a consistent, logical set of accounting principles, what one might call a theory of accounting.

Instead of being based on ad hoc responses to problems, GAAP should have been derived from a set of postulates or basic concepts. The profession has had difficulty obtaining general acceptance of FASB pronouncements; the FASB seems to reinvent the wheel each time it develops a new "principle." The profession needs to define circumstances or axioms from which certain rules would follow.

Attempts by the APB, educators, and certain CPA firms to develop a conceptual framework have been fruitless because they used a piecemeal approach. They have been unable to reach a consensus because of their fear of alienating certain segments of the economic system, too strong a commitment to precedents and tradition, failure to identify the information needs of users through empirical research, adherence to vested interests by large corporations, and honest differences among accountants. Not having underlying standards in the first place makes the solution of individual problems all the more difficult.

APB Statement 4, issued in October 1970, was a step toward developing a more consistent and comprehensive structure of financial accounting. But such pronouncements have limited effect because they do not change, supersede, or interpret GAAP. The October 1973 report of the Accounting Objectives Study Group did not lend itself to formal adoption by the accounting profession. The study group merely intended the report to be considered a contribution to the profession's literature. And then the profession created the FASB, which took too long to develop its statement, "Conceptual Framework for Accounting and Reporting." No exposure draft was issued, and priorities were soon directed to other areas. The FASB seemed to lose interest. Now it is dealing only with the problem's first layer, the objectives of accounting. It will have to follow up with a complete set of objectives, definitions of key terms (particularly income and assets), a set of broad principles deduced from the objectives, and standards and procedures. Complications are the tendency of auditors to demand precise, all-inclusive rules without regard to circumstances and the tendency of circumstances to be too varied to catalog in a rule book.

One respondent said the AICPA should have committed its entire resources to "polishing" and adopting Sprouse and Moonitz's ARS 3, "A Tentative Set of Broad Accounting Principles for Business Enterprises," written in 1962. Historical-cost accounting would then have given way to "current-value accounting with general price-level-adjusted or common dollars as the unit of measure." No longer would GAAP have been responsible for inconsistent and misleading financial statements, which would have exposed accountants to less legal liability and better press and given it more prestige. The profession should also have acted more promptly in defining the uses and purposes of financial reports and in developing a conceptual framework for solving accounting problems.

Another respondent thought the profession should begin immediately to draft a basic framework for accounting, resisting any pressure to divert attention to solving individual problems. It would be accused of ignoring other important problems and would have to face the possibility that new postulates might make present GAAP obsolete.

If the FASB should give the matter its highest priority, it should not take more than a few months to complete its study, "Conceptual Framework for Financial Accounting and Reporting: Objectives, Qualitative Characteristics, and Information." Robert Sprouse, a member of the board, has already developed a good set of broad principles. First, the FASB has to develop a set of objectives. Whatever they may be, a set of accounting principles would flow logically from them. The trouble is that some constituencies, such as management and investors, would be disappointed if their concepts were not adopted and could pressure the profession enough to scuttle the project.

Unless the FASB attacks the problem, it will go the way of the APB. It cannot succeed if it continues to provide ad hoc solutions. The FASB is the profession's last opportunity to keep the standard-setting function within the private sector. If it fails, the SEC would increase its influence over the profession and usurp the AICPA's leadership role.

The stature and prestige of the profession would suffer. The profession would continue to make a fool of itself, continue to "muddle through" with political compromises, continue to sanction more accounting alternatives. GAAP will remain conventional and will become generally accepted by tacit agreement rather than by formal derivation from a set of basic concepts and postulates. In a constantly changing environment each new GAAP runs the risk of contradicting existing principles. Each newly issued pronouncement will have to undergo the same critical analysis of possible alternatives rather than a mere test of the degree to which it fits the basic postulates.

4 Independence

Of all the critical problems that emerged in the survey, none raised hackles as much as the accusation—or even the implication—that accountants are not independent.

Highlights

Auditors may not be absolutely independent, but they are sufficiently so; the issue is not whether they are independent but how independent. Neither corporations nor their accountants see reason to change present arrangements except by slow, evolutionary increments.

Management retains significant control over the auditing process, choosing accounting principles to suit its purposes, determining the length and scope of an audit, and hiring and firing auditors. And competition pressures CPA firms to nurture existing accounts and gain new ones. Nevertheless, accountants claim that their primary allegiance is to the general public. No one doubts that that is what they want, but professing independence and being independent are very different. No change will result if accountants are intent on protecting special interests and the status quo in the short run.

Whether a conflict of interest exists when a firm provides both auditing and management advisory services to the same client depends more on the firm's attitude than on the facts of the situation. So long as accountants believe they are *serving* management when auditing it rather than *checking* its performance, the interest they serve will remain that of the company that pays them and not that of the unseen people who rely on the company's financial statements. The trend toward establishing audit committees composed wholly or mainly of outside directors to select the auditing firm and manage the audit engagement is a step in the right direction.

The Auditor-Client Relationship

The number of suits filed against major accounting firms, actions by the SEC, and statements made by district attorneys, state legislators, and congressmen all indicate that the profession lacks the required degree of independence in carrying out its attest function in behalf of third parties. Independence means

61

freedom from the influence of management during the audit engagement. Often management demands that the accountant present the company's financial picture to reflect most favorably on its trusteeship of the enterprise. Some firms resist such demands, though at the risk of losing the account.

Critics cite the high fees paid to public accountants as evidence of their dependence on the client; accountants thus have little financial incentive to change, they reason. Yet critics need to be reminded that when management and accountant disagree, the accountant does have influence derived from the SEC, which empowers him to perform independently according to accounting principles.

The profession's inaction has stemmed from its refusal to acknowledge that such dependence on the client affects the objectivity of financial reports. The APB failed to solve this problem, according to one respondent, because its members often pleaded the cases of their clients instead of their own convictions. The FASB will also fail unless it remains impartial and stands firm on its findings. One respondent pointed out, however, that the problem has less to do with accounting principles or auditing standards than with the quality of auditing.

The profession has also tried to police itself through greater emphasis on peer review. But it is hard to get a firm to change its procedures unless assurance is given that it will not be subject to penalties for prior infractions. Another mechanism for monitoring infractions has been the joint regional trial boards, composed of AICPA officers and certain state boards. They have fallen short of expectations because state boards, often resentful of the national institute's intrusion into their affairs, withhold full cooperation.

The profession has also imposed stricter requirements for continuing professional education on all accountants. That measure is criticized for not reaching the "offenders" and for not directly attacking the problem of independence. Higher ethical standards have been set regarding accountants' ownership of stock in client firms, but without any enforcement machinery. The AICPA has given verbal support to firms that when locked in dispute with a client have threatened to resign from the account and bring the problem before the SEC. But another CPA firm has always been waiting to take management's position on the controversy—and secure the account—and the matter has been dropped. Accounting firms are not wont to report even apparently unethical behavior of other firms, such as picking up an account resigned by the former firm to preserve its independence.

One respondent noted that the profession has recommended that an audit committee hire the auditor and monitor the results of the audit on behalf of management but independent of it. The recommendation has not been widely enough adopted, perhaps because many are still skeptical of such a committee's actual independence from management.

Although the respondents recognized that there are no simple answers, especially when the lack of independence is not acknowledged as a problem, they suggested various specific remedies that should have been tried. For example, the profession should have made it more difficult for a client to change its method of accounting or accounting procedures against the auditor's recommendation. An auditor should be able to render a qualified opinion without risk of losing the account; and more reports of client intransigence should have been reported to the SEC, to bring the legal power of the SEC on the auditor's side. A corporate financial executive suggested that the profession should have withdrawn its insistence that financial reports be prepared in accordance with GAAP. Audits should have been conducted, and reports certified, consistent only with the client's system of internal controls and current method of external reporting.

As for what the profession should do now, respondents made the following suggestions. The profession should

develop a strong lobbying body to press for legislation that will ensure independence. A lobbying effort cannot be mounted, however, until agreement has been reached on the problems.

require firms to separate their tax and MAS activities from their audit work. CPA greed is an obstacle.

disclose significant results based on management statements rather than on objective evidence. The result, however, would be excessive footnotes and objections by management.

limit the legal liability that accountants can bear, as has been done in some foreign countries.

improve public relations efforts, though the action might be thought self-serving.

persuade CPAs to distinguish their responsibilities from those of management and to secure an agreement, before the audit, about what happens in the event of a dispute. The profession might object that it would have to give up its prerogatives and authority.

fight nuisance suits vigorously and in the open. Accountants are too afraid of being sued; they settle suits they should fight. They are victims, like other professionals, of unscrupulous attorneys. Forceful legal actions such as slander and countersuits may be necessary against some.

One respondent urged the profession to shift attention from legal liability concerns to performing excellent audits for financial statement users. Another suggested that the profession stop trying to make all financial statements comparable among companies and instead point out the usefulness and fairness of the company's statements compared with the auditor's findings. Despite possible criticism that subjectivity rather than objectivity would thus dominate the preparation of financial statements, there is nothing wrong with subjective opinions so long as they are developed professionally and independently.

CPA firms should be more willing to resign from accounts. They should examine how clear management's information would be to a prospective user and be less willing to accept management's opinion. That might increase the expense to the client and the responsibility of the CPA. Because disagreements with management center on issues for which different interpretations lead to different solutions, disputes lend themselves to accusations by management that the auditor is infringing on its prerogatives. For that reason, when a firm resigns from an account because of disagreement, it should take pains to present the problem fairly to the SEC. It should also insist on verification from relevant people below the top management level.

Unless the profession solves this problem soon, the investing public will continue to lose confidence in it, and government agencies will attempt to control the profession. Malpractice lawsuits will continue to be brought against CPAs, preventing the extension of potentially useful services by accountants, who are even now afraid to undertake the preparation of forecasts or other innovations. Overall the accountants' effectiveness in producing financial statements will diminish. Conflict between corporations and their accountants will increase. CPAs will seek to protect themselves from greater exposure to legal liability, perhaps through defensive audits or by greatly increasing their legal staffs and internal control procedures. Companies may respond by disclosing too much material. As a result, financial reports will become so complex that even professional security analysts will have difficulty dealing with the amount of information being given them.

Allegiance to the Client versus Responsibility to the Public Interest

Accountants have yet to solve the conflict between the desire to serve their clients, including management and equity owners, and their responsibility to the public. The recent scandals involving corporations such as Penn Central, Equity Funding, and Goodbody & Co., and their accounting firms, the criminal sanctions imposed by the courts against individual accountants, and the increased government surveillance of the profession and intrusion into its historical policymaking prerogatives have raised the issue to a critical level.

The problem is complicated because maintaining independence depends on professional "integrity" and therefore cannot be legislated or ordained, the profession is reluctant to admit wrongdoing by acknowledging the existence of such conflicts, and the leading accounting firms do not want to offend their competitors. (This last reason is presumably a reference to the strong ties between the larger firms, such that a blemish on the reputation of any one reflects on all the others and could prompt new legislation that would limit the freedoms of all firms.)

In an effort to solve the problem the profession has created the semiautonomous FASB, but the FASB is too closely linked to the AICPA. The policy process is too far removed from the needs and participation of clients on the one hand and of the public on the other. Independence means that public responsibility and disclosure should override the concerns of the client. Yet the profession has not taken this stand. If it had, it would have taken disciplinary action against violations by its members and would have recovered some of the public confidence it has lost.

Being primarily responsible to the public is a concept difficult to realize in practice. While making public accountants truly public has a nice sound, the profession has been fighting it for years. Accountants continue to regard the companies they audit as "the client" while professing independence in serving the public. They should drop the pretense. Their interests are tied to the fee-paying abilities of their clients. Because this philosophy does not make good press, the pretense continues.

Two other suggestions are worth noting. One is that the profession establish a code of behavior for individual accountants and firms, even at the risk of hurting some big firms. It should also establish a board to police the code and adjudicate complaints. Because of the danger that the revelation of improper actions by a few will hurt the entire profession, it may not be realistic to take any action against any member. In any event the profession needs to periodically review the accountant's professional privilege—what it means to be a CPA. The other suggestion is that the profession should shift the burden of setting accounting standards to a public agency and concentrate more on lobbying, auditing standards, and technical development. There would probably be a strong reaction to this proposal from those who want policymaking kept in the private sector.

If the profession does not clearly declare its primary responsibility to the public, companies will continue to seek accounting firms that do not make trouble for them, and CPA firms will less often take a stand for fear of losing a client. The profession's self-interest would come under public scrutiny, possibly with open discussion of auditors' fees and their technical competence. Conflict of interest would continue to interfere with the setting of standards, in turn degrading the quality of financial information provided to the public. Legal actions against accountants will proliferate and result in costly settlements and higher insurance costs; confrontations with regulatory agencies will intensify.

It is just a matter of time before policies and laws will be made to clarify the profession's role and primary responsibility; by taking the initiative, the profession would buttress its autonomy and strengthen its reputation.

**Auditing and Management Advisory
Services for the Same Client**

So long as the profession sanctions the provision of auditing and management advisory services to the same client, it is promoting a conflict of interest. As beneficial as the dual role might be to an individual firm, it is detrimental to the profession's interests in the long run. The profession should forbid the independent auditor from engaging in any activity but auditing for an audit client. The auditor should be required to disclose in the 10-K filing the various peripheral services it performs for the client and the fees it collects. Third parties could then assess for themselves the degree of independence exercised by the firm. One respondent thought the accountant should be an independent referee or fact finder for the public. Providing peripheral services to management and stockholders impedes that role. Inaction with respect to the conflict will surely exact a toll of greater regulation by government agencies.

Perhaps the problem stems from the belief of CPAs that they, more than other professionals, provide the best management advisory services in the business. Critics contend that they have strayed too far from the traditional definitions of accountant and accounting. Nonaudit work has led the profession into areas in which its practitioners are not qualified and has heightened the conflict-of-interest problem. The profession has also failed to prescribe acceptable practice in management advisory services and has not recognized the need to do so. Computer analysis and management scientists, rapidly becoming more sophisticated than accountants, are intensifying competition with the latter for MAS accounts.

The issue cannot be drawn in black or white. It is as unrealistic to consider MAS a bona fide accounting function as it is to prohibit a CPA firm from providing MAS. Firms, fearing loss of substantial income (and inside information) will never give up their MAS units. Two main remedies were proposed: confining the scope of practice to auditing and bringing specialization into the profession.

Proscribing MAS would cause undue hardship among firms that derive much of their business from MAS and other nonauditing activities. They would inherit a large personnel problem; through no real fault of their own, they would be violating a "good faith" relationship with employees who do not meet the definition of auditor. Lawsuits would challenge the profession's right to eliminate aspects of practice. Career opportunities for many practitioners would be severely curtailed.

Possible specialties include tax accounting, auditing, SEC regulations, computer auditing, and information systems. For each one the profession would specify standards for qualification, practice, and continuing education. The strongest objection would come from those who felt unable to meet the standards. Objections would also come from lone practitioners or small firms whose business depends on their being generalists and having a variety of skills. They would argue that they could not compete effectively unless qualified in all specialties. CPAs are opposed to losing clients in any aspect of their practice and thus cannot take an objective view on any issue where loss of business is a possible outcome.

Another approach called for a new role and designation for the CPA—general practitioner of business management and consulting. He could then call on a multidisciplinary team of specialists to respond to client problems and opportunities. Such a radical change would probably destroy public acceptance of the CPA and his traditional image. It would also fragment and probably destroy the profession as we now know it.

The profession should conclusively decide to whom it is primarily responsible. Once that decision is made, others will follow naturally. The profession could organize itself so that auditors were paid by the SEC or the stock exchanges from a fund assessed on all publicly held companies and rotate firms or partners with respect to an audit engagement. The idea is radical, and the inbred conservatism of the profession and fear of new approaches would have to be overcome. Corporate managements would also resist it, and it might prove very costly to implement.

If the profession does not resolve the problem, resolution may ultimately have to come from the courts. The criticism that CPAs are not truly independent will continue, bringing with it a rash of lawsuits and heavy financial claims. Government agencies might force a separation of auditing and MAS, prohibit nonaudit activities by CPA firms, or even take over the auditing function entirely, thus nationalizing the profession to meet the SEC's requirement of independence in the audit function.

5 Technical Standards and Performance

Though the number of lawsuits accountants have lost has been growing steadily, those cases represent a very small percentage of all the audits performed. Still fewer can readily be traced to careless or shoddy work—"substandard performance." Respondents focused on the matter because it is a serious, rather than a pervasive, problem.

Highlights

The central issue is the definition of accountants' competence. No consensus has emerged, and the rapidly shifting technologies and environment of accounting have made it extremely difficult to distinguish competent from substandard work. Perhaps because of that difficulty, accountants have favored general solutions to the problem, such as mandatory continuing education, accepting graduates only from professional schools of accounting, and registering all firms that audit publicly held companies. Certainly they have had no standards for gauging competence.

Although many states now require continuing education as a condition for maintaining the CPA license, critics contend that the courses often do not address substantive issues and are uneven in quality. Those claiming that substandard work stems from an unprofessional attitude believe that only specialized schools of accounting can inculcate a professional identity. Critics of professional schools point out the disadvantages of narrow training compared with a business school's broader education. Respondents also criticized the profession for developing and accrediting professional schools of accounting without involving educators in the planning.

Audits often suffer from unrealistic time and budget constraints and from the assignment of inexperienced staff. Despite steps taken by individual firms to correct the problem, mandatory peer review programs seem inevitable.

Another reason for substandard performance may be that auditors have not fully exploited the computer as an auditing tool and are sluggish in responding to the demand for auditing computer-based systems. Neither subject has received adequate attention in the CPA examination or in continuing education courses.

Substandard Performance

The criticism aimed at the profession from within and outside stems from the feeling that accountants are professionally incompetent. As evidence, witness the increasing emphasis on continuing education by the various state boards and the legislative trend toward compulsory periodic renewal of accountants' licenses. Witness also the profession's effort to define a "body of knowledge" for accounting and its push for the establishment and accreditation of professional schools of accounting. Efforts to persuade the public of accountants' competence simply add insult to injury.

A corporate financial executive estimated that one-third to one-quarter of all CPAs in public practice perform substandard work. Public acceptance of the profession's technical standards cannot be expected until the profession's members subscribe to them more thoroughly; the whole profession is drawing criticism from the poor work of a few.

The profession should become more aggressive in monitoring and dealing with substandard work, in auditing and preparing financial reports. Yet identifying the less competent practitioners is not easy: substandard reports are hard to come by when creditors and others refuse to turn them over to the proper authorities for peer review.

The profession's encouragement of firms to develop and train their own staffs is a remedy that is "too little and too late." The long-term solution may be to raise the profession's entrance standards, which now require college courses, on-the-job experience, and passing the CPA exam. Again, because such standards are legislated by each state, nationwide change is difficult to implement.

The Roy-McNeill study attempted to determine the profession's common body of knowledge, and later the Beamer report recommended improvements in accounting education. But the field of accounting has become too broad, eclectic, and pluralistic to be represented by a single body of knowledge. If the profession had broadened the inquiry to embrace all relevant disciplines, it could have drawn more broadly from business schools and not just from the very narrow segment that specializes in accounting. The profession should consider expanding the CPA examination, following the example of the CMA exam, to cover a much broader knowledge base. This might force accounting subjects of long standing to give way to relevant material from other disciplines.

The profession should do nothing until it has thoroughly studied the requirements and attributes of competent CPA performance, and then it should restructure the profession accordingly. The results would improve the quality of the individual practitioner and over the long term would resolve the problem of substandard performance. Admittedly, achieving consensus on CPA competence would be extremely difficult.

The AICPA proposal now before the SEC to register firms instead of individuals would require a certain level of quality-control procedures in the firms registered. They would also have to undergo periodic field reviews. But unless the plan elicits wide acceptance and full support from participants, it may only divide the profession further. The profession would need to secure assurances by the SEC and other governmental agencies that they would accept such a registration program along with their own review programs. The SEC is often unwilling to accept any program that it can mandate on its own authority. Clients should also be persuaded that the expense of a high-quality audit will represent a large savings over the long run.

To monitor the quality of a firm's performance, the profession has developed peer-review programs. They are still very tentative, experimental, and limited in scope. The firm being reviewed has been given no opportunity to disclose the results of the review, so neither the firms nor the financial press are satisfied that the program will achieve its purpose. State societies and the AICPA have together established programs to review general practices and financial statement certification. Experience has shown, however, that the firms and individuals who need these reviews most do not volunteer for them.

Peer reviews could have a salutary effect on the practice of competitive bidding. Firms often promise more than they can deliver in the time or for the money, lowering audit quality. The profession should have ensured that firms adhered strictly to its injunction against competitive bidding.

The widespread offering of programs of continuing education has been a valuable step, though the quality of the courses is still very uneven. Many of them are inferior and unimaginative. Yet, on the AICPA recommendation, some state societies have made continuing education a condition for practicing. However, educational courses offered by state societies are not of high quality. To comply with the law (which varies from state to state), the courses must be general enough to be within the average (low) knowledge level of practitioners. In fact, as with review programs, those who need the education most (those who do the most substandard work) do not take advantage of it.

If substandard performance continues unabated, many present responsibilities will not be met, and future opportunities for the profession may be lost. Practitioners who fail to comply with standards will damage the profession's public image, degrade the profession's product, and lower average compensation levels for CPAs everywhere. For firms practicing before the SEC, it is just a matter of time before a quality-control review program is instituted. If the profession does not take the initiative, the federal government will. Critics look in vain for tangible evidence that the profession is seriously addressing the problem of substandard performance. Finally, members doing substandard work will find themselves much more vulnerable to legal liability as accepted standards become more precise.

Continuing Professional Education

The question of continuing education for members of the profession is a complex one. What should be the format? Is it desirable? Should it be voluntary or compulsory? Who should be the enforcing or regulatory body? No one doubts that continuing education is needed; a CPA cannot otherwise keep abreast of all changes in all related fields. The questions of whether credit should be given for in-house (within the firm) training and how reviews should be conducted are still undecided. While many CPAs object to mandatory continuing education, they do not attend the courses voluntarily.

The AICPA offers extensive voluntary professional education courses and self-study programs. Again, many CPAs do not take advantage of them; the internal programs of many large CPA firms compete and keep many away. Also, many courses are geared to the public accountant, not to the industrial or management accountant.

The profession is trying to cope with the "knowledge explosion" by dividing the AICPA into specialist groups, like the medical profession. However, the lone practitioner cannot say to a client, "I do only tax work," and survive. His small clients need all services—audit, tax, and MAS. Even within a firm, the accountant will call in his partner only on large or critical problems. In most dealings with the client, it is impractical to go to others for help; thus the accountant must draw on his own resources most of the time and must know about many fields. The trend toward specialization argues convincingly against retesting in a wide variety of subjects as a condition of maintaining one's license, as certain fields would have no relevance to specialists.

In short, the profession should recommend continuing professional education as a licensing requirement to state legislators over protests from many practitioners. It should require continuing education as a condition of membership in the AICPA by requiring the completion of, say, forty hours of study over a three-year period before AICPA membership would be renewed. Some CPAs might as a result withdraw their membership from the AICPA; it would also be a problem to decide which courses would meet the requirement. The AICPA should help organize a review committee in each state to examine selected financial reports issued by CPAs. If an inadequate report is found, the CPA should be required to defend it; if the defense is poor, he should be placed on probationary membership in the AICPA for a year. Whether such a committee could cope with the flood of reports that would be issued may be a problem; such enforcement could also cause CPAs to withdraw from their state societies and from the AICPA.

The profession should consider requiring its members to undergo a tough relicensing examination to maintain their right to practice and should impose tougher continuing education requirements. The majority of members would object. But the AICPA cannot write the laws; all it can do is pressure the state bodies to require continuing education as a condition for renewing a license. This could cause political repercussions in some state legislatures; pushing for tougher relicensing laws could be construed as persecution of some accountants by the others.

One respondent suggested that the profession launch an aggressive continuing education program aimed solely at the Big Eight leadership and not just their staffs. Rather than concentrate on existing or proposed rulings, the program could focus on the need for changes in matters where abuses had not appeared. As a result, the profession could make more headway in solving some of its fundamental problems and could repair some of the damage done to it by media headlines alleging extensive wrongdoing.

Because they have enforcement powers the profession lacks, the state legislatures, not the AICPA, may take the lead in requiring continuing education for CPAs. The AICPA may have to content itself with a consulting role in making such programs as uniform as possible among states.

Inculcating Professionalism

The profession should require that its prospective entrants be educated in a school of professional accounting. The CPA must absorb professional qualities and attitudes as well as acquire an arsenal of technical skills. Because many universities would probably not agree to form such specialized schools, however, such a requirement might have the effect of severely limiting the flow of prospective entrants.

The AICPA has already appointed the Board on Standards for Schools and Programs of Professional Accounting to set accreditation standards. The board's membership is drawn from academia and practitioners. Regrettably, neither group fully understands the aims and goals of the other, nor have the attributes of professionalism yet been defined to everyone's satisfaction. The AICPA's proposal regarding professional schools of accounting will probably not bear fruit because of the poor public relations job it has done to bring the proposal to a wider audience. The institute has muddled the issue by introducing the subsidiary matter of accreditation in the proposal.

The universities that have established schools of professional accounting have produced little more than old programs taught by the same faculty. To be effective, the curriculum must be fundamentally overhauled and the faculty "professionalized." If professional accounting schools (graduate schools built on a strong base of liberal education, like the schools of theology, medicine, and law) had been established, they might have developed a solid basis of profession-alism. As a result accountants might have a better understanding of the profession's social significance and a greater sensitivity to their responsibilities as professionals, as well as the necessary technical skills.

The AICPA also alienated its friends in academia by unilaterally calling for professional schools of accounting, rather than exploring the issues with accounting educators in advance. An auditor who favored professional account-ing schools suggested that the profession devote financial resources and its full support to the venture and enlist the cooperation of accounting faculties and administrators of schools where accounting is now taught. An accounting educator opposed to professional schools thought the AICPA should replace its director for professional education or reverse its resolution and reopen the issue. The profession might not adopt this suggestion for fear of losing face; on the other hand, academia resents the profession's insensitivity on the issue.

Schools and programs of professional accountancy should have been accredited by the public accounting profession. But to require prospective entrants to graduate only from such accredited schools would have entailed massive amounts of cooperation, support, and money, and probably would not have gained widespread approval.

Unless professional schools of accounting inculcate a sense of professional identity into potential entrants, public accounting will be "deprofessionalized." Business will be lost to more sophisticated disciplines, such as law and business consulting. Accounting will become increasingly isolated intellectually, eventually slipping to the level of vocational education. The best faculty and students will prefer other educational disciplines and career opportunities.

The profession will enter a prolonged period of antagonism with business schools and, in order to finance its own costly schools of professional accounting, will restrict the flow of financial resources that support most accounting education today. But unless the quality of entrants is raised substantially, possibly through professional schools of accountancy, accounting services may proliferate beyond the competence of those who provide them. Accountants without an understanding of professionalism seek to be all things to all people.

Ineffective Quality Control

Auditing practices have deteriorated at all levels, from the senior partner to the lowliest junior, as testimony in recent well-publicized litigation attests. At the grass-roots level, according to one respondent, the ignorance of most small practitioners is "pathetic." Perhaps the profession has expanded too rapidly, or perhaps entrants are inadequately trained.

Voluntary peer-review programs have operated without much success. The Big Eight firms have yet to agree on an acceptable program. Each firm's concern for its public image and its excessive competitiveness obstruct the programs. Standards are not yet specified. How do we know, for example, that a staff accountant assigned to an audit is competent? If he's to audit, say, a limited partnership, does he understand the partners' vulnerability? Does he know what "evidence" means? In the absence of standards, voluntary programs may give way to a registration program requiring firms to undergo peer review.

The firms' managements themselves have devoted considerable attention to quality control and have instituted programs of continuing education and quality review. Improvement has been seen in the better firms, but basic problems remain—the inadequate skill of the employees, a fear of the new by older practitioners, and the relentless pressures of completing an audit engagement on time and within budget. Even cross-firm or within-firm review procedures may be unable to deal with lack of skill and the effects of poor training. They can, however, expose such issues so that they can be faced. The AICPA's voluntary review program will not benefit the profession as a whole if its purpose is only to establish that a firm is applying its own procedures properly. This point also applies to continuing education. Unless the AICPA's proposal advocates a structured, comprehensive, periodic review of germane material, the profession as a whole will not benefit. In some states attendance at a chapter meeting to listen to a talk counts as one credit-hour.

Had the profession developed methods of testing individual competence, its attention would still be focused on the individual and not on the size of the firm. Excessive concern about legal liability has kept CPAs from reviewing and commenting on the work of fellow practitioners. On-the-job experience, a separate requirement for entrance into the profession, should have become part of the educational requirement in the form of a true internship. Substantial continuing-education requirements should also have been imposed. These changes might have improved the quality of auditing. Public accountants, particularly auditors, should be restricted to certain kinds of businesses for which the public would have greater assurance of their expertise.

The profession should move quickly toward a coherent program of education, review, and enforcement, with stricter continuing education requirements. It should reexamine all certificate holders over a five-year period, establish more detailed requirements for audit standards by industry, and begin to develop a framework for specialization within the profession. All these suggestions are fraught with difficulty. Besides the practical and legal ones of enforcement, one respondent graphically comments that "screams of anguish from present license-holders would fill the air. They would insist on something that Peter Sellers said in 'I'm Alright Jack' [an old British movie] —we cannot accept incompetence as grounds for dismissal!"

Small practice units would resent the large firms' ability to provide in-house continuing education. Firms would fear that other firms were gaining a competitive edge. Audit costs would rise inexorably. The profession again would experience difficulty securing agreement on the basis for stricter standards.

The AICPA should also try to couple accreditation of its educational offerings with the education requirements now compulsory in fifteen states and perhaps even develop new measures of learning. The problem of accreditation remains—who is to do the accrediting and on what basis, not to mention the extraordinary difficulty of developing measures of learning in nonacademic subjects.

To encourage excellence, the profession could try establishing academies within the AICPA that would name fellows to recognize special competence in parts of the audit. This would raise the problem of establishing criteria for fellowship status.

As the demand for accountants and auditors increases, the gap between what they can deliver and what is expected of them will also increase. Reform will become more and more difficult as vested interests close ranks to maintain the status quo. The best students will shun accounting in favor of law or other professional careers. The chances of governmental regulation (imposing auditing standards or even taking over the auditing function) will rise, possibly accelerated by the wishes of those CPAs willing to sacrifice the profession's autonomy in exchange for limited liability.

Insufficient Training in the Use of Computers

Had accountants become more skillful in working with computers, they could have not only performed audits more efficiently, but also extended their services to auditing computer-based accounting systems. The profession has only superficially acknowledged the problem of auditing with computers. Members' ability to audit using the computer has not kept pace with advances in computer technology. Too few professional development courses address the subject; those that exist are often too rudimentary. Undergraduate accounting programs do not place enough emphasis on computer auditing. Staff auditors do not have the knowledge; they may even fear the computer, believing that the computer will put them out of business rather than finding it a way to do a better job at less cost. Those with actual experience of small systems have not trained others; the majority have believed that they need not learn the techniques, as there will always be someone else to do it.

There ought to have been as much emphasis at the introductory level of EDP courses on small computer systems as on the more sophisticated software useful only on larger systems. Computer education should be an important part of accounting training, both at the undergraduate level and on the job. The profession should recognize the need to provide basic, audit-oriented training in small computer systems (such as IBM System 3, System 32; Burroughs B-700; Singer System 10) and should increase the number of EDP-related questions on the CPA examination. All levels in the profession lack knowledge about the computer. Severe time pressures associated with audit engagements allow no time for learning the necessary skills; neither are many CPAs willing to devote the necessary time.

So long as this state of affairs is allowed to continue, scandals such as the one involving Equity Funding will erupt from time to time. The profession will continue to give lip service to computer auditing without real competence, drawing bad publicity. Computer audit specialists will take business from the profession as business moves toward greater automation. Clients' confidence in auditors not familiar with EDP—the majority—will decline. Audit fees will climb to pay for personnel time rather than for cheaper computer time. The on-site auditor will continue to avoid using the computer as an auditing tool.

6 Litigation and Liability

With the exception of potential government intrusion into the rulemaking and functioning of the profession, the massive liability to which auditors are exposed is probably what the profession fears most and what limits it most. The magnitude of recent court actions, both in numbers and dollar settlements; the increasing difficulty CPAs have in finding insurers; evidence of defensive auditing; and the ease with which plaintiffs can bring multimillion dollar suits against CPAs—all are symptoms of the unprecedented vulnerability and exposure of accountants.

Highlights

Although some respondents regarded litigation and liability as a primary problem, others recognized it as the effect of more fundamental problems, such as poor work, inadequately supervised audits, skill obsolescence, weak guidelines for accounting decisions, and lack of independence. Nevertheless, the rash of lawsuits and accountants' fear of liability have spawned defensive auditing procedures at considerably higher cost to clients and have inhibited expansion of the CPA's societal role.

Some solutions suggested by respondents focused directly on legal issues—limiting accountants' legal liability, eliminating lawyers' contingent-fee remuneration policy, limiting monetary judgments, and requiring unsuccessful plaintiffs to pay court and defense costs. Other solutions included improving practice review procedures, enforcing compliance with the ethics code, and increasing the auditor's independence from his client.

The Causes and Effects of More Lawsuits

A decade or so ago only corporate management had to defend allegations of misleading financial information, but it is now common for aggrieved third parties to include the auditor in their allegations. As in the medical profession, the threat of malpractice suits has affected the attitude, judgment, and latitude with which auditors practice. Having become more vulnerable, they have withdrawn into conservatism. A corporate financial executive remarked that in recent years his independent auditors were doing more detailed work and were more concerned about materiality. Their legal liability is causing the profession to create additional accounting rules and audit standards in an effort to prevent malpractice.

The problem arises in part from an increasingly common tendency in our society to solve disputes by litigation. Only by changing the law or form of legal practice can the tide be stemmed. The AICPA's Liability Committee tried to limit Chapter 11 of the 1933 Securities Act but, according to one respondent, the effort was ineffectual. The legal profession may hold the key to solving the problem.

One respondent sees litigation as exacerbating some of the profession's other problems. For example, the tendency of regulatory agencies, plaintiffs, and lay juries to extend the legal responsibility of auditors reflects their ignorance of what auditing can reasonably achieve. Thus litigation is used to revive the unsettled issue of how fair financial statements are. Litigation has always provided a convenient means of placing blame; investors seek to recover losses, and government regulators seek to punish and possibly acquire more control over the profession.

In response to the problem the AICPA has customarily filed a brief as amicus curiae or otherwise participated in the defense without studying the merits of the case. One respondent criticized this as self-serving. Another wondered whether the AICPA was defending not a person but a concept of honor, perhaps in the fear that one sullied reputation sullies all.

Accountants being sued for negligence have often mounted vigorous defenses. In most cases, however, to avoid a long and costly trial, accountants have decided to settle out of court. That has denied them the opportunity of proving their innocence, which might have deterred potential plaintiffs.

The profession has attempted to work with the SEC to pass legislation limiting accountants' liability, but without much success. The only alternative is malpractice insurance. The AICPA has put together a plan providing malpractice coverage for a period of three years; the plan is too young for its effectiveness to be gauged. The profession has tried to educate the public, especially investors, about the meaning and limitations of the auditor's opinion on financial statements, but it has not been effective. Investors still look for someone to blame when investments go bad. Scandals such as those involving Penn Central and Equity Funding have made the public cynical. Under AICPA sponsorship, the profession is experimenting with quality-review programs and is developing new audit and control-system rules. Accountants have responded sluggishly to the quality-review programs. The first review of a Big Eight firm was halted by the reviewer's fear of being taken to court.

Advisory committees have been created to detect trouble spots before they become critical. But their members often put the interests of their own firms before those of the profession, inhibiting effective communication among competitor firms and aborting solutions to problems.

The larger firms have taken steps to put their own houses in order; many now require extensive documentation to support conclusions. Financial statements are more formally reviewed by successively higher echelons in the chain of command. Occasionally, however, undisciplined individuals ignore or circumvent the new rules, leading to errors, omissions, and eventual litigation. Investors and the public have come to consider the profession's attempts at self-control ineffective.

The economics of audit engagements leaves firms with little choice but to use inexperienced people, often inadequately supervised. Some of the really troublesome discrepancies are not noticed because junior accounting and auditing personnel rely too much on first impressions and not enough on independent investigation. Despite the greater attention given by the larger firms to supervision and continuing education, there is very little motivation to change. Most people ignore the problem, believing that it will not touch them—until it does! In addition, the carefully worded legislation on professional educational requirements that many states have enacted is difficult to change.

What should the profession have done when litigation became a serious problem? The respondents cited four actions. First, it should have mounted a public relations campaign to educate Congress, the courts, and the public about the inherent imprecision of financial statements, the role of the auditor in preparing them, and the complexity of financial reporting. Plaintiffs might then not have been so ready to include auditors as defendants in suits alleging management fraud. Such a campaign could have defined what "presents fairly" in the auditor's opinion means, as well as the differences between audited and unaudited financial statements. Investors and the general public would learn that complex business transactions cannot be distilled into a single index, earnings per share. They would learn that to assess the quality and prospects of a particular investment, they would have to study the company in more depth, examining the quality of earnings, balance sheet strength, and market outlook. No longer would investors regard reported earnings per share or the audit certificate as a guarantee of the financial picture of a company.

Second, the profession should have pushed harder for legislation to limit accountants' liability over a specified period to nonruinous amounts of, say, $1 million. The accountant could then have foreseen his risk over the period; he probably would have been willing to make difficult judgments and possibly to expand the range of his services (for example, attesting interim financial statements and forecasts). The AICPA could also have spearheaded a drive to prohibit lawyers' contingent fees in litigation, possibly by joining with other professions. Frivolous suits by individuals would have been prevented, saving great sums of money and much time. It might also have dissuaded opportunistic lawyers from moving in to create cases. Defending suits more aggressively instead of settling so many out of court would have produced more precedent-setting cases resolved in accountants' favor.

Third, the profession could have created the FASB sooner than it did and developed reasonable GAAP and a clearer definition of accounting goals. Accounting principles and auditing standards should have been written to permit more flexibility and subjective interpretation. Had this been done, the profession would have recognized potential trouble spots early on, preventing some of today's problems.

Fourth, instead of becoming defensive in the wake of early litigation, the profession should have learned a lesson and improved its self-regulation and quality control. The profession might thus have been spared the mass of new regulations, standards, and disclosure requirements that have been imposed by regulatory agencies. The profession could also have required quality-control reviews and more stringent enforcement of ethics rules; the former would have revealed shortcomings, and the latter would have eliminated some of the sources of problems.

What can the profession do in the present litigious climate? The respondents' suggestions included two external remedies.

Legal Action. The profession should seek relief from the harsh provisions of Section 11a of the 1933 Securities Act. It should also join with other professions in pushing for legislation to eliminate lawyers' contingent fees. That would generate strong oppostion from the legal profession, from certain antibusiness consumer organizations, and probably from the SEC. The profession should nevertheless enlist the aid of the SEC in support of the draft federal securities code sponsored by the American Law Institute, containing a $1 million limitation on liability. The AICPA could provide practitioners with sources of legal liability insurance. In time, however, what has befallen the medical profession may also befall accountants—such sources may dry up as lawsuits become too hazardous.

Reducing the Costs of Litigation. Legislation should be enacted to require an unsuccessful plaintiff to pay the costs of a successful defendant. Legislators might view this as a denial of the prospective plaintiff's rights; the legal profession would object to the possible loss of business through such a move; and the consumerist movement would oppose it. Alternatively, legislation should be enacted to limit monetary judgments. Trial lawyers would object, and it might cause a rift between the two professions.

Most of the respondents' suggestions for dealing with excessive litigation, however, focused on internal reforms related to the causes of litigation.

Practice Review. The profession should make public practice review mandatory for all firms associated with the AICPA. There is the risk that a review report indicating substandard work might itself result in litigation. Another approach would be to have every firm draw up its own quality-control procedures and then have peer review to insure compliance. Smaller firms might object on the grounds that their work does not expose them to the same risks as larger firms. And clients might object to paying higher fees for accountants' defensive measures. Whatever quality-review procedures the profession adopts, it should publicize them, though the public might view it as self-serving. Other suggestions included requiring all practice units to submit to a peer review at least every third year, with a follow-up to correct serious problems. Unless required, many firms would probably not be willing to participate.

Enforcement. The AICPA's Trial Board should take disciplinary action against incompetent members and should publicize the infractions. It should not rely on the SEC and the courts to take such action. This could, however, result in more litigation—the very thing it aims to reduce.

Support for FASB. The profession should demonstrate full support of the FASB and discourage individual firms from undermining it by setting their own standards and principles. Despite the SEC's impatience and its chief accountant's attempt to force the FASB's hand, the profession should stand up to the SEC more than it has in the past. One reason for the FASB's present lack of support is that the profession has not accepted its studies.

Public Relations. The profession should also mount a massive public relations campaign to restore public confidence in CPAs and CPAs' confidence in themselves. Historically the profession has found it hard to define important target groups, to agree on the right approach, and to get the right people to present its views. The attempt to convey the limitations of accountants' responsibilities might, however, be misinterpreted as an evasion of proper responsibilities. The profession needs to convince the users of financial statements as well as those who regulate the industry that CPAs are *not* guarantors. At the same time, pressures are mounting to increase the responsibilities of CPAs to include detecting fraud and preparing interim financial statements and forecasts.

Education for Small Firms. To avoid becoming the target of litigation, small accounting firms and lone practitioners should be educated in methods of good quality control. The individuals and firms involved would probably protest the implication, but some states are already requiring continuing professional education for all CPAs. The education should include the risks accountants run with respect to liability exposure. The danger is that too much emphasis on legal liability may give attorneys and their (plaintiff) clients additional ideas for litigation.

Competence at the Top. One respondent observed that CPAs in the larger firms rise to the top jobs more because of their relations with clients or sales skills than because of their technical expertise. The implication is that lack of technical control and adequate supervision at the top is a cause of litigation. The economics of an accounting practice make client-relation skills important in competing for business. In the long run, however, a firm's reputation for good work will suffer unless technically competent people can also rise to the top.

Independence. Finally the profession should work with the SEC to increase CPAs' independence from their clients. It should urge companies to establish independent audit committees, thus severing the economic link between company and auditor that many believe biases the results. However, many clients would prefer to retain their present freedom to exercise economic pressures on the auditor. The profession might also consider limiting the number of times that an audit firm may successively audit a publicly held corporation. This would raise the costs of the audit, however, and would confuse the reporting of successive periods because of differences of opinion among auditors.

Unless the AICPA acts to reduce the accountant's liability and the extent of litigation, lawsuits will continue; and an increasing proportion of them will be class-action and nuisance suits having little merit. Judgments against CPAs will increase, and court awards and settlements will become much more costly. Potential entrants into the profession will be scared away, as will qualified people presently in practice. The profession's reputation will deteriorate more rapidly.

The profession will be deterred from extending the range of its services. For example, it will not risk further legal exposure by being associated with value-based statements or forecasts. Auditing will become more mechanical, and reports will provide more limited information. As the profession's standards decline, fewer "professional" personnel will be involved.

To reduce the individual liability burden, firms might merge. The necessary insurance coverage will become so expensive that small firms will have to manage without any or cease practicing. Insurers may require the scope of audit work to be expanded to cover more detail, again forcing longer and more costly audits. Both the profession and the capital markets will suffer. The profession will find itself pushed against the wall, as recently happened to the medical profession in San Francisco. Many firms will go bankrupt. Auditors may refuse to work, prompting insurance companies, other professionals, or government agencies such as the GAO to assume the auditing function. The SEC may develop its own (unnecessarily restrictive) rules of conduct for the profession. And small firms would not be able to practice before the SEC if the risk of litigation became unbearable.

7

Threat of Government Intrusion in Setting Standards

Underlying respondents' concern over standard setting by the government was a fear that the profession might lose its autonomy, its right to regulate, discipline, and perpetuate itself in the public interest.

Highlights

Respondents cited the FASB's slow pace in standard setting and the profession's weak attempts at holding its own against the SEC as tantamount to an invitation for government to assume the standard-setting function. Yet those may not be the underlying reasons.

The profession is unable to solve its own problems because opinion is divided on virtually every issue. Each faction—industrial and management accountants organized under the NAA, accounting educators under the AAA, financial executives under the FEI, accountants in government under the NSPA, and public accountants and CPAs under the AICPA—puts its special interests above those of the profession and the public. The result is frequently a stalemate or at best slow progress beset by controversy.

Many CPAs claim that the FASB has set the wrong priorities, dealing only with the problems of the largest firms and neglecting emerging problems. FASB effectiveness is further retarded by the litigious and regulatory climate in which it operates, where the government tends to solve problems only by enacting more laws. However, the SEC is mandated by Congress to oversee the adequacy of accounting rules made in the private sector, and it is empowered to act in a variety of ways if the profession does not measure up to expectations.

Legitimate Oversight or Control through Legislation?

Respondents cited the intrusion of the government into the profession's standard-setting role as a critical problem in its own right, not a consequence of more fundamental problems. The increasingly assertive role of the SEC can be judged from the flow of its releases (ASRs) and rules affecting the profession. Congress, through its investment tax credit and other legislation, and the CASB are also contributing more heavily to accounting standards. The decisions of those bodies carry the force of law.

An auditor saw this phenomenon as part of a government tendency to nationalize many businesses and services. When the private sector is judged to have performed unsatisfactorily, the public looks to the government to intervene and pass legislation protecting consumers, the poor, users of financial statements, and so on. An accounting educator said that his research had suggested that if the FASB lost its public and professional support, the government would probably take over that body's standard-setting function.

Another aspect of the problem is the SEC's tendency to act before the FASB reaches a conclusion on an issue, thus undermining the FASB's role. The FASB's slow pace was likened to "the barn door [that] gets closed after the horse has gone." The releases expressing the SEC's impatience with disclosure requirements have been followed quickly by numerous APB and FASB pronouncements, in an effort to have the rules appear to emanate from a single source. The pressure to react to a strong and activist SEC has further delayed the FASB's other important work.

The AICPA and FASB have tried to keep up with the SEC's actions and releases by issuing prompt commentaries on them, though there is little else they can do given the SEC's legal authority. SEC staff exploit the fact that the balance of power is tilted far in the SEC's favor. They even take advantage of the disarray of the profession to expand SEC influence. The AICPA meets regularly with SEC staff to discuss mutual problems, and partners of major firms often participate. But because of their own lack of consensus, the profession's representatives have so far been unable to convince the SEC that the profession will eventually solve its problems if left alone. Vigorous, early action by the profession could have prevented many of the SEC incursions.

A respondent pointed out that a professional organization lacks the ability to move as quickly as a government agency and the power to force compliance. Its snail's pace is probably the fault of divergent views among the large firms. For example, if CPAs had united and more aggressively opposed the SEC disclosure requirements, they could have eliminated or at least reduced the number of releases the SEC has produced in recent years. The confrontation regarding disclosure first came to a head with the famous investment credit controversy. Instead of presenting a united front, the profession split on the issue when some of its members championed the causes of important clients. Similarly, by having policed itself more vigorously, the profession could have won the respect of the SEC and defused much of the SEC's initiative. It should have systematically reduced the accounting alternatives open to management and thus made many of the SEC's releases unnecessary. The IRS might even have adapted the profession's definition of income for measuring and computing income taxes.

The AICPA has created a special ad hoc committee to make the profession more responsive to emerging problems and to facilitate consensus among the major firms. The AICPA has also opened a Washington, D.C., office to monitor government activities and to lobby for the profession. Congress has tended to give short shrift to the lobbies of professional groups, and it believes that problems can be solved simply by more regulations and laws.

CPAs have begun appearing at congressional hearings to present well-prepared statements. But they face the lobbying strength of any industry group that opposes the proposed legislation. CPAs have generally failed to convince legislators that piecemeal legislation often precludes solutions to the larger problems.

With a larger staff, the FASB could have gone through its work load much faster and would not have accumulated the backlog of unsolved problems it now has. The profession should obtain the funds to provide the FASB with a larger staff, then press it to define one set of accounting standards. The FASB itself should try to find a way of overcoming the deep differences in opinion between individual practitioners and among firms, corporate officials, and the academic community. It should attend to unsolved problems as quickly as possible. At the same time the profession should resist any efforts by government agencies to legislate rules or to set standards. Given the extent of SEC involvement already, such efforts may be too late.

The profession should immediately improve its auditing standards and appoint a special task force to develop new wording for the auditor's report. It should also tackle the serious problem of not having accounting measurement rules that are definitively comprehensible and widely accepted. Obviously much dissatisfaction will be expressed by business, investors, and others. But the profession must recognize that its constituency is ultimately the marketplace where values are set. More vigorous and less equivocal enforcement of its accounting standards would make accountants more independent. Firms might lose some clients, but they would only be marginal clients. The profession might also become even more fragmented, possibly a desirable consequence, depending on one's viewpoint.

To retain its control over auditing, the profession must enhance its image with the SEC and with the investing public. It must show that it can get the job done without outside interference. It must agree to accept more nationally standardized accounting for reporting. Clients adversely affected will suffer in the short term, but if the profession sets the rules *and is supported*, the client will have no recourse but to accept. Educating the investing public about why standards are necessary and how they will be implemented would help restore confidence in the profession. Clearly certain changes will affect the price of some stock; there will be short-term losers. If the implementation is handled properly, however, as in the case of a new tax law or regulation, needless suffering can be avoided.

The profession should establish stronger ties with the SEC and a more forceful lobby in Washington to present the profession's point of view to regulatory authorities. The lobby could also try to forestall the involvement of any government agency in setting accounting principles and auditing standards. However, the best way to do this might be to expand the FASB or create an alternative mechanism for it. The profession should improve its public relations. It should publicize more of its deliberations and decisions. It should gain the support of nonaccountants in its decisions about the accountant's role.

Accountants should be encouraged to critique all future SEC exposure drafts, and the AICPA should evaluate all current SEC releases to determine their usefulness to investors. The profession should require that business and the accounting profession be represented in SEC decision making, though the nature of such representation is not clear.

CPAs should be prepared to rebut proposed legislation reflecting adversely on the profession's credibility. They should testify constructively on pending legislation affecting accounting principles or their application. (CPAs in various constituencies differ in their views, so a unified presentation on behalf of the profession is impossible.) The profession should oppose bills that unnecessarily regulate business activity. The call for individual involvement may not be heeded because of the time and money it would take and the natural tendency to let someone else bear the responsibility.

If the profession made changes in anticipation of possible requirements of regulatory authorities, it would alleviate potential criticism. A prerequisite is agreement among members and constituencies on the required areas and directions of change. Most of all, it should strive to upgrade the quality of work done by its members, thus reducing the need for greater SEC involvement.

Increasing dominance by SEC rules could make financial statements less useful and less representative of economic reality. Accounting would become a "cookbook" procedure, with no flexibility, choice, or judgment. Other regulatory agencies such as the FTC, CASB, and IRS would feel freer to set more and perhaps conflicting rules, further weakening the profession's ability to govern itself. It could eventually become the mechanical arm of the SEC. A struggle for power between the SEC and CASB could ensue. At the very least, the profession could find itself deferring to the government in crucial areas of policy. Government would audit individual firms and examine their audit procedures. Accounting standards would be developed to meet governmental objectives, not the needs of preparer or user. The standards represent even less the consensus of those affected. The profession's only hope of avoiding regulatory control is to restrict its own freedoms with additional rules and regulations.

CPAs may find themselves working for the government. The auditing function will be taken over by GAO auditors, and all reports will follow the dictum "in the public interest." Pronouncements of the profession will no longer have any force. The large national CPA firms will expand their small-business departments to replace the auditing business lost; the result could be fierce price cutting with local practitioners, which might force them to merge or go out of business. CPA firms will become primarily management and tax consulting firms rather than auditing firms.

The profession's stature would suffer. It would lose the respect of clients, become less attractive to students of accounting, and lose its leadership in setting international standards. It would be charged with being unresponsive to a changing environment. Financial statements would become less useful, business enterprises less productive, problems would be solved less effectively, companies would be burdened with excessive or unwarranted expenses, and the profession's legal problems would continue.

8 Detection of Management Fraud

Highlights

Though a number of audit procedures are designed to detect fraud or other management impropriety, the profession has traditionally taken the stand that management, not auditors and accountants, is responsible for detecting fraud. The reason, some respondents suggested, is that accountants are unwilling to bear the liability for failing to detect fraud; if they are not responsible for detecting it, how can they be liable? Further, accountants say that if top management wished to perpetrate a fraud, not even the most exhaustive inquiry could detect it. Much fraud detection relies on personal testimony and cooperation; auditors cannot constantly look over management's shoulder, and they sometimes have to rely on what they are told.

Nevertheless, the courts are now requiring accountants to assume that responsibility, on the grounds that users of financial statements cannot otherwise be sure that the figures accurately reflect management's stewardship. Attestation, then, implies using audit procedures designed to uncover fraud.

Respondents considered some cost-effective ways of detecting fraud, how material a finding should be before it constitutes fraud, how the profession can institute reforms while lawsuits are still pending, what assurances a firm can have that exposing fraud will not lead to loss of the account, to what lengths an auditor can go in his investigation before the client will balk at the increased costs, and to what extent the internal control system of the corporation itself should be audited.

Responsibility for Detecting Fraud

While auditors insist that fraud detection is not an audit objective, they adhere to certain audit procedures designed to detect the presence of fraud. Fraud includes matters beyond the fairness of financial statements, such as political contributions or illegal foreign payments, conflict of interest and dishonesty in top management, and any other illegal activities or improprieties. The public expects the annual CPA audit to be a guarantee against fraud in the audited company; it also expects the auditor to keep management honest. But providing such a guarantee for a large company would be prohibitively expensive; all inventories would have to be physically checked, all assets verified. Consequently, the auditor is forever vulnerable to a dishonest management.

The profession is avoiding its responsibility for detecting and disclosing management fraud, particularly at the highest levels. Recent headlines about kickbacks, bribes paid to foreign government officials by multinational corporations, and illegal political contributions have all reflected adversely on the profession. The public is not satisfied with the uncertain stance of the profession and demands an accounting of the illegal or questionable activities of companies. Moreover, the courts have ruled in many cases that the accountant *is* responsible for detecting all types of material fraud.

The profession has often reiterated its position that detecting fraud is not a legitimate audit function but purely a management concern. SAS 1 formally denied responsibility for fraud detection. On the other hand, the investing public needs assurance that massive fraud is not present, and auditors are the likely group to provide that assurance. One auditor suggested that the AudSEC denied auditors' responsibility for detecting fraud because it feared increasing their exposure to legal liability. Since fraud is often difficult to detect, no CPA is eager for greater liability.

After the famous McKesson and Robbins case in 1939-1940, CPAs were required to confirm receivables and physically count inventories as part of a company audit, even though they continued to insist they were not responsible for detecting fraud. Auditors still rely on certain management representations and use sampling and spot checks to verify inventories or check the accuracy of a company's control system. A dishonest manager who knows the nature of the sample or spot check can camouflage some impropriety. Accountants can always devise more sophisticated and elaborate checks, but the costs would mount accordingly. Such escalation has its limits. Management will resist what it considers an unduly expensive procedure. CPAs do review the internal control system in the audit, but they do so to determine whether GAAP have been followed, not to detect fraud.

A government-sector respondent pointed out that management fraud is not a new problem for auditors. Testimony in the McKesson and Robbins case disclosed that accountants had scrutinized the internal control system too casually and uncritically. Since then, the respondent believed, accountants should have developed more skepticism; yet, large frauds have become commonplace in recent years. Detection of major fraud involving top management should have been made a part of auditing standards and objectives.

Another respondent agreed, declaring that the profession should have educated the public about the costs and benefits of applying such standards. The public would thus have gained a better understanding of the profession's role and a healthier respect for CPA firms as independent examiners. Accountants should have been more frank in explaining to the public that the ordinary audit is not a guarantee against fraud. Though the public would still tend to blame auditors for any fraud that came to light, the profession's legal liability might have been better defined.

The AICPA and the larger firms have promoted peer-review programs and better quality-control procedures to raise the quality of audit work. The SEC, for one, expects such measures to aid in detecting management fraud, but it is too early to tell. The Commission on Auditors' Responsibilities will probably recommend further measures.

The AICPA has formed a committee to study certain fraud cases (such as Equity Funding) to determine to what extent the auditors should have been responsible for detecting fraud. An auditor complained that the task force, not wanting to infringe on anyone's legal rights, would probably not issue its report until all litigation stemming from the cases had been settled. By that time, no one would care about the issue.

The profession should have accepted limited liability (for example, five years' fees or $1 million) for failure to detect material fraud (say, 5 percent of sales or 10 percent of profits). It could thereby have restored the public's faith in the profession and might have stimulated Congress to specify liability limits for CPAs and provide them with legal recourse when management intentionally misrepresents facts. Since the quantitative tools for detecting fraud have been available for five to ten years, the profession should have devised a fraud detection program for the use of all CPAs. It would have reduced the incidence of fraud and enhanced the image of the profession.

The professional, legal, moral, and practical aspects of the issue, in addition to the widely varying views it elicits among regulators, prosecutors, lawyers, investors, and CPAs, make it difficult and complex to resolve. Nevertheless the profession should accept its responsibility for detecting fraud. It should propose audit procedures designed to uncover fraud, including ones to extend the audit outside the company's records on all questionable transactions. Such requirements would increase the cost of auditing substantially, and clients would object. There would not be enough qualified auditors to fill the demand; a different auditor-client relationship would be necessary to maintain the fact and appearance of independence. The profession should draft guidelines delineating CPA responsibility for fraud detection. Of course, new vistas of auditing would be opened and auditors would require more rigorous training, while auditors resistant to change would protest.

Means of Detecting Fraud

If the profession officially accepted fraud detection as a responsibility, adhering to the generally accepted criteria for a careful review of the company's control system should uncover the major problems. In this regard, the profession should see that CPAs are trained in the use of the appropriate quantitative tools now widely available. Agreement would be needed on the standards and methods to be used. Using such tools would extend the scope of the audit and increase its cost. Moreover, audits are always distracting to company personnel; if carried too far, the company's productivity could drop and its overhead increase.

The profession could require a statement of the auditor's responsibility for fraud detection in all accountants' reports. The SEC might object, leaning as it does toward rather stringent requirements on CPAs. It would be constructive for the profession to promptly complete the Audit Standards Bulletin on related-party transactions. The draft discusses just the kind of undetected relationships that have been part of many management frauds.

Minimum guidelines for the disclosure of material fraud could be developed. One government-sector respondent urged that the FASB establish criteria for reporting fraud and that the AudSEC promulgate auditing procedures for such cases. This move would require educating the profession; it would also cause clients to protest increased audit costs, and it would add to the burden of key client personnel subjected to such guidelines.

The profession should propose legislation imposing greater penalties on any management that perpetrates a massive fraud. It should also state unequivocally that it will not be a party to questionable business ethics, such as the $1.25 million bribe paid to a Honduran official. Relations with management may have to become less friendly if the profession is to earn the respect of the investing public.

The profession should sponsor research classifying various types of management fraud, developing methods for detecting them, and assessing the costs and benefits to the profession if auditors accept greater responsibility for detecting fraud. Obstacles include the difficulty of obtaining empirical data and accountants' fear of liability. Research on various types of fraud should be widely disseminated, despite past difficulties in publicizing sensitive or controversial issues. Case studies showing the use of audit procedures to detect fraud could be developed for continuing education seminars to educate CPAs themselves. If made public, however, such case studies might succeed in training the perpetrators as well as the detectors of fraud.

The AICPA could negotiate with the SEC a policy on auditors' responsibility for detecting fraud that would be acceptable to both sides. However, each side's unwavering position blocks progress, and disagreement over the issue within the profession compounds the problem.

Another respondent suggested that rotating auditing teams apply different checking techniques each year to catch dishonest employees. However, it would be inefficient to train a new team each year, and there is no assurance that one technique would reveal fraud any better than another. Practitioners found derelict in applying fraud-detection procedures could be disciplined. That action, however, would unduly influence the legal strategy of the parties bringing suit against the accountant and would no doubt draw adverse publicity to the profession. The disciplinary actions appropriate to particular situations would also be difficult to decide.

An accounting educator suggested that CPAs take cases of alleged management fraud to the courts to determine the extent of auditors' responsibility for developing procedures specifically to detect fraud. He acknowledged that CPAs might be required to assume a degree of responsibility they are probably unwilling to bear.

Unless the profession faces this problem, the public will continue to lose confidence in it. With the issue unresolved, the public will take too broad a view of auditors' responsibilities, which will be reflected in adverse decisions by juries in court cases. The accountants' image will continue to deteriorate as each new fraud undetected by auditors surfaces in the press. Sensationalist media could undermine the profession by intimating that CPAs' failure to uncover fraud causes stockholders and investors to lose money (as in the Equity Funding case).

The government would step in to establish standards for fraud detection or might even take over the auditing function. An auditor speculated that the government would promulgate unworkable standards. Regulatory agencies and licensing authorities would be free to take disciplinary action against CPAs. Other auditors, such as employees of federal or state auditing agencies, might assume responsibility for detecting fraud. The SEC might dictate rules regarding fraud detection that would burden both CPAs and clients and thus not serve the interests of investors, clients, or accountants. The SEC would unilaterally establish disclosure policy and measurement principles, virtually ensuring the demise of the FASB.

Alternatively, the courts might define the extent of auditors' responsibility and thus preempt resolution within the profession. The courts would render decisions or adopt rules unpalatable to the profession and assign it responsibilities it could not handle.

Management fraud itself might become more widespread. CPAs might become wary of issuing reports without testing extensively for fraud; they might refuse to accept engagements if a company's internal controls have been found less than excellent. Unnecessary lawsuits for undetected fraud will continue to be brought against CPAs who exercised due care in performing the audit. Class-action suits for damages will continue. Expectations placed on an auditor will continue to outstrip his unrealistic capabilities. The cost of litigation and liability insurance will rise and may drive many from the profession. The scope of the audit will widen, and the higher audit fees will provoke client protests. The combination of increasing legal judgments and government interference could wipe out accounting as an independent profession and break down the entire investment process.

9   **Concentration of Firms**

Highlights

Some respondents were bothered by the existence of huge accounting firms that audit giant corporations. Such firms, they believed, are prone to anticompetitive behavior that could draw the censure of government agencies and lead to heavier regulation of the entire profession.

Can the Large Firms be Controlled?

The accounting profession is not a unitary body but two or more professions, each with diverse interests and divided according to firm size. The large firms serve publicly listed companies and major governmental groups, with regional, national, and often international practices. Local firms serve the much more numerous small companies, including most privately held ones. Among the first group, the eight largest (the Big Eight) also dominate the formulation of **GAAP** and reporting standards. Divisiveness is created within the profession not only because large and small firms pursue different interests but also because even the large firms do not have a common viewpoint on problems. The larger the firm, the greater its tendency to pursue its own interests rather than work through the AICPA.

The growing size of public accounting firms has paralleled the growing size of businesses in general. When companies go public, they often believe it necessary to retain a "name" accounting firm as auditor. That has aided the growth of the large firms and the development of specialists in all aspects of public accounting.

According to a corporate financial executive, certain large accounting firms harbor an adversarial attitude toward the FASB and are impatient at its slowness in handling critical issues. These large firms have in fact been devising their own accounting standards with what appears to be the tacit blessing of the AICPA and SEC. Organizations that could do something about this problem, such as the AICPA, the SEC, and the state professional societies, do not regard it as a problem. The AICPA is dominated by these large firms, so AICPA policies reflect the needs of large firms and neglect the small ones. A great portion of accounting academia is grossly ignorant of how accounting is actually practiced in a small firm.

The AICPA has attempted to involve the smaller firms in its deliberations, but it has not done so effectively. Because large firms are more involved with the SEC and the government, the AICPA reacts more to their fears of government regulation. The work performed by very large firms and that performed by individual practitioners differ enormously in complexity and use of the information: contrast the reliance on audited financial statements for long-term investment decisions with the one-time need for an individual tax return.

The profession's emphasis on continuing professional education has helped increase the competence of smaller firms. But the gains do not offset the strong trends that widen the differences between large and small firms. Auditing a large company demands a sizable staff; the growing complexity of the business and tax structure demands specialists, who can operate profitably only in the large firm.

The profession is studying the advisability of a separate set of accounting standards for small businesses. Would the public or financial statement users understand why different accounting standards were being used for business entities of different size?

When the excessive concentration of firms first became noticeable, the profession should have taken the steps that it is now taking—getting leaders of the major firms together to discuss the problem. It should have explored whether different kinds of users of financial statements existed and whether different reporting standards would be needed for companies of different sizes (publicly held versus private). The public would thus have been better served, and there would be fewer disgruntled small practitioners.

In the late 1950s and early 1960s, when mergers and buyouts produced an almost geometric expansion of large firms, the AICPA should have been alerted to the long-range consequences of allowing a very few firms to be responsible for accounting and auditing the vast majority of American companies. Instead of having fifteen to twenty-five giants, the profession might now have one hundred sizable firms. Of the 17,000 firms now in the AICPA, the largest eight or twelve have as many AICPA members as all the rest of the firms put together. Given the consumerist trend, the government may someday accuse some firms of conspiring to restrain trade. If that happens, the profession as a whole will surely suffer. It should have discouraged the mergers of twenty years ago so that more rather than fewer firms could have participated in the booming corporate growth. The AICPA would thus have been able to provide its members with stronger leadership. As things are now, it has no choice but to follow the lead of the big firms.

Had the AICPA been less dominated by the Big Eight firms, there might have been less "idealizing of greatness" and more emphasis on quality. The public should have been told that the size of the firm bore directly on its attractiveness to a company. As a result, competition among auditing firms would have been enhanced, and smaller firms would have had the opportunity to expand.

The profession needs to recognize and confront the problem and to foster communication among the opposing factions. It needs to enlist the cooperation of leaders of the major firms to make the AICPA a stronger, more responsive entity. But how does one get strong-minded individuals to act for the greater good rather than for their own firms? A national committee needs to study and delimit the problem and then take steps to solve it. Obstacles to be overcome include disinterest on the part of the larger firms, fear of a possible split into two or more professions, and fear of legislative recognition of non-CPA accountants, who have persistently sought licenses to practice as CPAs.

One auditor urged that larger firms encourage smaller firms' efforts to expand their business. Acknowledging that his opinion was heretical, he asserted it for the benefit of the entire profession. Larger firms should moderate their aggressive sales programs and refer business to the smaller firms. That practice is followed in the legal profession; few firms have found it necessary to establish an office in every city over 300,000 in population.

The roles and scope of practice of CPAs should be reevaluated and nonexpert services such as tax preparation and bookkeeping eliminated. Small firms would oppose the measure to the extent that their revenue is derived from such services.

The profession should more strictly enforce its code of ethics against anticompetitive actions. Size as a virtue should be discouraged. The profession should muster the courage to dictate policies and principles to the very large firms instead of the other way around. A risk is that one or more large firms might withdraw from the AICPA and chart their own course.

The AICPA should throw its full support behind the FASB as the single standard-setting authority. The FASB intends to provide more flexible procedures to handle emerging and current issues, and the AICPA and the large firms should cooperate. It is potentially ruinous for firms to be forced to act on the basis of obsolete or nonexistent standards (possibly bringing on a lawsuit) just because the FASB has not been able to work quickly enough. To achieve a consensus in support of the FASB, firms and the AICPA's AcSEC should be prepared to reverse positions already taken. The AICPA was instrumental in establishing the FASB in the first place, and the reasons for its creation are still valid.

Arguments about large national firms versus the independents will continue unabated. The big firms will continue to get the business, the lawsuits, and the public attention. The smaller firms will continue to feel impotent and neglected in state and national professional organizations. The prognosis for solving the problem is poor, and the respondents were almost resigned to it.

The most common scenario envisioned a more distinct division between the large and small firms, as the profession becomes increasingly less effective in maintaining any semblance of unity. The AICPA will eventually split into several groups, such as the Big Eight firms (over five hundred members), large firms (fifty to five hundred members), other firms, academia, and industry and government. The initial split will evolve into a bifurcation—local practitioners and very large firms. The large firms might leave the AICPA. The smaller firms might also become alienated and leave the AICPA's influence and control, the quality of their services declining as a result.

The AICPA will become weaker and in time ineffective, leaving the profession unrepresented except by the individual firms. Its membership and hence financial support will decline, as has been happening to the American Medical Association. The Big Eight firms will gradually create eight unique sets of accounting standards (if the SEC has not by then begun setting standards itself).

The FASB's authority will be undermined as various other bodies (AICPA committees, firms, IASC, CASB) set standards, often conflicting ones. Comparability among financial statements would be lost. The auditor's opinion would frequently be qualified, unnecessarily subjecting that company's financial reports to suspicion. If the FASB were to fail, setting accounting standards would almost certainly become the responsibility of a government regulatory agency, probably the SEC. In fact, increased and possibly excessive regulation is now more than a possibility.

Users of financial statements, particularly those who own small businesses would be dissatisfied. Clients would refuse to pay high fees for work they considered neither desirable nor necessary and would become accustomed to less professionalism. Young people would be discouraged from choosing accounting careers. Stockholders and other financial statement users would continue to bring suit against accountants. The public would experience great confusion trying to understand financial statements, and the reputation of the profession would deteriorate even further.

10 Personnel Problems

Most of the personnel and staff problems that concerned the respondents are manifest at the level of the individual accounting firm. However, all have implications for the profession as a whole and can be ameliorated by the AICPA.

Highlights

The litigious climate is blamed for poor recruiting prospects, and boredom and stress for the high turnover among partners and auditors, respectively. The poor educational preparation of staff accountants is due to the lack of professional schools of accounting.

Recruitment and turnover problems would virtually disappear if the qualifications demanded of entrants were tailored to match immediate challenges, and if an accounting career were made truly satisfying (to include public service opportunities as well as monetary rewards). The obsolescence of skills could be prevented by regular continuing education and training courses.

Recruiting

The profession seems unable to attract, for lifetime careers, the talent needed to meet public expectations of CPAs. Personnel trained broadly enough for the smaller accounting firms are difficult to find, and the recruitment and retention of minorities are general problems. Perhaps the hostile legal climate makes a CPA career unattractive; perhaps the greater number of rules and regulations pertaining to financial reporting have caused frustrations that outweigh the satisfactions traditionally associated with a career in accounting; perhaps doubts about universities' effectiveness in preparing today's recruits for their careers have made them insecure. Most potential accountants are attracted to the world of big business and to the big firms that can provide opportunities to work on sophisticated computer-based accounting systems. The result is a greater need for accountants with either broad experience or special skills and less need for those who expect to undergo a traditional apprenticeship.

What can the profession do to make accounting a more attractive career opportunity while giving equal opportunities to the small firms and to minority applicants? The profession should seek a more precise definition of the extent of

CPAs' legal liability; it should press for creation of separate schools of professional accounting at the major universities, despite resistance to change and low budgets. At the same time the AICPA should offer more practical training in specialized auditing techniques (using the computer and mathematical methods such as statistical sampling) and broader financial analysis and forecasting. To pay for the training and the greater skills produced, client fees would have to be raised or profit margins cut. Supervising the new breed would require a specially trained cadre of senior staff, also costing time and money.

Smaller firms should be encouraged to subsidize additional formal training for their employees despite the high immediate costs of time lost and tuition expense. An obstacle would be the persistent belief that on-the-job training is the only worthwhile kind. The larger firms need to retain minority CPAs long enough for them to become partners. The usual period of eight to ten years will have to be shortened. The AICPA could strengthen its existing programs on minority recruitment and try to find more funds for scholarships. Although the profession is trying, it is a slow process.

If the present difficulties persist, class distinctions could develop between the smaller and larger firms; small firms may disappear for lack of new blood; and minorities will probably never be appropriately represented as partners in the larger firms. Entrance examination standards may have to be changed, possibly even lowered, to admit more minorities. To cope with the rising legal risks of practice, CPAs may have to curtail certain kinds of services. Lacking the talent needed to meet its great potential, the profession will diminish in stature.

High Turnover

The profession is finding it hard to keep its conceptual leaders throughout their careers, perhaps because the profession resists change and people with vigorous minds become bored. Such leaders should be put to work investigating new ways the profession could contribute to society and should be offered new roles such as serving as professional members on boards of directors. A risk is that conflicts of interest could develop and make it more difficult for auditors to maintain their independence.

There is also high turnover among top auditors, those who spend long hours trying to complete audits on time. Firms should add staff to help such burdened auditors. But overtime periods are concentrated at year-end audits, not distributed evenly though the year, so the rest of the time the extra employees would be underused. In any case the present situation is causing an exodus of qualified auditors and is discouraging potential entrants to the profession.

Education and Training

Educational institutions have lost touch with the profession and the world of the accounting practitioner. Recruits are not as well prepared now as they were a few years ago. Business schools are not keeping pace with the growing demand for accountants. One reason may be the lack of professional schools of accounting and the general nonpractice orientation of university education today.

The profession should pursue the efforts begun by the AICPA to establish professional schools of accounting, by prescribing standards for such schools and maintaining some control over the curriculum and faculty appointments. Educators will oppose professional schools and any AICPA involvement in matters of curriculum and faculty. Deans of business schools are also vehemently opposed to the idea of professional schools and seem thereby to discount the profession's needs.

A foundation could be established to pool the funds that large CPA firms now contribute to universities and use these funds to accredit and support professional schools, though firms might object to the lower visibility their contribution would receive under a pooling arrangement.

Another respondent urged that the profession establish graduate schools of accounting and economic theory and require that all CPA candidates attend. As undergraduates, prospective CPAs should take no accounting courses but only "impractical" ones like English literature, philosophy, and political science. Conventional thinking and the fact that today's accountants were not educated that way would make this suggestion difficult to implement. And because state requirements for a CPA license vary widely, such a change might require federal legislation, not to mention substantial financial support. The profession could provide internships for undergraduate students. However, firms might not be able to accommodate the internees satisfactorily.

If the situation remains much as it is now, the firms may have to continue their inefficient and inadequate efforts to provide on-the-job training for accountants. A college degree in accounting would diminish as an advantage to a prospective accountant, and the number of students enrolling in accounting and business studies would decline. Students would find other careers more desirable.

With inadequate educational preparation, the profession will become increasingly unable to cope with the complex array of problems confronting it. Accounting standards will continue to decline. The profession's image will be damaged and its self-esteem lowered. The accounting profession may ultimately cease to exist.

11 Specialization

Highlights

It was difficult to make sense of the often contradictory and disparate remarks of the respondents who cited specialization as a critical problem for the profession. The issue seems to be whether non-CPA professionals specializing in management advisory services for CPA firms should be formally recognized by the profession—if not as associate members of the AICPA, then as genuine specialists. While CPA firms recognize their value in enhancing the firm's skills and profits, such persons experience second-class treatment simply because they are not CPAs. A related issue is whether CPAs themselves should achieve greater competence in certain areas that would be formally recognized as specialties. One respondent suggested that the profession be divided into sections of specialists, as in the medical profession.

How would officially recognized specialists affect the profession or the business prospects of their firms? Small practitioners, who sell primarily general services to clients, would feel threatened. It would be difficult to reach agreement on the details of implementing such a scheme—what constitutes a specialty, how it can be tested, and whether people can be registered for more than one specialty at a time. Yet if the profession is to rebut accusations that accountants' skills are not keeping pace with advances in business and technology, it must give serious thought to dividing the burden of keeping current among its members. Just as the division of labor revolutionized manufacturing at the turn of the nineteenth century, the division of skills might make accounting more up to date and efficient.

A Narrowly Defined or Pluralistic Profession?

The profession needs to recognize specialists within accounting. For years firms have recognized three or more separate disciplines, and the AICPA's Committee on Scope and Objectives is recommending professional status for them. Full-time professional but non-CPA employees should be accorded the same stature as CPAs, giving MAS greater legitimacy within the firm. Respondents disagreed whether MAS and non-CPA professionals should be allowed membership within the AICPA.

Specialization is inevitable. Because of the rate at which new rules and regulations are being developed, and because accounting is still more art than science, a practitioner can no longer practice competently in more than one field. However, limiting a CPA's practice to one field would make it almost impossible for the sole practitioner to earn a living.

The AICPA has long been considering whether to admit non-CPAs as members. All studies to date have recommended denying membership to non-CPAs. Accountants claim that though management advisory services, which employ the bulk of non-CPA professionals, have been extremely profitable, they are not consistent with auditing, accounting, and tax services. Nevertheless the profession has permitted some non-CPA members of CPA firms to serve as committee members in professional institutions. The gesture has been half-hearted and smacks of second-class citizenship. MAS could have been identified as a function clearly subordinate to accounting or even as a separate entity, as in Canada and the United Kingdom. MAS specialists would then be freer to define their own markets and engagements, and a firm's MAS capability would not be a significant factor in evaluating its competence.

One accounting educator noted that in the past the profession rejected the advice of its leaders and refused to distinguish levels of competence, that is, specialists. The second Beamer report called for a continuing education requirement, which implies labeling competence. Although the Beamer proposals have received wide acceptance, the fifty states have to decide separately whether to adopt any of them.

Another respondent suggested dividing the profession into specialist sections, as the medical profession has done, strengthening individual elements of the profession. The report of the Scope and Structure Committee should be approved and specialties formally recognized. The large national or regional firms and the small practitioners may split on the issue. Members who wish to remain generalists will object; some fear the creation of a bureaucratic "jungle." Leaders of the profession, especially those in the Big Eight, should obtain public support for labeling higher degrees of competence as specialties. The issue has been raised so often that attitudes may have hardened to the point where no change is possible. Unless the question is raised repeatedly, however, no action will ever be possible. The public also might perceive a move toward recognized specialties as self-serving in view of the profession's troubles with litigation.

The profession could develop a realistic referral program whereby work beyond the competence of a generalist CPA is referred to a specialist, possibly in a different firm. It would probably be necessary to assure that the referrer would not lose his client. Even so, smaller firms would probably feel their client relationships jeopardized.

The CPA examination should be modified to emphasize basic skills such as business management concepts, logical ability, and information systems; a specialist examination should demand greater competence in one aspect of practice. This scheme would have to be ratified by the general membership and would require redesigning the examination (always a complicated, controversial activity) and getting it approved by the state boards.

One respondent asserted that CPAs should be restricted to matters in which they are most competent, meaning matters to which they are as skilled as the technicians they use. Firms, however, would be unwilling to forego the profits from assignments that require skills they do not possess.

CPAs will discredit themselves and the profession if they stray too far from basic accounting and auditing services. Those practicing more than one specialty will find they cannot adequately keep up with developments even in one. As the competence of small practitioners wanes, they will lose more business. Tax work, for example, will be lost to non-CPA tax-preparing services. In time new groups would encroach on the profession's current territory, and the profession as a whole would become less confident and innovative. Specialists, if unrecognized in their own profession, might join other professions, taking services they had provided CPA firms. Clients would no longer be served as well. The public would eventually rise up against the profession as it discovers the profession's labeling of competence to be unrealistic. The profession would cease to lure prospective entrants who expect to practice their specialty and to be designated accurately. As CPAs lag in the struggle to keep current in too many complex fields, the quality of their work will deteriorate. The growing obsolescence of skills will damage the reputations of firms and the profession, and will increase accountants' liability exposure.

Finally, if CPAs and non-CPAs involved in MAS are unable to resolve the issue to their mutual satisfaction, it will fall to the SEC to define the legitimate role of MAS practitioners.

12 Social and Nonfinancial Accounting

Should accountants expand their role to include social and other forms of nonfinancial accounting for clients? Only a few respondents singled out this issue as a critical one for the profession, and their views are sharply divided.

Highlights

Proponents asserted that there is great public demand for social accounting, especially from consumer activists, and that accountants in their objective role as auditors are well-suited to it. Social accounting would also be a source of profitable new business for auditing firms. One respondent warned, "If we don't do it, others surely will." Depending on the interpretation, that statement could imply a weak rationalization for the idea, or it could suggest that social accounting is inevitable and that accountants had better prepare for it.

Opponents contended that the measurement and audit techniques have not yet been refined enough to give consistent or comparable results; much more research is needed. A conceptual issue is whether a corporation should be required to be socially responsible. By making a profit, rewarding investors, and providing employment, a corporation is fulfilling its proper social role. Opponents were also fearful lest accountants, in their zeal, began practicing in a matter that is beyond their technical competence, thus doing the profession a disservice.

Social Accounting—Opportunity or Trap?

Social and other forms of nonfinancial accounting include evaluating a company's measures for alleviating environmental problems; extending the attest function into the social impacts of corporate actions; and auditing the social performance or social responsibility of private enterprises and nonprofit agencies. Even proponents wondered whether reasonable measures could be developed so that corporate performance could be reported through the accounting system. Should such social factors be included in financial statements? How?

The SEC is currently holding hearings into the desirability and feasibility of auditing for social responsibility, prompted by consumerist pressure to require some form of social-measurement reporting by publicly held corporations.

The profession should begin to delineate what can and cannot be done, and then develop methods for doing what is possible. Environmental problems, for example, could be divided into smaller areas such as health, safety, recreation, and aesthetics for discussion and possible action. This approach could run afoul of differing goals of government commissions. Many practitioners would resist tackling such a difficult subject. They fear exposing themselves to further liability, feel they have plenty of work already, and object to committing the resources necessary to retrain their staffs.

The profession should sponsor experiments on measuring social impact realistically. There are no standards and definitions as guidelines. What should be measured? How to go about it? The FASB could appoint a high-level task force to devise workable methods, though CPAs and corporate financial executives might remain skeptical that social factors and their impacts cannot be measured.

One advocate of social accounting urged at SEC hearings that the AICPA appoint a committee to study what had been learned so far and be prepared to participate in any rulemaking on the subject. It is unlikely that such a committee will be formed because of accountants' traditional inertia. But even if the AICPA's Social Measurement Subcommittee endorses the idea, questions of attesting such results and disclosures will arise. What quantity and quality of information are needed? Ways of auditing management policy statements could be developed, say, by categorizing statements as testable or not and then devising methods for testing. If management asserts, for example, that it practices equal opportunity, the auditor should be able to ask what that implies and determine whether the evidence supports or negates the assertion.

One corporate financial executive vehemently opposed the notion that an accountant or anyone else is entitled to evaluate management's social responsibility. He believed that companies have no social responsibility. The profession should refuse to have anything to do with the subject and, if necessary, call a CPA strike. The SEC, the general public, and the investor need the CPA to do what he is now doing. CPAs have more power than they realize but lack the courage to use it. The possibility that the government would threaten to take over CPAs' functions if they went on strike left the respondent unfazed: "As old John L. Lewis said of the government takeover of the coal mining industry, 'You can't dig coal with bayonets'; nor can one render an accountant's opinion with bayonets."

Expanding accountants' functions to embrace social accounting will require more manpower with more skills than is now available. If the profession does not act now, advocates of social accounting may turn to other professions or other bodies to help them implement their proposals, bodies such as the GAO, consumerist organizations, and Common Cause. Assuming responsibility for social accounting could be the first step in taking over the entire attest function. CPAs are also blind to the potential financial gains at stake.

If the profession does not resolve this issue, the public will have no way of evaluating a corporation's performance against its social obligations. By legal decision or self-assertion, the SEC could in effect assign the task to the profession by laying down certain disclosure rules to which companies and their auditors would have to adhere, with CPAs attesting to the accuracy of those reports. If the profession, on its own or by government fiat, began auditing for social responsibility, then government, corporate management, and other public groups might be misled into making unrealistic decisions because of the poor evaluation methods used.

Either way, public confidence in the profession would erode. If it does not carry out social auditing, it could be accused of not meeting public demand; and if it does, it could be accused of substandard work that is sure to occur before the profession has had time to set realistic and uniform standards.

13 Problems, Remedies, Opportunities, and Consequences

This chapter summarizes the results of the second survey. In the highlights they are summarized by key problem; the subsequent text is organized along the lines of the questionnaire itself—the relative importance and solvability of problems, remedies, and opportunities and consequences in the future.

Highlights

Setting Accounting Standards. Among the problems the profession has been giving the most attention to, the setting of accounting standards and principles is the most critical. The consequences of inadequate or not widely accepted GAAP are gravely injurious to the profession and to society. Furthermore, the tendency of existing standards to quickly become obsolete straitjackets is one of the least solvable problems. Despite the importance the respondents attached to the matter, however, none of the remedial actions they thought the profession ought to take pertained to formulating and revising standards. One opportunity— making accounting, auditing, and reporting standards uniform throughout the world—was paradoxically judged both highly desirable and unrealistic and difficult to implement.

Auditor Independence. The second most critical problem is auditing firms' lack of independence from their clients. Analysis showed that solving this problem would aid the solution of other critical problems. Nevertheless, the respondents opposed two actions designed to make accountants more independent. Predictably, the public accountant respondents asserted that they are sufficiently independent. The respondents overwhelmingly agreed that the profession should recognize the public as client; in viewing that action as an opportunity, they implied that there is much room for improvement.

Quality of Work. The profession's technical standards, ethics, and work performance have deteriorated. Underlying respondents' dissatisfaction was a concern that the profession has no real standards for distinguishing competent from incompetent work. For example, the scope of accountants' activities keeps expanding, new techniques applied unevenly make their work standards difficult to discern, and existing standards are now being openly challenged in the courts. Opinion is so diverse on these issues that it may be a long time before a

113

consensus is reached. The profession has been relatively ineffective in its disciplinary procedures, although severely limited in its punitive powers (denying a person membership in the institute does not prevent him from practicing as a CPA). Respondents urged the profession to elevate CPA competence and to develop the machinery for enforcing standards of work performance.

Role Uncertainty. Coupled with accountants' characteristic lack of consensus on issues, their uncertainty about the profession's role in society probably accounts in large part for the public's misunderstanding of the role of the auditor and the meaning of his opinion. Most respondents believed that solving this problem would help solve many other problems. They were optimistic about determining the proper scope of the audit and attest functions before 1985, probably because they hoped that the profession would act on the findings of the Commission on Auditors' Responsibilities.

Relative Importance and Solvability of Problems

From an analysis of all responses, four problems emerged as most crucial for the profession:

1. Inadequate, not widely accepted GAAP and the lack of an underlying framework for GAAP.
2. The auditor's lack of independence from his client.
3. Deficient technical standards, ethics, and work performance.
4. Uncertainty about the profession's role in society, which in turn exacerbates the "expectation gap" and CPA claims of public misunderstanding.

Profession's Attention to Problems

The respondents were first asked which problems they thought the profession had given the most attention to (hence thought were the most important), which it had given least attention to or ignored, and which it should now consider top priority. Of the five problems respondents thought the profession had given the most attention to:

Two appear to be symptoms: the likelihood that the SEC will define accounting standards, and the threat of litigation and liability.

Two are not considered as important as the crucial ones noted above: problems with unaudited and interim financial statements, thought likely to be solved in the coming decade, and the problem of recruiting, educating, and training accountants, thought to be intractable before 1985.

One seems to be fundamental: defining and reaching consensus on GAAP.

As for problems the profession had given the least attention to (without regard to whether the inattention was good or bad), the respondents most often cited the following:

Public misunderstanding of the auditor's role.

The dominance of a few large firms.

The validity of nonfinancial accounting.

Overcomplicated financial reports.

Auditors' responsibility for detecting management fraud.

The following headed the list of the problems that should be given top priority:

Public misunderstanding of the role of auditors and of the meaning of the auditor's opinion.

The CPA's growing dilemma of whom to serve.

Developing an underlying framework for GAAP.

Determining and applying the objectives of financial statements.

The increasing likelihood that the SEC will define accounting standards.

Public accountants, both auditors and nonauditors, were primarily responsible for the top ranking of the first problem; no other group ranked it as high. Of the four crucial problems mentioned above, only two survived the synthesis process. As we shall see, two others—public misunderstanding and the likelihood of the SEC's setting accounting standards—are thought to be symptoms rather than fundamental problems.

Solvability of Problems

The respondents were asked to estimate the problems' solvability by giving a percentage estimate of the chance that each problem, considered alone, would be resolved or greatly remedied by 1985.

Next the cross-impacts of the problems were examined. Each respondent was asked to estimate for each of the three problems he considered most critical the effect on the other twenty-four in the list if the one in question were solved by 1985. The result was a group of impact estimates of problem pairs. For each pair, would solving the one promote, leave unaffected, or inhibit solution of the other? The controlling assumption was, of course, that the profession would strive to solve all the problems in the list at once and vigorously. The results, therefore, speak to the relative solvability of the problems taken as a group.

Changes in the solution probability of each problem over a ten-year period (resulting from equal efforts to solve all other problems) were also estimated by means of a cross-impact simulation model, described in appendix A.

Of the four problems they considered crucial, the respondents thought that solution of the profession's role uncertainty and auditors' lack of independence would foster the solution of many of the other problems. The other two problems were not considered pivotal. None of the four was thought likely to be solved before 1985; improvement of GAAP was judged especially intractable. It seems intuitively reasonable that respondents would not cite easily solved problems as the most important ones faced by the profession. Other problems cited as unsolvable by 1985 help explain why solution of the key ones seems so difficult. For example, the lack of professionalism and rise in commercialism that apparently characterize the behavior of large CPA firms might well lead to a lowering of standards and the quality of accountants' work.

On the premise that a problem whose solution aids the solution of other problems is a fundamental problem and more worthy of the profession's attention, the following problems turned out to be *not* very important: public misunderstanding, the likelihood the SEC will define accounting standards, and the threat of litigation and liability. The first two, in fact, are among those whose solutions are shown most helped by the solutions of other problems. Rather than being real problems, then, they seem to be symptoms or consequences of other more fundamental problems.

The five problems most likely to be solved by 1985 are almost all within the FASB's jurisdiction. Three have to do with financial reporting: problems with unaudited and interim statements, price-level or other attempts to achieve current-value financial statements, and the definition and application of objectives in financial statements. The other two are deciding the proper scope of the audit and attest functions and the FASB's inadequate handling of emergency problems and its slow reactions to a changing world. None of these appeared in the list of the profession's key problems.

The problems regarded as least solvable include two pertaining to the way accounting firms are structured and operate: the dominance and influence of a few large firms and the loss of professionalism and a concurrent rise in commercialism, including unfair competition and bidding. Also near the top of that list are the restrictive nature of GAAP (where rules increasingly preempt the exercise of judgment), the overcomplication of financial reports, and whether social and other nonfinancial forms of accounting should be used.

Constituent Group Opinions

An examination of how each constituent group voted reveals much about the groups themselves. A group's choice and ranking of problems reflected its special interests. For example, corporate financial executives ranked the threat of the SEC's defining accounting principles as a greater problem than did auditor CPAs. In general, the groups most intimately involved in preparing and auditing financial statements (CPAs and corporate financial executives) were least consistent in their view of which problems were important. Those who use and rely on financial statements most or who are most removed from the issues (educators, investment company executives/financial press, and government-sector respondents) were the most consistent, especially investment company executives and members of the financial press, who before the survey appeared the most critical of the profession. As later results attest, they were also the most pessimistic in their outlook for the profession.

Remedying the Problems

Obstacles

The problems suggested by respondents in the first survey were by instruction continuing problems,[a] ones that have been evident for some time and are likely to remain critical in the near future. Why hasn't the profession been able to solve them? What in the profession's institutional arrangements, its style, and its idiosyncrasies is keeping it from being more successful?

Many respondents to the first survey criticized the profession's past efforts. The criticisms generally appeared as reasons for the profession's inaction or ineffective action with respect to a particular problem or as obstacles that might be encountered in attempts to solve a problem. Forty such comments were taken from the first survey, and the respondents were asked whether they were true or false.[b]

The key findings—comments rated true by over 75 percent of the sample—are that the profession has not presented a united, forceful, and visible front to its constituencies or to the external world and that it has not kept pace with the stream of problems confronting it. Neither has it been able to police itself adequately. Of the 40 generally unfavorable comments, 28 were rated true, 13 of them true by every constituent group. Thus respondents think these criticisms still apply.

On ten comments the respondents as a group were ambivalent; the criticisms

[a]Respondents were also asked to suggest a new problem, one without any historical precedent that might become critical in the years ahead. Disappointingly, the "new" problems were so similar to the "continuing" problems that the two were merged and discussed together.

[b]The results were analyzed only for the respondents who made a determination; "don't know" responses were ignored. The chief interest was which comments the respondents considered true and which false; whether there were differences among the constituent groups; and what implications those differences may have for the profession.

were ones that a majority would have declared false if the profession were in a state of good health, for example:

Not disciplining members who violate ethics and standards because they are sheltered by their firms.

Inadequately clarifying the distinctions between accounting and bookkeeping.

Not being aware that the purposes of accounting are obscure to many users.

Not being able to agree on what the problems really are.

Some constituent groups disagreed with the mainstream on certain issues. Auditors agreed with the statement that the profession is not afraid of a confrontation with the SEC, while all other groups disagreed; public accountants denied that the profession is run by the large national CPA firms, counter to the opinion of all other groups; and public accountants and corporate financial executives all said the profession acts objectively, unlike the remaining groups.

Nonauditor CPAs denied that the profession strives for unanimity of opinion among its members, rather than being content with a simple majority, and that it compromises and takes noncontroversial positions to achieve consensus; all other groups claimed the opposite.

Educators were the only group to maintain that the profession does not have a set of GAAP that has wide acceptance, that it is too busy to tackle really important matters, and that it has not recognized that many of its problems are interrelated.

The investment company executives/financial press group believed that the profession does not give sufficient support to the AICPA on fundamental issues and that it gives lip service to the FASB while undercutting it, both contrary to the opinion of all other groups.

Lawyers were the only group to say that the profession has been able to get those who need it most to engage in continuing professional education; that it is not reluctant to make its rulings mandatory; and that it is unable to confront the SEC on issues that impede the profession's effectiveness or that run counter to its objectives.

Constituent groups other than auditors sometimes differed strongly among themselves, contrary to the expectation that they would differ mostly with auditors or public accountants. In three instances the investment company executives/financial press and the lawyers found themselves at opposite ends of the spectrum, with the lawyers defending the profession's success with its continuing professional education programs and asserting that the FASB and AICPA enjoyed the profession's full support for their positions on fundamental issues. In two cases government-sector respondents and lawyers found themselves opposed, the former claiming that the profession is reluctant to make its rulings mandatory and cannot control its own destiny, and the lawyers again coming to the profession's defense. Where the voting discrepancy was over 50 percent, the investment company executives/financial press and government-sector respondents virtually monopolized the critical end of the spectrum, and the lawyers—not the auditor CPAs—mainly supported the profession.

Remedies

Respondents cited the following as the most desirable actions for the profession to take:

Educate the investing public to understand the limitations of independent audits.

Work closely with the SEC to improve the quality and relevance of financial disclosure.

Establish a more effective mechanism for identifying, evaluating, and taking action on incompetence and unethical behavior.

Review the public practices of all firms associated with the AICPA.

Detect and report management fraud.

The respondents were asked which actions would alleviate the most problems. Three of their highest-ranked choices were identical to the first three most-desirable actions. They thought the most widespread benefits in that respect would come from clarifying and enforcing standards of competence.

Three of the desirable actions were judged difficult to implement: educating the investing public, establishing better ethical and quality-control mechanisms, and determining what constitutes competent CPA performance. Working closely with the SEC to improve the quality of corporate financial disclosures was judged one of the easiest actions the profession could take.

The action regarded as least desirable by all constituent groups but the lawyers was to shift the burden of accounting standards to a public agency so that the profession could concentrate on lobbying, auditing standards, and technical and professional development. Among the other actions thought least desirable were two measures to improve the independence of auditors from their clients: limiting the number of times that a firm can successively audit the statements of a client and forbidding an auditor to engage in any other activity for a client while auditing that client. The reason may be that the respondents, particularly auditors, felt either that CPAs were already independent enough or that those restrictions were not appropriate solutions to the problem.

Finally, respondents were asked to indicate which remedies would be most effective for the high-priority problems each had selected. Their highest-ranked responses corresponded to the list of most desirable actions, with one addition—"take positive and swift disciplinary action."

How do these findings relate to findings about the relative importance and solvability of problems? Of the four problems that emerged as the most critical, only one was thoroughly addressed by the desirable actions: deficient technical standards, ethics, and work performance. Another action, the detection and reporting of management fraud, only partially addresses the problem of the profession's role uncertainty. Two actions designed to improve independence were discarded as among the least desirable of all actions. Nothing emerged to address the problems the profession has with GAAP. None of the top-ranked actions directly addressed the problems that were found to be particularly intractable, that is, those with the lowest probabilities of solution in 1985.

Opportunities and Consequences in the Future

This section examines respondents' views of the opportunities open to the profession and the consequences of inaction or ineffective action that the profession may wish to avoid.

Opportunities

The perceptions of opportunities were elicited by an optional fantasy question in the first survey, which 44 percent of the respondents completed. It asked them to imagine the American scene in the year 2000 and to describe everything about the public accounting profession that pleased them. The question was a device to draw forth respondents' present concerns in the absence of current institutional constraints. The assumption was that respondents, when asked what would please them twenty-five years in the future, would use the interim period to solve the problems that concern them most today. That assumption generally proved valid.

Some responses were fresh and imaginative (several respondents created full scenarios), but most resembled the inventory of problems cited in the rest of the survey. (For a summary see appendix B.) Role problems predominated: the need for better self-regulation in the profession, ways of broadening the accountant's role, and improvements in accounting practice. The probable reason for the predominance of role problems is that more than half of all contributions came from CPAs, both auditors and nonauditors. Financial reporting problems were cited next most often: reporting standards, the extent of disclosure, and the appropriate format and reporting medium.

Five respondents, among the oldest in the sample, envisioned the demise of the profession by the year 2000. Several other respondents saw the profession carrying out primarily extensions of existing functions, such as the attest function extended to other areas, or foresaw functions without a precedent, such as a new tax-practice profession. A common theme was a greatly enlarged role for the computer.

In the second survey thirty-three of the most provocative and specific ideas among those responses were rephrased as actions and presented as opportunities for the profession. The respondents were asked to rank them in potential importance, estimate how soon they could be realized if vigorously pursued, and indicate which were most unrealistic.

The following opportunities emerged as highest in priority for the profession: devising better accounting systems, including better measures of the effects of corporations on society; recognizing the public as client; extending the profession's role in society by regularly auditing all public companies; making accounting principles and auditing standards uniform throughout the world; creating an independent institution to perform long-range planning for the profession; and establishing a federal accounting court. Curiously, the standardization of GAAP throughout the world was also rated one of the most unrealistic opportunities, a clear expression of the simultaneous appeal of that goal and the intrinsic difficulty of attaining it.

The opportunities favored by the lawyer constituent group departed radically from the other respondents' choices. Five of its top seven choices were ranked no higher than twenty-second by the respondents overall, and three of them were judged most unrealistic by the respondents overall. On the contrary, as the lawyer-favored opportunities had to do with details of audit practice and work-related issues, they appear more realistic than the grandiose and overly ambitious measures favored by the other respondents.

All of the top-ranked opportunities (except making GAAP uniform throughout the world) were believed achievable by 1985. The long-range planning institute could be established by 1979, and the others between 1981 and 1985. Creating a set of international accounting, auditing, and reporting standards was possible by 1985 according to the lawyers and corporate financial executives, while the nonauditor CPAs, investment company executives/financial press, and government-sector respondents estimated 1995, with 11 percent judging beyond 2000 or never. The assumption underlying these estimates needs to be stressed again: that the profession *would* pursue these opportunities vigorously. To the extent that it does, the estimates have some validity; if it does not, they should be considered extremely optimistic.

In all these estimates, it is not clear whether respondents are making factual judgments as requested ("When may it reasonably happen if the profession were to pursue it vigorously?) or value judgments ("When would I want this to happen?"). The resulting estimates lead one to suspect they may have been contaminated by respondents' value judgments.[c]

Consequences

Respondents were asked what would befall the profession if its problems remain largely unsolved. The negative outcomes most frequently mentioned in the first survey were rephrased as specific events and assembled in a list in the second survey. From that list the respondents were asked to check three outcomes that, if they occurred, would most hurt the profession, three that would most hurt society, and three that would most benefit the profession. They were also asked to indicate which of the critical problems they identified earlier might contribute, by their persistence, to the adverse outcomes selected. Finally they were asked to estimate, by contemplating the worst possible scenario, the earliest year in which those outcomes could occur.

Their responses could reveal either incentives the profession would have to resolve the problems that cause the unpleasant outcomes or outcomes the profession would want to avoid. Thus these imagined outcomes are surrogates for problems. They were found to elicit stronger responses from the constituent groups than the problem statements. Simply by being phrased as future events they appear more dramatic.

The respondents conjured up a grim picture of the consequences of unresolved problems:

By 1981 lawsuits against CPAs could triple, and financial statements could become so complex as to be unintelligible to users and prevent useful comparisons between companies.

Substandard work could become the norm by 1983 (though 12 percent of the respondents denied that outcome before 2000 if at all).

By 1984 the accounting profession could drop from near the top to tenth in attractiveness to potential entrants, and the public could reject the FASB.

Accounting could cease to be useful in making investment decisions by 1988, and the profession could lose its autonomy to the government by 1990 (though 18 percent, mostly public accountants, estimated beyond 2000 or never for that outcome).

---

[c]The problem could be resolved with further questioning and refining of the estimates using, for example, the Delphi method, characterized broadly as "a method for structuring a group communication process so that the process is effective in allowing a group of individuals, as a whole, to deal with a complex problem" [Harold A. Linstone and Murray Turoff, eds., *The Delphi Method: Techniques and Applications* (Reading, Mass.: Addison-Wesley, 1975), p. 3].

These are the worst scenarios, and the estimated dates are mean figures (that is, many thought these outcomes could occur even sooner). Many more respondents gave specific dates than indeterminate ones, adding weight to the probability that these outcomes will occur. Some estimates were only a year or two away. Taking 1985 as a reasonable planning horizon, no fewer than six of the eight top-ranked outcomes could occur. New light is also cast on the responses to the first survey. For example, the reliance on the FASB to solve many of the profession's problems, often expressed in the first survey, is shown to be accompanied by the belief that such reliance is futile.

Not all outcomes were perceived as negative. Respondents overall ranked the following highest in benefiting the profession:

The courts define the extent of the auditor's responsibility and liability in detecting fraud.

An accounting court, like the U.S. Tax Court, is created to settle accounting disputes and claims.

CPAs render unqualified opinions only after having performed extensive testing geared to fraud detection, and they may refuse a client whose internal controls are found wanting.

The federal government requires a financial information quality-control program for firms practicing before the SEC.

The SEC requires the CPA to assume greater responsibility for the client's financial reports.

The most surprising finding is that all constituent groups agreed that the first outcome might benefit the profession most. CPAs have always fought hard to maintain autonomy in this matter, yet here they are approving that the courts make this decision for them. Given the increasing amount of litigation, such an outcome may be inevitable. But that was not the question asked. One possible explanation is that the respondents may be focusing on the fact that defining the limits of auditor responsibility is beneficial for the profession. Yet they may have forgotten momentarily that the AICPA commissioned a special task force to make recommendations on that very topic.

The adverse outcomes, while not tied directly to the four crucial problems, give those problems particular urgency. The prognosis could be bleak if the following synthesis of respondents' perceptions of current problems and future consequences is borne out:

The profession's inability to develop an underlying framework for and reach consensus on GAAP leads to public rejection of the FASB and standard-setting by a government agency and to overly complex and unintelligible financial statements, preventing useful comparisons between companies.

Weakened technical standards and ethics, and hence substandard performance, bring an end to accounting as a useful factor in investment decisions, and lawsuits against CPAs triple.

Auditing firms' lack of independence from their clients and the profession's continuing uncertainty about its proper role in society lead to governmental administration of the profession. All CPAs work for the government. Accounting drops to tenth place as a career choice.

**Part II
The Turbulent Present**

Part II
Introduction

The pace of change is now so rapid that events in 1975, when the two surveys were conducted, seem distant. The respondents did more than reveal the important issues troubling the profession; they predicted increasing intervention in its affairs and intensifying pressures to reform its standards and practices. The picture they painted was of a profession so frantically busy reacting to its environment that it had lost the ability to independently manage its affairs.

Since the survey many of their predictions have come true. Especially current are their views that the profession has a number of specific and continuing problems, that their solution is hampered by severe dissension within the profession, and that accountants and their main constituencies cannot agree on which are the most important problems.

Until recently the profession had not had to answer in public for its actions. But over the last decade or so, cumulative court decisions and a more activist SEC have combined to change the situation. Instances of negligent auditing have received notoriety; and critics, both accountants and others, have fundamentally questioned the role and functioning of the auditor with increasing boldness. Alarmed at the implications, the AICPA in 1974 commissioned a panel to study the issue (it did not release its report until mid 1977). In the meantime two congressional subcommittees conducted their own inquiries. Their reports, issued in October 1976 and January 1977, unequivocally called for more governmental control. Chapter 14 summarizes the criticism leveled at the profession from those sources.

The barrage of criticism has galvanized the profession into activity, the most activity since accountants pressed for the authority to manage their own affairs in 1934 when Congress established the SEC. Chapter 15 gives a broad picture of the profession's demonstrated efforts to counter its critics and institute needed reforms. It describes the FASB's accomplishments and problems in setting standards, the steps that the AICPA and firms have taken to improve auditing practice, and the attempts by the AICPA to adapt its organization to operate more effectively. The picture is but a snapshot at a moment in time; the efforts are continuing, for the profession has been given until July 1978 to show significant progress or face a heavier controlling hand by the SEC and possibly new legislation.

Chapter 16 synthesizes the survey results with the events observed during the two years following the survey to give an independent assessment of the profession's current problems and its likely efficacy in solving them. It concludes that a gap still exists between the progress the profession has made and the expectations of Congress and others. Chapter 17 outlines some steps that the profession could take next to close the gap.

14 Forces Impinging on the Accounting Profession

At no other time in the history of the accounting profession have so much attention and criticism been focused on it or so many changes taken place within it. Its relationship with the SEC, while not quite adversarial, has become tense as the SEC has assumed a more aggressive role in overseeing accounting principles, auditing standards, and auditing independence. The profession cannot ignore the SEC's initiatives or its wishes because they carry the force of law; yet the commission's actions often prompt quick reactions from the profession, scarcely allowing it to settle into steady, productive work. Since many of the SEC actions pertain to matters already on the agenda of the FASB or AudSEC, their deliberations cannot have a truly independent outcome (if the profession's conclusions differ, two standards are set in competition; and the profession ultimately risks loss of face if overridden by the SEC on an issue). While the commission may disagree, the record shows that it has been very active in setting accounting principles and has moved much faster than the FASB. The FASB has been wrestling with far weightier topics, including rethinking the conceptual framework underlying accounting principles, but the SEC is fulfilling its obligations under the Securities Acts of 1933 and 1934 by taking action whenever it judges that accountants have failed to do so. Thus its injunctions and disciplinary actions logically proceed from its functions as overseer. Under a new chairman the SEC plans to tighten its control over the profession in the future, and this control will limit the freedom of action the profession has enjoyed.

Perhaps the single most inhibiting force in accountants' lives these days is the fear of litigation. It has stifled innovation and risk taking; it has encouraged defensive auditing; and it has raised audit costs. The greater expense stems not only from the cost of defending litigations, of settling cases out of court, and of higher malpractice insurance premiums, but also from more thorough audits and tighter controls and peer review. The hidden costs may be even more severe: loss of credibility and prestige, a fear of being unable to attract highly qualified people to the profession (at present unfounded, for the supply of accounting majors continues to outstrip demand by about three to one [1, p. 22; 2]), and possibly worst of all, a growing body of law and legal opinion by which accountants have to conduct themselves.

Since the late 1960s the courts have been writing accounting principles and auditing standards. They have compelled changes in those to whom the auditor is liable, the behavior that can cause liability, and the extent of that liability.

Until the 1976 *Hochfelder* decision, auditors were liable for negligence (both ordinary and gross) and fraud, to a degree beyond that required by adherence to generally accepted accounting principles. They were liable to third parties, even to those who could not prove that their loss resulted from misguided reliance on certified financial statements. And class action suits were de rigueur, which raised the liability ceiling astronomically. *Hochfelder* gave auditors temporary relief by ruling that negligence was generally not enough to make auditors liable, that the plaintiff had to prove intent to defraud.

By 1974 the profession must have sensed a growing confusion among its ranks and the public about the proper role and responsibilities of auditors. The confusion was no doubt exacerbated by a rash of litigations against accountants, widely reported in the financial press. In response the AICPA sponsored and empaneled the independent Commission on Auditors' Responsibilities, chaired by the late Manuel F. Cohen, a former SEC commissioner, to advise the profession. The job proved to be complex. The commission took at least a year longer than planned and did not deliver its findings until May 1977.

The study naturally took into account the litigious climate surrounding accountants and even made use of data from the Metcalf report without passing judgment on it. On the whole its findings were predictable; more importantly, many of them were palatable and feasible enough to ensure rapid implementation. It clarified a number of persistent misconceptions, such as the difference between accounting and auditing and the division of responsibility in preparing and publishing financial statements. Though the commission's recommendations are not binding on the profession in the same way that an SEC action or a court decision is, the profession is seriously considering them and plans to implement many of them soon.

As if that were not enough to keep the profession involved in self-improvement, Congress decided to take a closer look. Several congressmen and subcommittees have been particularly active in their scrutiny and have demanded the reform of accounting practices and a stronger and more direct government role in setting standards.

Representative John E. Moss (D-Calif.), chairman of the House Subcommittee on Oversight and Investigations, recently urged the SEC to prescribe accounting principles and auditing standards and sought to negate the *Hochfelder* decision by urging Congress to make accountants liable for negligence regardless of intent. Those criticisms, which surprised accountants, were made in the subcommittee's study of regulatory reform, published in October 1976.

The January 1977 staff report of the Senate Subcommittee on Reports, Accounting, and Management unleashed an even more blistering attack on the profession in its report, the Metcalf report, after subcommittee chairman Senator Lee Metcalf (D-Mont.). It charged the Big Eight accounting firms with unduly influencing the profession's standards on behalf of their large corporate clients. The Metcalf report shocked the accounting world, not so much because of its thesis, which accountants were quick to counter, but because it represented a powerful threat to the profession's autonomy. One is hard put to determine which fear predominates for accountants—litigation or government control. The criticisms in the Metcalf report have forced constructive thinking in the profession as no other recent event has, probably because the criticism came from a congressional body, with a strong threat of legislation if constructive change did not follow. The final, posthearing version of the Metcalf report, issued in November 1977, considerably moderated its criticisms of the profession; however, that fact does not alter the impact of the January 1977 version.

The profession has been the target of a barrage of steady criticism from within its ranks and from concerned observers. Numerous articles in professional and academic journals and in newspapers have assessed the profession's actions and nonactions, the effect of court or SEC decisions, and the proper course of action in the future. The brief account of these comments given at the end of this chapter should communicate the intensity and bite. Many of them come from CPAs themselves, and the controversies they have engendered are undoubtedly a sign of the profession's health.

Prodding from the SEC

The Securities and Exchange Commission, created in 1934 to monitor and enforce compliance with the 1933 Securities Act and the 1934 Securities Exchange Act, has the central mission of protecting investors and ensuring the proper functioning of the securities system. In addition, the commission is responsible for enforcing four other laws: the Public Utility Holding Company Act of 1935, the Trust Indenture Act of 1939, the Investment Company Act of 1940, and the Investment Advisers Act of 1940. One of its major tasks is the review and improvement of financial and related information disclosed by business corporations. Accountants, of course, play a crucial role in preparing and certifying that information [3].

From the beginning the SEC has chosen to let the accounting profession set accounting rules and auditing standards and to remain essentially autonomous, subject to SEC oversight.[a] This section discusses recent SEC actions with respect to accountants in matters of corporate disclosure, setting accounting standards, and regulating the profession through disciplinary procedures. In focusing on SEC functions directly related to the accounting profession, this section excludes consideration of other commission activities in the securities markets and with analysts and brokers, mutual funds and their advisers, and newer

[a]The commission oversees the practices of the accounting profession through the Office of the Chief Accountant. For a history and critique of the SEC's relationship with the profession, see refs. 4 and 5. Annual reports of the SEC are published as U.S. House documents.

matters of corporate disclosure such as determining where corporate responsibility lies, public participation in corporate decision making, reform of proxy rules, executive disclosure, protection of minority shareholders, and reform of state corporation laws [6-9].

Disclosure

To frequent criticisms of its requiring corporate disclosure information,[b] the SEC has replied that the traditional practice of corporate accountability to shareholders has weakened, for "many of the institutions that dominate today's stock market have no interest in this responsibility—leaving a gap that has to be filled" [6], and that the SEC filing gives corporate information a higher degree of integrity, the requirements imposing some discipline on companies. If mandatory requirements are lifted, the quality of information will deteriorate, a fact that analysts have already confirmed.[c]

In part because of the increasing complexity of business transactions and in part because of the rising amount of litigation, the SEC seems dissatisfied with the present role of the accountant in disclosure and with the types of information disclosed. Much of the dissatisfaction stems from the SEC's concern for the independence of auditors, the appearance of which is as important as the fact. As SEC chairman Harold Williams has said, "The crux of the whole problem is independence. . . . Most of the other pieces fall into place as ways to safeguard and assure the existence of independence" [16, p. 42]. Not only is independence important as an assurance of the validity of financial reports, but in view of the recent spate of illegal payments and bribes, the obligation to search for and report any suspicious circumstance is now greater than ever.

[b]Professor George Stigler, of the University of Chicago business school, maintains that the market has many sources of information and strong incentive to obtain it; compelling companies and analysts to widely disperse information can dry it up, not increase it. Professor George Benston, of the University of Rochester business school, reports research findings of share prices for NYSE companies before and after the 1934 Act (requiring disclosure) that show no significant reevaluation. Another of his studies showed no narrowing of bid-asked spreads that would have occurred if increased disclosure had had any impact on investors in those companies. Finally, Homer Kripke, former SEC staff member and professor of accounting and securities law at New York University law school, sees disclosure as meaningless when the numbers being reported refer exclusively to past transactions that cannot guide future investment decisions [10]. Kripke also questions whether the benefits of required disclosure justify the costs [11].

[c]A.A. Sommer, Jr., chairman of the SEC Advisory Committee on Corporate Disclosure, in a talk at the UCLA Graduate School of Management [12]. The Committee had conducted a survey of 14,000 investors owning less than 1000 shares each, and it had obtained a 45 percent response. The results were insufficient, however, for determining the value of the SEC's reporting requirements. Sommer maintained that analysts do not pay attention to firms whose market value is below $50 million and thus would not need information on those firms from the SEC, but individual investors might need it and would have no other source. (For brief reports of the committee's ultimate findings, see refs. 13-15.)

Unless auditors are independent, they cannot meet this new demand. Once accountants take a more subjective view of materiality and begin judging the preferability of accounting methods, the need for them to be independent becomes even more vital [16, p. 44].

Primarily to help investors assess the independence of auditors, then, the commission is proposing to stiffen disclosure rules involving relations between CPAs and their corporate audit clients [17, 18]. First, any company switching accounting firms would be required to report the reasons and whether the change had been approved by its board or audit committee. The requirement would go beyond the present rule requiring an 8-K report to be filed when the disagreement is over accounting principles or practices, financial statement disclosure, or auditing scope or procedures. Second, independent accountants would have to disclose in proxy statements the services they provide and the fees they are paid for them. Clients would have to state whether the services had been approved by the board or the audit committee and whether any revenue was derived from the CPA firm.

The commission has been wrestling with four related issues. The first is the timing of disclosures. Former Chief Accountant John C. Burton favors a concept of continuous disclosure, one that "recognizes the responsibility for continuous public disclosure of significant events." He sees it extending to management analysis, interim financial reporting, forecasting, and disclosure of liquidity [19]. The second is the extent of the auditor's responsibility. Burton believes that the auditors should involve themselves in all a client's financial reporting, even if they are not legally responsible for such reporting [19]. More specifically, it is held that public accountants should be more closely associated with all the financial information that a corporation releases to the public [20]. (Now they are responsible just for the audit of the certified annual financial statements.) Third, differential disclosures should be made. Average investors should be given an understandable statement, and more sophisticated stock market analysts should be given the kind of data they need to reach professional judgments about a company [19]. Fourth, the impact of inflation on individual businesses should be revealed [19].

Finally, the SEC is still actively considering the value and feasibility of requiring the reporting of earnings forecasts. Its Advisory Committee on Corporate Disclosure has suggested a trial period to see whether companies will voluntarily provide such forecasting information [12]. The commission has proposed a rule to protect persons who disclose such subjective data from legal liability that could result if third parties claim to have been misled [21].

Setting Accounting Rules

The SEC has placed itself in a dilemma [5, pp. 268-269]. On the one hand, it has accepted authority from Congress to develop the accounting rules for disclosure and the proper functioning of the securities markets. On the other, it has largely delegated that authority to the accounting profession. Chairman Harold Williams has said that "the federal government should not be setting accounting and auditing standards—except where the private sector proves itself unwilling or unable to do so" [16, p. 43]. Nevertheless, between 1973 and 1976, the SEC issued about seventeen ASRs each year [22], whereas during the same period the FASB, the accounting profession's rulemaking body, published only twelve standards and offered four more for comment [23, 24]. The SEC believes that it saw a need and fulfilled its obligation to oversee the profession's activities. It was neither interfering with nor undermining the FASB, as many critics in the profession have claimed. Indeed, when the FASB or the AICPA's AudSEC has eventually produced a ruling already covered by an ASR, the SEC has withdrawn or modified its regulations "in deference to the profession's rulings."[d] Of course, a prior SEC ruling virtually forces subsequent compliance in the private sector, which causes one to wonder whether accounting standards are really set in the public or in the private sector. For example, Leonard Savoie has written, "For sentimental reasons I still prefer to see accounting standards set in the private sector, but I can no longer advocate this position with great conviction. My reasons are that standards are now being determined largely in the public sector and inevitably the function will be taken over completely by the public sector" [24, p. 321].

When particularly controversial and difficult questions are under study, the SEC sets up special oversight procedures to guide the formation of standards. It established an advisory panel of twenty-nine accountants and industry executives on implementing the new replacement cost rule [25, p. 67]. Special liaison procedures were established for the financial accounting and reporting in the extractive industries, after the Energy Policy and Conservation Act of 1975 authorized the commission to determine, by December 1977, accounting practices by companies engaged in the production of crude oil or natural gas [25, p. 65].

The SEC has not always had its way. In a precedent-setting action, Arthur Andersen & Company, one of the largest accounting firms in the nation, first contested [26, 27] and then sued [28] to enjoin the SEC from delegating its rulemaking powers to the FASB [29]. The action was unpopular with most other large accounting firms [30] and many in the profession. They believed that unless the FASB received the SEC's formal support, it could not survive and standard setting would transfer to the public sector. On the other hand, other firms shared Andersen's objection to ASR 177, over which it has also sought

---

[d]As an example of the SEC's deference to the FASB, John Burton cited ASR 188, dealing with the New York City debt moratorium, and the commission's intention to amend Article 4 of Regulation S-X in compliance with the FASB's treatment of business segments disclosure [19]. The commission also withdrew its proposed standards for review of interim financial data (ASR 189) after the AICPA issued SAS 10, "Limited Review of Interim Financial Information" [25, p. 67].

injunctive relief (decision still pending) [28, 31]. They believed accountants lacked the necessary criteria to judge one accounting principle as preferable to another. While the debate over preferability promises to continue, the SEC's position seems clear enough.

Such actions, openly challenging the SEC's position and judgment in the federal courts, have affected but not deterred the commission.[e] The net effect could only be in the pace—not the direction—of SEC-imposed change in the accounting profession.

Regulating Accounting Practice

The SEC's chief accountant may recommend disciplinary proceedings against an accountant or accounting firm. Through injunctive and administrative actions, the SEC can censure a firm, order it not to accept engagements for a certain period, disqualify an accountant or attorney from practicing before it temporarily or permanently, require remedial training, or take other appropriate action. For example, in 1975-1976, the commission imposed sanctions on eight accountants and accounting firms subject to disciplinary proceedings under Rule 2(e) of the commission's rules of practice [25, p. 68].

Recently, the SEC has tried to avoid costly and time-consuming court battles by using the consent decree, whereby a firm agrees to remedies proposed by the commission while neither admitting fault nor guilt. For accountants, the remedy preferred by the SEC has become the peer review. Depending on the circumstances, the commission may require the firm to employ consultants to review and evaluate its audit procedures and to report the results to the commission; to participate in a peer-review program conducted by the AICPA; to have its professional practice examined by a committee of individuals named jointly by the commission and the firm; or even to submit to a review by another accounting firm [25, p. 68; 34-37]. Such settlements have indeed avoided protracted and costly arguments, and the auditor's role will never be the same. Firms now operate with tighter procedures and a heightened sensitivity toward keeping meticulous workbooks, carrying out independent checks on both derived information and the quality of a company's internal control system, and pursuing any leads about suspicious activity. Thus, although the SEC does not directly regulate the practice of auditing, it does influence its development.

---

[e]The SEC lost a case brought against it by the National Resources Defense Council and other public interest and church organizations, forcing it to reconsider its decision against requiring expanded corporate disclosure of environmental and job-discrimination matters. Existing disclosure was ruled insufficient to reveal capital expenditures and expenses for cleaning up pollution and rectifying environmental harm [32]. In another instance, Arthur Young & Co. successfully challenged an SEC injunctive proceeding in the *Goetek Resources Fund* case [33, pp. 75-76].

The SEC would like to shore up accountants' independence from their clients by barring accounting firms from recruiting and placing executives for client firms [38], and it is studying whether to prohibit firms from performing management advisory services for their audit clients. Chairman Williams has declined to say whether any prohibitions would result but has predicted firms will probably have to disclose the fees they receive from both auditing and MAS in proxy statements [16, pp. 45-46].

The Future

In a recent interview Chairman Harold Williams revealed his thoughts on the commission's work in the future [16]. He expressed a commitment to ensuring a vital and self-governing profession with adequate procedures for establishing accounting standards, assuring auditors' independence, and disciplining itself. To help him, he is seeking a chief accountant who is primarily an activist and who cannot be considered a handmaiden to the profession. (Until he does, he plans personally to assume control of the commission's accounting profession policy [39].) He believes that peer reviews should be conducted by a reviewing body that is independent of the profession, industry, and government; reviews conducted by another accounting firm lack credibility.

The chairman was sympathetic with the FASB in its effort to set accounting standards. "It's very difficult to provide direction to a profession as diffuse as accounting. There has been a lot of uncertainty as to whether the FASB is going to survive. It's hard to be effective if you don't know if you're even going to be here tomorrow." Nevertheless he believes the FASB needs to address issues more promptly and provide better leadership than it has to date.

For the profession to govern itself more effectively, it may require a new institutional arrangement. (Representative John E. Moss (D-Ca.) has suggested a legislated system of oversight by a new body of the profession, responsible to the SEC and through the SEC to the public [16, p. 42].) At a hearing on the Metcalf report in mid 1977, Chairman Williams said that legislation was not yet necessary, that the accounting profession was capable of putting its own house in order. But he gave the profession one year to do so. In July 1978, he said, he would report back to the Metcalf subcommittee. It could then "review whether the profession has demonstrated the capability to unite voluntarily behind constructive responses . . . or whether legislative action is necessary [38, 40, 41]. Williams and the SEC will be carefully watching the profession's progress during the coming year.

A Hazardous Legal Climate

Accountants are being taken to court more often then at any time in the history of the profession.[f] Not only are there more cases to fight, with their attendant

---
[f]This section draws on material in [42-44]; see also [45].

costs in money and time, but the profession is affected in numerous other ways. By their judgments in these cases, the courts are setting standards that increasingly define the extent to which accountants must bear responsibility for their actions. And the fear of litigation has inhibited accountants' willingness to meet the rising demands placed on them by society.

The enormous amount of litigation experienced by accountants has derived largely from the so-called expectation gap, the difference between the expectations of those who rely on financial statements and other accountant services and what accountants can and do deliver [46]. Accountants were once liable only to their clients, with whom they had a contractual relationship. Gradually the common-law doctrine of privity was replaced by a liability that extended to "foreseen" third parties only for fraud, which one court ruled could be inferred from gross negligence. The accountant became progressively more liable, first to third parties for ordinary negligence and then to "ordinary" third parties rather than sophisticated investors. He also became subject to individual and class-action suits by third parties under Rule 10b-5 of the 1934 Securities Exchange Act.[g]

---

[g]Several significant cases have expanded accountants' liability toward clients. In *National Security Corp.* v. *Lybrand* (1939, 256 App. Div. 226, 9 N.Y.S.2d 554), the judge ruled that an engagement to perform an audit implied a duty to verify all that can be absolutely verified, especially cash. The SEC investigation for *In the Matter of McKesson & Robbins, Inc.* (SEC ASR 19, 1940) eventually resulted in the requirement that the auditor have physical contact with clients' inventories and confirm the accounts and notes receivable. *L.B. Laboratories* v. *Mitchell* (Supreme Court of California, 1952, 39 Cal.2d 56, 244 P.2d 385) established that the late filing of a client's tax return constituted a breach of contract, not a violation of tort law. In *1136 Tenants' Corp.* v. *Max Rothenberg & Co.* (1971, 36 A.D.2d 804, 319 N.Y.S.2d 1007), it was found that any work performed by an auditor, whether auditing or "write-up" work, carries an obligation to inform the client of any suspicious circumstance, including missing invoices or suspicious actions by company employees.

In *Glanzer* v. *Shepard* (1922, 233 N.Y. 236, 135 N.E. 275), a public weigher was held liable to a third party for certifying a weighing on the order of his client "with the very end and aim of shaping the conduct of another" [42, p.181]. As the weighers were pursuing an independent calling, they owed their diligence "not only to him who ordered, but to him also who relied." The case that first cracked the doctrine of privity was *Hedley Byrne & Co., Ltd.* v. *Heller & Partners, Ltd.* (House of Lords, 1964, A.C. 465 [1963]), which involved a negligently stated accommodation credit report by a bank on which a third person relied, to his damage [44, p. 1208]. A *foreseen third party* is one who may rely on an audit opinion, specifically identified to the auditor by class though not known to him individually.

Fraud is the intentional misstatement or concealment of a material fact; *ordinary negligence* is oversight, inattention, or an error in judgment or perception; and *gross negligence* is an extreme, flagrant, or reckless departure from standards of due care and competence in performing or reporting upon professional engagements [43, p. 8]. That fraud could be inferred from gross negligence was established in *Ultramares Corp.* v. *Touche* (Court of Appeals of New York, 1931, 255 N.Y. 170, 174 N.E. 441), in which auditors failed to discover an overstatement of capital and surplus that management had concealed by recording fictitious accounts receivable and other assets.

In *Rusch Factors, Inc.* v. *Levin* (United States District Court for the District of Rhode Island, 1968, 284 F.Supp. 85), the auditor was held liable to a third party for certifying financial statements that showed a corporation to be solvent when in fact it was insolvent.

Herzfeld v. *Laventhol, Krekstein, Horwath & Horwath* (Federal District Court of the Southern District of New York, 1974, CCH Fed. Sec. L. Rep. §94,574) established that a

Several cases clarified—and expanded—the obligations of fair disclosure that auditors have under the legislative intent of the 1933 and 1934 acts. To protect investors, financial statements must portray economic reality. *Gerstle* established that adhering to generally accepted accounting principles is not enough if the resulting information turns out to be misleading. By the *Fischer* decision, if subsequent information is discovered that invalidates a prior report, that fact must be reported immediately to the SEC and to affected investors even if, as *National Student Marketing Corp.* held, the prior report was unaudited. Disclosure of hitherto confidential audit processes and judgments may be required if they materially affect the financial statements.[h]

As a result of the landmark *Continental Vending* case, the critical test of the adequacy of financial statements is whether they "fairly present" the financial position of the company. An accountant cannot rely on the general acceptance of each principle employed in the preparation of a financial statement to support his certification of a statement that is not fair *as a whole* [48, p. 204].[i]

Court decisions have often addressed generally accepted accounting principles because adherence to them has often been advanced as the accountant's principal defense. *BarChris* held that accountants could be held to standards no higher than those recognized in their own profession, though the same case held

---

company's financial reports must show the true position of the company to the "untutored eye of the ordinary investor."

The precedent-setting cases subjecting accountants to suits by third parties were *Drake* v. *Thor Power Tool Company* (United States District Court for the Northern District of Illinois, 1967, 282 F.Supp. 94), where accountants misrepresented financial statements; *Heit* v. *Weitzen* (402 F.2d 909 [2d Cir. 1968], 395 U.S. 903 [1969]), where accountants understated income in financial statements; and *Carpenter* v. *Hall* (CCH Fed. Sec. L. Rep. § 92,729 [S.D. Texas, 1969]), which held that a trustee in bankruptcy can sue derivatively on behalf of the bankrupt corporation under Section 10(b). In *Ernst & Ernst* v. *United States District Court* (439 F.2d 1288 [5th Cir. 1971], 457 F 2d 1399 [5th Cir. 1972]), it was further held that the trustee in bankruptcy can sue for claims on behalf of the class of persons who purchased or made loans against the company's stock, provided the court designates "an additional representative of the class to appear as plaintiff along with the Trustee" [42, p. 97].

[h]*Gerstle* v. *Gamble-Skogmo,* 298 F.Supp. 66 [E.D.N.Y. 1969], 332 F.Supp. 644 [E.D.N.Y. 1971], brought under Sec. 14 of the 1934 Act; and *SEC* v. *Bangor Punta Corp.,* 331 F.Supp. 1154 (S.D.N.Y. 1971), brought under Sec. 11 of the 1933 Act.

Fischer v. *Kletz,* United States District Court for the Southern District of New York, 1967, 266 F.Supp. 180, also referred to as *Yale Express,* after the company whose auditor was later found to be negligent.

SEC v. *National Student Marketing Corp.,* CCH Fed. Sec. L. Rep. §93,360, 1972. Lawyers were sued in addition to NSM and its auditors.

[i]*United States* v. *Simon,* U.S. Court of Appeals for the Second Circuit, 1969, 425 F.2d 796. For a penetrating analysis of this case, see ref. 47.

SAS 5 appeared substantially to adopt the *Simon* position, as the end of paragraph 7 shows: "The auditor should recognize, however, that there may be unusual circumstances in which the selection and application of specific accounting principles from among alternative principles may make the financial statements taken as a whole misleading" [48, p. 205]. As long ago as 1942, the SEC warned that "in addition to following accounting principles, financial statements must be informative on an overall basis." See *In The Matter of Associated Gas and Electric Company,* 11 SEC 975, 1058-1059 (1942) [42, p. 39, n. 43].

auditors liable for certifying a principle that did not fairly account for the transaction being described [48, p. 202]. *Gerstle* established that information additional to that called for by accounting principles may be required to avoid misleading investors [49]. To clarify their judgments, both the courts and the SEC have defined more broadly the concept of "materiality" of information in financial reports.[j] Finally, by the *Simon* case, auditors can be found negligent if they do not disclose any known misconduct of their clients or their officers that may reasonably affect the audited financial statements. The *Continental Vending* case was perhaps the first to add the threat of criminal liability to the legal hazards of accounting.

With *Hochfelder*, the most recent landmark decision, the Supreme Court ruled in favor of the accounting profession [52]. Overturning a 1974 ruling unfavorable to the profession by the Seventh Circuit Court of Appeals, it concluded that for accountants to be liable for damages under Section 10b and Rule 10b-5 of the 1934 Act, investors had to show that the accountant intended to "deceive, manipulate, or defraud"—a mental state termed "scienter" [53]. A footnote to the decision (dubbed the "hole in Hochfelder" [54]) left open the possibility that in certain circumstances, liability can extend to include recklessness in the absence of scienter, so ignorance or gross negligence, despite the *Hochfelder* ruling, may not shield the auditor from legal liability.[k] The trend is toward a standard of liability amounting to more than negligence but less than scienter, with an "emerging legal principle . . . to find liability when an auditor evidences recklessness or a willful disregard of facts that he should know through the normal exercise of his function" [55, p. 54].

What are the implications for accountants? What are the courts telling the profession? Clearly, they have found accountants' standards wanting when the interests and financial safety of investors are considered.[l] They have found it

---

[j]In *Escott* v. *BarChris Construction Corp.*, United States District Court for the Southern District of New York, 1968, 283 F.Supp. 643 (1968), auditors were found to have exercised neither due care with respect to audited statements on which they expressed an opinion, nor due diligence in conducting the S-1 review covering events between the audit date and the effective date of the registration statement.

The courts have defined "materiality," a prerequisite to liability under Sec. 11 of the 1933 Securities Act, as having an effect on an investment decision (the *BarChris* case) and on the market price of the security (*SEC* v. *Texas Gulf Sulphur Co.*, 401 F.2d 833 (2d Cir. 1968) [42, pp. 92-93]. According to Causey, "accountants and auditors tend to consider materiality in terms of the relative importance of an item to the firm's profits and financial position. However, courts approach materiality in a qualitative sense of whether the misstatement or omission is likely to affect a reasonable person's conduct. *The legal test is, thus, not whether the item is material in amount, but rather whether its probable effect will be to mislead in terms of one's decisions and conduct*" (italics in original) [50, p. 23]. The Supreme Court, in *Affiliated Ute Citizens* v. *United States* (406 U.S. 128, 153, 154 [1972]), speaks of material facts as those that "a reasonable investor might have considered . . . important in the making of this decision" [51, p. 30].

[k]*Bailey* v. *Meister Brau, Inc.*, May 6, 1976 (1976 CCH Fed. Sec. L. Rep. § 95,543) was a post-*Hochfelder* decision that took advantage of the loophole.

[l]Melvin Eisenberg writes, "This is perfectly illustrated by the *BarChris* case itself, because the possibility that there was more than one fair way to describe the transaction clearly does

necessary to define what constitutes adequate disclosure, what is meant by materiality, and how to get financial statements to portray economic reality [42, pp. 118-120]. They have also set the extent of auditors' liabilities.[m] Thus both the SEC and the courts have put increasing pressure on accountants to detect and report the presence of fraud or other suspicious circumstances and to be sensitive to their danger signals. Yet they offer no guidance about the conditions under which the auditor's confidential relationship with his client should be overridden in favor of a broader public or social interest [57, p. 92].

The mass of litigation against auditors has been the consequence of a number of forces that have developed over the last decade. The consumerist movement has fueled much of this activity [49, p. 152]. "Militant watchdog groups . . . see legal action as a way to impose interminable delays on projects they oppose" [58]. The surplus of practicing lawyers, created in part by the curtailment of the no-fault insurance laws in the once-lucrative auto business, has spurred "speculative damage" or nuisance suits, taken on a contingent fee basis in hopes of fat out-of-court settlements [58]. Such suits cost defendant corporations and accountants as much to defend as legitimate actions and thereby inflate their legal expenses.[n] Add to those factors the ease with which those who buy or sell securities can bring suit against accountants without having to prove reliance on financial statements [69], liberal rules of discovery adopted by the courts [60, p. 31], and "accommodating judges who stretch the old laws far beyond their original scope" [58], and it is clearer why the legal activities of the larger accounting firms have swelled.[o] The evolution of new concepts of auditor liability to third parties centers on two key issues: an expansion of the class to whom the auditor owes care (the required relationship between the plaintiff and the defendant auditor) and a redefinition of the level

---

not mean it could be accounted for in any way management chose. No one would claim, for example, that the transaction could have been accounted for as a gift, and it was equally inappropriate to account for it as a sale yielding sales income. An argument that accounting for the transaction as a sale was permissible because others were doing it and the APB had not forbidden it simply demonstrates the moral and intellectual poverty of the term 'generally accepted accounting principles' as interpreted by the accountants" [48, pp. 193-194].

[m]Reiling and Taussig believe that the profession and not the courts should set accounting principles: "[A]ccounting procedures should be generalized from the experience of going concerns run by ethical managers, not failing companies run by wrongdoers" [56, p. 180].

[n]Though few claims against accountants result in the award of large damages to plaintiffs, the cost of defending them is considerable. One case in which a plaintiff sued for $3 million was settled for $10,000, but the accountant's defense cost $72,000. In another a plaintiff sought $600,000 and settled for $7000, but the accountant spent $124,000 in the action [60, p. 32].

[o]Liggio estimated that in 1974, between 500 and 1000 cases were still pending against accountants and that over 200 had been decided [61]. Jaenicke believes that "cases brought by third parties related to alleged audit deficiencies may have peaked in 1975 and early 1976" [43, p. 2].

of care that the auditor owes to third parties (the definition of intent and its necessity) [43, p. 8].

The rise in class-action suits and the resulting increase in the magnitude of potential damages has given impetus to new concepts of insurance [43, pp. 4-5].P *Rusch Factors* possibly opened the way to unlimited damage claims on auditors, as the court's opinion suggests:

> The wisdom of the decision in *Ultamares* has been doubted . . . and this court shares that doubt. Why should an innocent reliant party be forced to carry the weighty burden of an accountant's professional malpractice? Isn't the risk of loss more easily distributed and fairly spread by imposing it on the accounting profession, which can pass the cost of insuring against the risk onto its customers, who can in turn pass the cost onto the entire consuming public? [43, p. 14].

That largess was diminished by Hochfelder's narrower interpretation of liability under Rule 10b-5 of the 1934 act. The high court observed in a footnote that to have found the auditors negligent (it did not) would have extended "to new frontiers the 'hazards' of rendering expert advice under the securities acts, raising serious policy questions not yet addressed by Congress" [53].

Litigation against accountants is part of the larger social phenomenon of increased lawsuits against business and the professions generally [65, 66]. Business faces complex and increasing regulatory actions [67], and between 1969 and 1970 lawsuits against business increased fivefold [68]. The legal profession may share the blame. In the eyes of many, lawyers have gone beyond their advocacy role in the best tradition of the profession to engage in unnecessary actions to make a lot of money through contingency fee arrangements against defendants who have high insurance coverage. One editorial called for lawyers who bring suits without merit to pay the defendant's costs, including the fees paid to defending counsel, and for bar associations to disbar lawyers who repeatedly bring such suits [58]. A more balanced view is that, despite the many adverse effects on the accounting profession, "the present legal climate has not had an overwhelming negative effect on either the accounting profession or society [43, p. 81]. If the changes brought about by the courts in the profession can be viewed as beneficial, then such a claim has some substance.

PIn one case, a federal judge approved a record $60.5 million settlement of class-action lawsuits stemming from the scandal surrounding the demise of the Equity Funding Corp. of America [62]. In another historic case (*SEC* v. *Mattel, Inc.,* CCH Fed. Sec. L. Rep. § 94,807 [D.D.C. 1974]), Arthur Andersen, the former independent auditor for Mattell charged with being negligent in auditing financial statements filed in and after 1971, settled its litigation by payment to the class of $900,000 cash [63]. See also ref. 64.

Griffin accounts for the so-called "deep-pocket factor" as follows: "[W]hen a company becomes bankrupt, the auditor is one of the few parties left with any financial resources, and his principal resource is his malpractice insurance coverage. In many instances of client failure, the accountant finds that his indemnity insurance policy is the prime target of demands for recovery" [60, p. 31].

The impact on the profession of recent litigation can be summarized as increased pressure to (1) tighten accounting and auditing standards so as to enable an incontestable defense in any court action; (2) extend the audit and attest functions respectively to detect fraud and to give directors, underwriters, creditors, and attorneys more "due diligence" protection [56, p. 179]; and (3) disabuse the investor of the notion that accountants can guarantee the accuracy of financial statements [61, p. 24].[q] As Griffin notes, "Accountants' responsibilities under the law are being developed and undertaken much more quickly than the boundaries are being drawn" [60, p. 34]. The more quickly the profession can draw those boundaries—with or without the help of the SEC and the courts—the less liable it will be.

Findings of the Commission on Auditors' Responsibilities

Established in October 1974 by the AICPA, yet functioning independently of the Institute, the Commission on Auditors' Responsibilities was ordered to define the role of auditors. It found that charter sufficiently taxing that in September 1975 it published a statement of issues and requested more time to complete deliberations. Its tentative conclusions were delivered in May 1977 [69]. Most of the forty or so recommendations were directed at auditors, but also concern the SEC, the courts and corporate management. A brief summary follows.

Distinctions between Management and Auditor Responsibilities

For the most part, financial statement users have reasonable expectations about what auditors can and should do for them, but they should not expect more services without weighing their additional costs and they should recognize that management, not the auditor, has ultimate responsibility for the data reported in financial statements. Auditors and management are in the best position to narrow the gap between unreasonable expectations and reality.

The auditor is an independent intermediary between the issuer and users of financial information. While accountants prepare financial information, auditors (also called public accountants) check it; the primary function of public accountants is auditing. It is the responsibility of the auditor to evaluate management's choice of accounting principles, the appropriateness of their application, and their cumulative effect. "Fairness" is inappropriate as a standard because it

---

[q]According to Reiling and Taussig, "auditors should not express an opinion on financial statements without qualifications as to the level of confidence for the estimated amounts in those statements," and "confidence limits should be published for the principal items along with their expected values" [56, p. 177].

is too subjective, and should be eliminated from the auditor's report; auditors' responsibilities are better defined by specifying criteria for the selection and application of accounting principles. Any reference to consistency in the auditor's report should also be deleted; it is management's responsibility to disclose changes in the accounting principles used. The auditor's report should be expanded to include a separate paragraph of standardized wording on every major element of the audit engagement [69, pp. 77-78]. To clarify the division of responsibility between auditors and management, management should, in the annual report, formally acknowledge responsibility for the statements, the operation of the internal controls, and so on, and state that its legal counsel is satisfied with the information given the auditors regarding the company's claims, litigations, and assessments [69, p. 79]. Auditors should be present at the annual meeting of shareholders to answer questions.

The auditor has the duty of searching for material fraud (materiality is not defined) and of reporting it in the financial statements. In conducting the search, he should exercise "due professional care," familiarizing himself with the controls designed to detect and prevent fraud. He should be basically skeptical and prepared at any time to question management's honesty. Since not all fraud can be detected, an auditor should be evaluated on whether he exercised due professional care. Nevertheless, management should bear the primary responsibility of corporate accountability. Management should issue policy statements specifying the required standards of conduct and the procedures for ensuring compliance with them. The auditor could monitor compliance and report on it. Illegal or questionable acts should be considered without regard to materiality.

Users do not appreciate the degree of uncertainty to which all financial statements are subject. A separate note should be included in financial statements to explain the significance of all material uncertainties for earnings and financial position, replacing the "subject to" qualification in present reporting.

Should the auditor's present role be expanded? The answer is a qualified yes. Auditors should attest to all corporate financial information produced by the accounting system and within the auditor's competence to verify. The auditor should evaluate the controls over the accounting system and assess management's description of them in the annual report, noting especially any uncorrected material weaknesses in the system not disclosed by management.

An audit should be conceived as pertaining to a period of time rather than to a particular set of financial statements (resembling the SEC's auditor-of-record concept). The audit should gradually expand to embrace all important elements of a company's financial reporting process, including the process used to prepare quarterly financial reports. Shareholders should be given an interim report on the progress of the audit.

Auditor Independence

Although independence is an essential attribute of an auditor, absolute independence is impossible because an auditing firm is selected and paid by the very company it audits. The source of funds for paying the audit fee is not as important in maintaining independence as is the source of the power to select the auditor and approve fees. Thus to improve the degree of independence an auditor must have from his client, there should be an independent audit committee or board of outside directors to select, appoint, set fees for and, if necessary, change a company's auditor. Providing MAS for an audit client does not necessarily impair the auditor's independence, but to avoid the appearance of a conflict of interest it would be prudent for the nature of an auditor's MAS to be disclosed to users. The board or audit committee should determine whether a conflict exists in each instance. Executive recruiting should be limited to positions below board entry levels so as not to compromise any decision about selecting or retaining an auditor. Auditors should not be barred from engaging in "accounting advocacy" on behalf of clients, but when they do so they should make it clear to users that their work and opinions are not presented in their capacity as independent auditors.

Finally, all firms should remove any unnecessary time and budget pressures from the audit staff because such pressures reduce the independence with which the engagement is carried out. Excessive price competition to attract and retain clients can lead a firm to accept an underfunded engagement and then to be tempted to take shortcuts or sacrifice diligence in order to complete the audit within budget. Most audit failures have stemmed from mistakes in judgment, which are often caused by overreliance on client representations. The tendency to take client representations on faith increases as time and budget pressures increase. Under such pressures, some auditors have signed off on audit steps they have not actually completed and audit managers have been spread too thin supervising too many audits in too short a time for a thorough review.

Other Issues

The AICPA's AudSEC should be restructured as a small full-time group (between five and nine members), and it should encourage participation from outside the profession. With respect to the profession's disciplinary procedures, secrecy should be removed from both the actions and penalties imposed; actions against ethics violations should not be deferred until litigation is settled unless there is an explicit connection; and action should generally not be postponed to await the outcome of an appeal in a litigation judgment.

The AICPA should publish analyses of cases involving significant audit failures. The courts and the SEC, as appropriate, should limit the extent of damages for which auditors can be liable, assess defense and court costs against unsuccessful plaintiffs whose cases lack merit, use court-appointed "masters" with accounting, auditing, and legal expertise comparable to that of an SEC administrative law judge to help resolve complex technical cases, and legislate "safe harbor" rules protecting auditors whose responsibilities are significantly extended or who are asked to assume new ones. (A safe harbor rule stipulates that the person seeking to establish liability must prove that a certain specified standard was not met.)

Accusations from Congress

At one time Congress was quite content to let the SEC monitor the profession's development of accounting principles and observance of securities disclosure laws. Recently, however, perhaps because of a heightened awareness of the crucial role played by accounting in the corporate information stream, Congress has been taking a closer look at the profession. It has not generally liked what it has found. As a result, proposals for stronger and even direct federal control have emerged.

The most specific proposal for direct government control occurred in the draft Title VIII to energy bill HR 7014, introduced in July 1975. Its sponsors, angered over alleged excess profits amassed by oil and gas companies and the failure of the FPC to collect adequate financial data on their activities, called for the GAO to determine accounting practices for the petroleum industry and audit the companies. The SEC and GAO swiftly and firmly rejected the staff report. It would undermine the role of the FASB, sanctioned by the SEC; it would duplicate the independent audits already being performed on the companies; and it failed to consider the opinions of accountants in the industry. Both agencies favored keeping accounting rulemaking in the private sector and urged House members not to adopt Title VIII. There was another instance of congressional intervention in the affairs of the accounting profession through energy legislation. In response to lobbying efforts by the petroleum industry to persuade Congress to overturn an FASB ruling requiring oil and gas producers to adopt the "successful-efforts" method of accounting, the Senate in October 1977 issued an amendment giving the oil companies, in effect, license to use two different kinds of accounting [70].

The two most grievous attacks on the profession and threats to its autonomy have come in the form of subcommittee staff studies. The first was the Moss report, a detailed study of nine regulatory agencies by a House subcommittee, released in October 1976. While commenting favorably on the SEC, it unleashed a "slashing attack on accounting and accountants," charging among other things that the FASB had "accomplished virtually nothing toward resolving fundamental accounting problems" [73]. The second, the Metcalf report, was a voluminous report on the accounting establishment itself, prepared by a Senate subcommittee and released in January 1977. It focused on the concentration of power in the profession and asserted that the eight largest accounting firms constituted an oligarchy ruling for private interests.

The Moss Report

In October 1976 the House Subcommittee on Oversight and Investigations (Chairman John E. Moss, D-Ca.) published a report called *Federal Regulation and Regulatory Reform.* The product of nearly two years of investigation, it was based on the oral testimony of over 200 persons from the public and private sectors and on over 3500 pages of written testimony. The Securities and Exchange Commission was one of the nine regulatory agencies studied in detail. The report was critical of the accounting profession and the SEC's regulation of it.

First, it expressed dissatisfaction with the profession's accounting principles and auditing standards and recommended that the SEC prescribe those principles and standards in detail. It also urged Congress to amend Section 10b of the 1934 act "to protect the public against negligence by accountants and others, regardless of intent to deceive or defraud" [51, p. 52]. That recommendation was prompted by the subcommittee's examination of the *Ernst & Ernst* v. *Hochfelder* decision, which held that the language of Section 10b clearly connotes intentional misconduct. Blackmun dissented, arguing that "auditors should be held responsible for negligence, particularly because of their critical role in the issuing and trading of securities" [51, p. 39]. In testimony before the subcommittee, Professor Abraham Briloff was also critical of the majority decision:

[T]he court has decreed that negligence by a professional person is not sufficient to hold him liable to those who are victimized by his negligence even though the person professes competence, expertise and responsibility (and where he is paid on the basis of such professions). For me, this very pretentious profession is the perpetration of fraud if it is known that negligence is a hidden factor in the profession's tool box [51, p. 39, n. 83].

The report goes on to say that "the negligence standard implies a failure to meet a standard of care appropriate for the person in question. Thus, the standard that a professional such as a certified public accountant should meet would be expected to be higher than the standard applicable to a person making ordinary transactions in securities" [51, p. 40].

The report also censured the accounting profession for its reluctance to require auditors to attest that the accounting principles used by management are the fairest, given the conditions, and for defining "fairness" so inadequately in SAS 5.[r] It is not surprising, then, that the profession has not yet resolved the basic preferability issue.[s]

---

[r]That judgment was based substantially on the testimony of Professor Briloff alone. The subcommittee's exclusive reliance on a controversial critic of the profession angered accountants and businessmen and drew a protest from the chairman of the FASB [71, 72].

Professor Briloff inveighed against the weak wording of SAS 5, noting such phrases as "have general acceptance," "appropriate in the circumstances," "classified and summarized in a reasonable manner," and "within a range of acceptable limits." "Considering the awesomeness of the problem with which it was wrestling, could any set of standards be more pusillanimous than the foregoing? Where do we find a mandate to the auditor to determine and apply the *fairest* of the alternative GAAPs which may be available in the particular circumstances?" [51, p. 37]

[s]The SEC's ASR 177 requires that when management changes an accounting principle, the auditors state that the new one is preferable; otherwise the auditor should veto the change.

Other testimony by Professor Briloff cited the uneven disciplinary actions of the SEC. Actions against individual accountants typically result in expulsion from practicing before the commission; actions against smaller accounting firms usually result in suspension for an extended period. The major accounting firms, however, are usually let off with "consent decrees" of limited effect [51, p. 39].

The Moss report recommended that the SEC assure that boards of directors (and their nominating and audit committees) are independent from management; that they are sufficiently compensated and staffed to perform their duties responsibly; that they review and approve the corporation's code of business conduct and system of internal controls; that the board's audit committee have independent expert advisers available to it; and that the board retain the authority to hire and fire the independent accountant, legal counsel, general counsel, and senior operating executives. Finally, it called on the SEC to ensure that independent auditors assess the quality of internal controls and their enforcement in the annual report.

The Metcalf Report

In January 1977 the release of a Senate subcommittee staff report *The Accounting Establishment* sent shock waves through the accounting and financial worlds. Climaxing a year-long inquiry by the Subcommittee on Reports, Accounting, and Management (Chairman Lee Metcalf, D-Mont.), the 1760-page report fundamentally criticized the structure of the accounting industry, charged the Big Eight CPA firms with controlling and exploiting the profession's rulemaking powers to protect the special interests of their corporate clients, and blamed the SEC for acquiescing in that state of affairs and restricting itself to "a mere oversight role."

Three arguments underlay the second criticism.

1. Former partners of Big Eight firms have served as members or heads of various policy committees in the AICPA and the FASB and hence by inference favored the interests of those firms over other smaller CPA firms and the interests of their clients over the public interest [73, pp. 10-11, 15, 26].
2. The FASB and the AICPA depend heavily on contributions of money and staff time from the Big Eight firms [73, pp. 14-16, 153-157].
3. None of the first twelve accounting standards issued by the FASB has "seriously threatened the accounting prerogatives of various special interest groups in the established business community" [73, p. 17]. Corporations still have the freedom to choose from several accounting principles in preparing their financial statements. "A study sponsored by the AICPA has listed 31 separate kinds of business transactions with an aggregate of 80

That ASR raised a storm of protest from accountants and even resulted in a suit to nullify the requirement [28].

different accounting alternatives for reporting the transactions" [75, p. 17]. Such flexibility can mean "the difference between reporting healthy profits or severe losses to investors and the public" [73, pp. 6, 38, and 188-189].

The Big Eight firms were also accused of anticompetitive practices in the supply of auditing and accounting services to private industry. They dominate the profession because of their size and the concentration of the corporations they audit. No professional partnership comes close to the size of these large CPA firms. Each has several hundred partners and supports a staff of from 4000 to 8000, with branch offices in every major city in the United States and affiliations or branch offices in most major cities in the rest of the world [73, p. 4]. Though they employ only about 12 percent of all CPAs, their clients account for 85 percent of the 2641 corporations whose shares are traded on the New York and American Stock Exchanges and generate 84 percent of the roughly $75 billion in profits after taxes. Fully 92 percent of the NYSE corporations are Big Eight clients. Other concentrations are found by industry (for example, Price Waterhouse audits six of the nation's ten largest oil and gas companies). The five most influential firms of the Big Eight collectively audit clients that account for 74 percent of the total sales and 79 percent of the net earnings for all corporations listed on the New York Stock Exchange. The same five firms count as their clients forty-two of the fifty largest American corporations in terms of sales, and forty-four of the fifty largest in terms of net income [73, pp. 4-5, 39, 42-43]. All of the fifty largest corporations in five categories—sales, income, taxes, employees, and assets—are audited by one of the Big Eight firms [73, pp. 39-40].

Observers of the business scene corroborate that "small and medium-sized accounting firms lose clients to the Big Eight when smaller companies go public or are acquired by major corporations" [73, pp. 7, 45]. Many underwriters, banks, and lawyers maintain that having a prestigious accounting firm as auditor is essential to success in the capital markets and that large accounting firms possess the "SEC experience" that a publicly held company needs.

The third strike against the Big Eight firms is what the report called their "alarming lack of independence and lack of dedication to public protection." The Big Eight firms openly promote their clients' interests in public forums, for example on tax issues or accounting methods for oil and gas extraction, which severely compromises their objectivity and hence their independence [73, pp. 8-9, 52-64, 65-67]. About 12 percent of their total revenues is derived from performing management advisory services for audit clients. MAS includes executive recruitment, marketing analysis, plant layout, product analysis, actuarial services, and financial management services, among others. Since such tasks help a client manage its business, they impair the firm's ability to audit independently [73, pp. 8, 34-35, 50-52]. The close relationship fostered over long periods by the Big Eight with the managements of client companies jeopardizes objective thought and action. To retain their wealthy and influential clients, the CPA firms are probably often willing to go along with management's choice of accounting principles, so long as basic tenets of GAAP are not violated. Such corporate "influence" over the auditor affects his independence [73, pp. 6-7].

The Metcalf report's solution to excessive control of the accounting establishment by private special interests at the expense of the public interest was total government control over the profession and far stricter oversight by the SEC. The report seriously questioned whether the accounting profession was capable of regulating itself in the public interest. Specifically it urged Congress to exert stronger oversight of accounting practices and to restore the right of individual investors who had suffered losses to sue independent auditors for negligence under the fraud provisions of the securities laws. Those exhortations were tantamount not only to overturning the Supreme Court's *Hochfelder* decision [54], but also to denying any accountant-client privilege and any limit on the liability of independent auditors.

Laying much of the blame for the current state of affairs at the door of the SEC, the report suggested that financial accounting standards be set by a federal board similar in operation to the CASB or even by the GAO and that auditing standards be set by the GAO, the SEC, or by federal statute. The report rejected the retention of standard-setting functions in the private sector: "The inability to divorce private influence from private control impairs all efforts to achieve public confidence in a system which invests public authority in private organizations" [73, p. 19].

The GAO was suggested as an appropriate federal agency, along with the SEC or a special federal audit inspection agency, to make periodic, mandatory inspections of the work of independent auditors. The report scoffed at the possibility of restoring public confidence in the profession by a quality-control program in which one large CPA firm would review the practices and standards of another.

Without specifying which agency should carry out the task, the report urged the federal government to define the responsibilities of independent auditors to meet the expectations of Congress, the public, and courts of law. Those responsibilities were characterized as follows: "The independent auditor's certification included in corporate reports should be understood by all auditors to mean that financial information is presented fairly and that corporate records are complete and accurate" [73, p. 23].

The report recommended that Congress consider means of increasing competition among accounting firms, particularly in the choice of independent auditors for major corporations. Instead of placing only one firm, nominated by management, on the ballot at the stockholders' annual meeting (thus almost assuring the retention of that firm), the report suggested amending the federal security laws to require more than one firm on the ballot, permitting holders of a limited number of shares to vote for their own representative on the company's audit committee, and forcing a change of accountants after three years or whenever the SEC finds that a firm has failed to exercise independent action to protect investors and the public.

The third suggestion was also considered a step toward making the auditing firm more independent of its client. Going further, the report called on the SEC to promulgate and enforce strict standards of conduct for auditors that would prohibit any activities that might impair their independence in fact or appearance. Specifically it urged prohibiting direct or indirect representation of clients' interests and nonaccounting management advisory services for audit clients. The report recommended that the SEC monitor and evaluate the performance of the large accounting firms by annually collecting basic operational and financial data from the nation's fifteen largest CPA firms. The SEC was also instructed to treat all accountants alike in its disciplinary procedures and not favor the large firms. Neither should it use private organizations to conduct compliance reviews but should undertake the reviews itself.

The final major recommendation was intended to relieve the allegedly excessive concentration in the supply of accounting and auditing services to large publicly owned corporations. It called for the Department of Justice and the FTC to determine whether such concentrations violated federal antitrust laws.

As he convened the open hearings of the subcommittees three months after issuing the report, Senator Metcalf declared that the purpose of the hearings was to give accountants and others a chance to respond to the report. (A staff aide said that the aim of the hearings was to put pressure on the accounting firms and on the SEC to correct accounting problems [74].) Senator Metcalf called for reforms that would "assure Congress and the public that accounting practices will report corporate financial results accurately and clearly." Senator Charles Percy, the ranking Republican on the committee, echoed that concern by sharply criticizing accountants for producing financial statements the public could not understand or rely on [75]. Senator Metcalf cited three essential reforms: (1) opening up the accounting standard-setting process to small businesses, smaller accounting firms, and the investing public; (2) establishing an effective system for reviewing the work of independent auditors; and (3) increasing the independence of auditors from their clients and making accountants more responsible to the public [74]. He expressed the hope that improvements could be made without additional legislation.[t]

---

[t]In a unanimous twenty-five-page final report released 14 November 1977, the Metcalf committee did not vote to introduce any new legislation, but instead concluded that the accounting profession can be relied on largely to police itself subject to close SEC oversight and the possibility of stricter legislation later. Accountants' efforts all year long to ward off legislation and increased government control over the profession have thus proved highly successful, though the pressure for it to reform itself has in no way dissipated.

The committee in this final report held firm to a number of its former recommendations: (1) all firms auditing publicly traded corporations should be required to join a self-regulatory organization with appropriate disciplinary powers, itself subject to SEC

A Steady Stream of Public Criticism

Hardly any facet of accounting activity has remained untouched by sharp criticism—sometimes from disgruntled practitioners or firms whose private interests are threatened, but more often from public-spirited persons. This section summarizes that criticism under the headings of auditor independence, validity of financial reports, and self-regulation.

Auditor Independence

Though accountants and accounting firms have long proclaimed their independence from their clients, such independence is difficult to achieve in practice [48, pp. 196-209]. The auditor is dependent on management for his selection, tenure, and dismissal. The auditor's only power stems from his discretion to qualify or withhold a clean certificate from the corporation's financial statements; he does not even select the accounting principles used—management does. Should he balk at management's insistence on using a particular principle, a more flexible auditor can always be found. An accountant who resigns or is dismissed has not only lost the client but has also been unable to correct the client's financial statements. Thus the very structure of the accountant's role places real pressures on the auditor to succumb to management's wishes. Only unusually strong people are able to resist them [77].

Eisenberg [48] contends that the structure of the accountant's role is seriously if not fundamentally flawed. It is not possible to expect objective reporting where the power to select accounting principles resides with the very managers whose activities are being accounted for, who also may hire and fire the auditors whose job it is to judge the acceptability of the selections.[u] The

oversight; (2) firms that audit public companies should be required to divulge financial and other data on their own operations; (3) auditing firms should divest themselves of management advisory services, such as executive recruiting services, that are not directly related to accounting; (4) the SEC should pursue as a major goal the development and application of uniform accounting standards and by so doing eliminate the immense flexibility inherent in the current set that allows companies to report different financial results for the same events just by using different accounting methods; (5) negligent auditors should be held legally liable for damages suffered by private parties as a result of their mistakes (in disagreement with the recent *Hochfelder* decision); and (6) the problem of industry concentration, hit hard in the earlier staff study, could be addressed indirectly by lifting bans on professional advertising and direct solicitation of clients and not, as advocated before, by forced rotation of company auditors [76].

[u]Management can also control the extent to which an auditor probes into the company's affairs: "the thoroughness of any audit is limited by how large a fee the client is willing to pay" [78]. Reporting on the results of a survey conducted by Professor John Grant Rhode for the Commission on Auditors' Responsibilities, Frederick Andrews writes that "about one-fourth of the sample said their firm's relationship to a client company—either the regard for the importance of the fee or fear of losing the client—impaired their firm's independence. Not entirely consistently, however, more than one-half contended that the mere fact of being paid by the client company did not hurt an auditor's ability to resist pressure" [79].

answer, he argues, lies in making two structural changes, changes toward which the profession has indeed been moving. First, the power to select appropriate accounting principles should be shifted from management to the independent auditor. Second, the auditor should be hired, paid, and fired by—and at all times answerable to—an audit committee composed primarily of outside directors.[v]

Professor Abraham Briloff, long a dogged critic of the profession, believes that auditors' independence is impaired if they perform management advisory and other consulting services for audit clients [88, pp. 418-420, 282-290; see also ref. 89]. He would ban the performance of nonaudit work for an audit client. It is the advocacy stance of the other services that gets in the way of truly independent auditing. Briloff cites the role of Peat, Marwick, Mitchell & Co. in the *Stirling Homex* case [90], criticizing the auditing firm for showing the client how to get around a problem that was preventing a clean certificate, and then giving it [88, pp. 419-420].

How can an accountant be independent if his professional association—and often the firm he works for—takes an advocacy role with respect to proposed federal legislation or court action?[w] The answer hinges on which interest predominates, the client's or that of the broader public. Clearly any advocacy for a client or industry diminishes even the appearance of independence. In some cases, however, auditors find it difficult to decide when the public interest becomes paramount. For example, what extent of client malfeasance justifies breaking the confidential relationship between the auditor and his client? Causey's criterion is that where "the matters involved are of great materiality and importance to investor decisions, the auditor must blow the whistle." In fact, where he has failed to do so, the auditor is liable "as an aider and abettor by allowing the firm to trade on his reputation and credibility as an auditor" [50, pp. 28-29].

---

[v]See refs. 80-84. In a letter to the Chief Executive Officers of Exchange corporations dated 3 September 1976, the New York Stock Exchange proposed requiring "every domestic listed company, as a condition of continued listing after December 31, 1977, to maintain an Audit Committee composed entirely of independent directors who are not part of current management. . . . Under the proposal, the Audit Committee would consist of at least three independent directors, two of whom must be outside directors. No upper limit is placed on the size of the Committee, but in all cases, the majority of the Committee must be outside directors." (See also ref. 85.) Frederick Andrews considers outside directors and accountants a "natural alliance. The outside director is hungry for information—he wants to know what's going on—and the accountant is hungry for some sort of person to whom he can report that is outside the ongoing stream of management. So that's a very congenial fit and has a lot of promise" [86, p. 18]. The *Wall Street Journal* reported that "Data compiled by and for the [New York Stock] exchange in internal and outside studies indicate that most of the Big Board's 1,550 listed companies already have a majority of outside directors and independent audit committees" [87].

[w]For an example of an advocacy position taken by the AICPA, see the comments of Frederick Andrews about the IRS hearings on proposed regulations under Sec. 861 of the Internal Revenue Code [86, p. 33]. The proposed regulations would have reduced the foreign tax credits that American corporations could claim; the AICPA testified in opposition to it. As example of an advocacy position taken by a firm, the Metcalf report accused Big Eight firms of client advocacy in numerous matters [73, pp. 52-64].

Validity of Financial Reports

The critics' perennial challenge, "What do the numbers mean?", is echoed in professionals' debates over the fairness of corporate financial disclosures, the amount of creative accounting permissible, and the validity of the numbers that result from the auditor's efforts [91].

Stringer has stated that accountants deal with two basic kinds of uncertainty in assessing financial statements: (1) the uncertainty inherent in the accounting process itself and in the accounting model on which it is based and how best to communicate those uncertainties to the reader and (2) the fallibility of auditors and of the auditing process and how best to communicate those uncertainties to the reader [86, p. 28]. The inherent uncertainty precludes an objective presentation of financial statements; a more appropriate goal for accountants would be to produce a fair statement [86, p. 28]. That is what the courts these days are demanding of accountants. The problem, of course, lies in deciding what is fair.

Though no satisfactory definition yet exists, several critics have suggested ways of making financial statements fairer. Kripke and others urge the greater use of forward-looking information such as earnings forecasts (under the protection of safe-harbor assurance from the SEC) [16; 92, p. 315]. Information based on the current accounting model of historical costs, says Kripke, does not help an investor make his "buy, sell, or hold decision. When he makes that decision, he wants to know whether his proposed or his present commitment of new cash or of the existing value of his present investment is a wise investment. . . . He wants to know what is happening to his own prospective commitment or to his own opportunity cost to sell out if he already has the investment" [92, p. 298]. Kripke essentially argues for replacement-cost accounting, though it is known to be difficult and problematic to apply: "After 50 years of awareness, 25 years of intensive research, and 10 years of steady and sometimes rapid inflation, accountants have yet to agree on a common-sense way to report the effects of inflation" [93]. During the last two years, debate raged about this topic, both in the United States and Great Britain [94-111].

Accountants are also assailed for giving financial statements an aura of precision they do not possess. Accountants themselves complain that the public thinks financial reports are accurate and that a clean certification guarantees the truth of the financial information. Andrews observes: "Accounting is the only form of measurement I know that doesn't indicate the range of its own accuracy" [86, p. 28]. There has been no published effort to present financial information in probabilistic terms, and efforts to do so could have the effect of further complicating the report. Burton has stated that writing something like "This audit is based upon a sampling process and has a .05 confidence interval," even if true, would communicate little to the reader [86, p. 27]. Reiling and Taussig advocate publishing confidence limits "for the principal items along with their expected values. For example, earnings per share should be reported as

$4.02 with the probability that they are between $3.90 and $4.14 at the 95 percent level of confidence" [56, p. 177]. Burton also believes that much of the wording of the accountant's opinion confuses the lay reader and serves only as a defense against lawyers; he would like to see new "tools of communication" used [86, p. 27].

Of course, the way the financial statement is put together depends in large part on the accounting principles used. In contrast to the AICPA's official position that the accounts of a company are primarily the responsibility of its management (together with responsibility for selecting the underlying accounting principles), Eisenberg presents a strong case for having the accountant select the appropriate principles [48, p. 188]. He also criticizes the principles themselves, arguing that the criterion of "general acceptability" for an accounting principle is a myth; it simply means the principle has been used in other financial statements by management without objection or has appeared in the literature. It is no wonder, he says, that "an accountant may certify a statement even though he believes that the principles employed in its preparation do not account for the underlying transactions as fairly as competing principles that management has rejected. This certification in turn provides even further support for the principles . . . [providing] great pressure for inferior principles to spread throughout an industry" [48, p. 190]. The loophole that permitted such a state of affairs was an APB ruling that substantial authoritative support could exist outside its own opinions. Until *BarChris* and *Continental Vending,* the prevalent attitude of the accounting profession (and the official position of the AICPA) was that "an accounting principle can be considered generally accepted if it is in use and has not been specifically disapproved by an authoritative institution, whether or not it fairly accounts for the transaction it describes" [48, p. 193].

Eisenberg gives another illustration of that attitude by analyzing the wording of the auditor's opinion that the company's financial statements *"present fairly* . . . in conformity with generally accepted accounting principles" its financial position and operating results. "To read this language as satisfied simply because each principle employed in the preparation of the financial statements is generally accepted would be to read the term 'fairly' right out of the certification: if a statement prepared in accordance with generally accepted accounting principles is presented fairly by virtue of that fact alone, there would be no difference between 'present . . . in conformity with' and 'present *fairly* . . . in conformity with' " [48, p. 194]. Harvey Kapnick writes: "The real test is not the general acceptance of the accounting principle, but the fair presentation of the financial data resulting from the application of the principle" [112, p. 376].

Finally, the absence of an explicit framework or underlying rationale for accounting principles will continue to frustrate the FASB, just as it did the APB before it. As Moonitz points out, "Some of its pronouncements will be inconsistent with other pronouncements. Individual pronouncements will be incomplete or vague, leaving the way open for new variations that will call for additional pronouncements. Partial solutions will parade as general standards and special interest groups will have a field day as loopholes are discovered and exploited" [48, p. 200, n. 34]. The FASB is now trying to develop such a comprehensive framework [113, 114, 115].

Self-Regulation

As a whole the accounting profession seems conservative, defensive, reactive, and self-protective. In a private address (not speaking from his position as former chief accountant of the SEC), Burton declared that the profession "has tended to be responsive rather than innovative. Where they have moved, it has been in areas where there were pressures brought upon them to move, rather than areas which they have identified and set forth on their own. Most of the significant auditing standards or pronouncements and professional developments in the past four or five years have been in response to some stimulus rather than representing an innovative stance on the part of the profession." He went on to deprecate the profession's inadequate efforts at policing conformance with its standards and disciplining erring accountants [86, p. 23]. Briloff has cited the profession's failure to ferret out incompetent work and take disciplinary action without prodding by the SEC, the courts, and the state boards [88, pp. 350-360].

One reason for the AICPA's reluctance to discipline its members could be the defensive and self-protective posture that has resulted from the current rash of lawsuits against accounting firms and individual CPAs. Its amicus curiae brief filed in the *National Student Marketing* case, asserting that auditors should not be held liable even when they know that financial information is not accurate, was self-serving and greatly harmed the profession [86, p. 23]. The profession has also been self-protective in regulating the ethical conduct of its members. Savoie comments: "Most ethical codes are designed first to protect members from outsiders, second to protect members from each other, and third to protect the public from unethical members. The AICPA Code of Professional Ethics is enforced quite effectively in matters dealing with protection of members. But disciplinary machinery works very slowly in matters affecting the public" [24, p. 319]. Briloff was even harsher when he called for as much time to be given to the principles of the accountant as is given to the principles of accounting. [88, p. 422] Frederick Andrews maintains that the profession's standards ought to be the strictest of any, given that it lacks the power to revoke licenses. Even though practitioners are acquitted of criminal violations, they should nevertheless be censured if they have violated professional standards [86, p. 40]. That the accounting profession represents the special interests of accountants is well-known; at issue is whether the self-interest is exercised at the expense of the public interest [86, p. 43].ˣ

That self-interest is nowhere more evident than in what Burton calls the profession's reluctance to accept responsibility. Accountants have avoided judging the preferability of accounting principles; they have tried to limit the extent to which they must report on interim financial statements, advocating disclaimers and nonassociation; and they have resisted improving reports on internal controls. They have declined to accept responsibility for taking action if information discovered during an audit could have material consequences; instead they advocate seeking the advice of the company's legal counsel [86, p. 23; also 116]. When auditors define their role narrowly to protect themselves, they exact a heavy cost in their long-term social interests [86, p. 43]. A salutary effect of the current litigious climate (especially the volume of class-action suits) is that accountants now have a greater economic stake in serving the public than a private client [86, p. 17].

Finally, the very structure of the profession's institutions and firms is seen as a major cause of its problems. The Metcalf report accused the Big Eight firms of harming the profession and accused the FASB of being too closely linked to the AICPA. When the FASB has occasionally lacked a sufficient majority for a decision, the SEC has stepped in. The SEC's action corroborates the general observation that "industry dissension often opens the door to more aggressive federal action" [117].

One critic, Eli Mason, has for some time been advancing a centralized organizational structure for more effective operation [118, 119]. He claims that the present hodge-podge of disparate elements impedes the profession's progress. As it now stands, the AICPA is the dominant professional group, yet not all CPAs are members, and it has no say over who may practice as a CPA. Each state board of accountancy reserves the prerogative of granting and revoking licenses. Although the AICPA administers a uniform national CPA examination, different rules and standards apply in each state. The FASB has the authority with respect to accounting principles, but the AICPA's AcSEC makes interim judgments in matters the FASB has not had time to address; and AICPA's AudSEC sets auditing standards. All are subject to oversight by the SEC. In addition, accountants must observe standards set by the CASB for clients that do business with the government (or who are government agencies) and will increasingly have to follow IASC standards, particularly for multinational corporations or those with foreign affiliates. Not only does the risk of conflicts between standards arise, itself slowing the standard-setting process, but the burden of complying with standards from such diverse sources inevitably raises the cost of accounting services.

ˣJohn C. Burton cites auditors' reluctance to investigate new practices such as auditor of record, continuous auditing and reporting, reports on controls and on forecasts, and replacement costs—all because of the immediate out-of-pocket costs (litigation, protecting self-interest) at the expense of their opportunity costs (in the public interest) [86, p. 43].

The Mason plan, in contrast, calls for a federally chartered national accounting institute. It would replace the various state boards in licensing and disciplining accountants. New state institutes would administer the rules, examinations, and the licensing process. They would also replace the individual state accounting societies, which now disseminate information, set up programs of continuing education, and advise the state boards. The twelve-person executive council of the national institute would include the chief accountant of the SEC, the U.S. Comptroller General, and the ranking technical official of the IRS. The plan is revolutionary but is a rational option lying somewhere between what now exists and complete federal control of the accounting profession. Another equally radical suggestion, from Briloff, is that Congress establish a corporate accountability commission to determine and enforce national and international standards pertaining to corporate morality, antitrust activity, and accountability. It would be empowered to protect the public by overseeing all professional work and penalizing any infractions [88, pp. 422-427]. Like the Mason plan, this scheme could reflect the frustration that members of the profession are experiencing with the present system. The very presence of the Mason plan underscores the dissatisfaction with the profession's present institutional arrangements, which has intensified over the years in response to political, legislative, legal, and economic pressures.

References

[1] AICPA, *Annual Report, 1976-77.*
[2] Edward B. Fiske, "Job Outlook Good, Students Jam Accounting Courses; Colleges, Overwhelmed, Strive to Curtail Enrollment" *New York Times,* 9 August 1977, p. 25.
[3] Charles B. Hellerson, "Accounting under SEC Regulations," *Accountant's Encyclopedia,* vol. 3 (Englewood Cliffs, N.J.: Prentice-Hall, 1962), pp. 1211-1260.
[4] Robert Chatav, *Corporate Financial Reporting* (New York: Free Press, 1975).
[5] John C. Burton, "The SEC and the Accounting Profession: Responsibility, Authority, and Progress," in Robert R. Sterling, ed., *Institutional Issues in Public Accounting* (Lawrence, Kan.: Scholars Book Co., 1974), ch. 7, pp. 265-275.
[6] "Chairman Williams Digs In at the SEC," *Business Week,* 30 May 1977, p. 69.
[7] Robert D. Hershey, Jr., "SEC Plans Review of Rules Governing Corporate Proxies, *New York Times,* 28 April 1977, p. 53.
[8] Judith Miller, "Making SEC Listen to the Public," *New York Times,* 29 September 1977, p. 61.
[9] "Corporate Governance—New Heat on Outside Directors?" *Forbes,* 1 October 1977 p. 33.

[10] "What Are You Up To, Mr. Hills?" *Forbes,* 1 March 1976, pp. 51-53.

[11] "Is Forced Disclosure 'Inefficient'?" *Forbes,* 1 June 1977, p. 78.

[12] Ed Moosbrugger, "Corporate Disclosure," *Santa Monica Evening Outlook,* 15 September 1977, p. 28.

[13] "SEC Corporate Disclosure System Found by Panel to be Sound; Changes Proposed," *Wall Street Journal,* 4 November 1977, p. 7.

[14] "The Disclosure Rules Survive," *Business Week,* 14 November 1977, p. 86.

[15] Judith Miller, "Cost to Companies of SEC Filings Listed by Agency," *New York Times,* 5 November 1977, pp. 27, 29.

[16] "The Profession's Future: New SEC Chairman Harold Williams Speaks Out," *Journal of Accountancy,* September 1977, pp. 42-46.

[17] "SEC Asks Stiffer Audit Disclosure," *New York Times,* 28 September 1977, p. 63.

[18] "SEC Proposes Rule Forcing Public Firms to List Reasons for Switching Auditors," *Wall Street Journal,* 28 September 1977, p. 12.

[19] "Hills Announces Reassessment of Disclosure at SEC Conference," *Journal of Accountancy,* February 1976, p. 28.

[20] Clarence Sampson, quoted in "The SEC-A Close-Up," *Business Lawyer,* November 1973, p. 299.

[21] Securities Act Release 5696, 23 March 1976, 9 SEC Docket 245.

[22] *Annual Report of the SEC,* fiscal years 1973-1976.

[23] *Annual Report of the FASB,* 1976.

[24] Leonard M. Savoie, "Accounting Attitudes," in Sterling, ed., *Institutional Issues in Public Accounting,* pp. 317-327.

[25] *Annual Report of the SEC,* 1975-76.

[26] Frederick Andrews, "Arthur Andersen Raises Scathing Protest to the SEC's Policy on Accounting Rules," *Wall Street Journal,* 22 June 1976, p. 8.

[27] "Debating Who Sets Accounting Standards," *Business Week,* 5 July 1976, pp. 19-20.

[28] "Arthur Andersen & Co. Sues to Enjoin Two SEC Accounting Pronouncements," *Wall Street Journal,* 2 August 1976, p. 7.

[29] Accounting Series Release 150, December 20, 1973, 3 SEC Docket 275.

[30] "Several Big Accounting Firms Criticize Andersen's Challenge of Standards Unit," *Wall Street Journal,* 24 June 1976, p. 8.

[31] Carol Falk and Charles Stabler, "Three Big Auditing Firms Balk at SEC Bid to Expand Their Role in Ledger Changes," *Wall Street Journal,* 15 July 1976, p. 32.

[32] "SEC Is Told by Court to Restudy Decision Not to Ask More Data," *Wall Street Journal,* 24 May 1977, p. 13.

[33] "Why the SEC's Enforcer Is in over His Head," *Business Week,* 11 October 1976, pp. 70-76.

[34] Leonard Sloane, "SEC Settles an Accounting Case," *New York Times*, 22 September 1977, p. 41.

[35] "SEC Says Firm Didn't Uncover Fraudulent Acts," *Wall Street Journal*, 22 September 1977, p. 6.

[36] "SEC Finds PMM's Auditing 'Generally Satisfactory,'" *Journal of Accountancy*, July 1977, p. 24.

[37] "Peat Marwick Says It Got a Good Rating in Quality Review Done by Arthur Young," *Wall Street Journal*, 24 November 1975, p. 10.

[38] "SEC Plans to Pressure Accounting Firms to Regulate Themselves, Be Independent," *Wall Street Journal*, 14 June 1977, p. 11.

[39] Note in "Capital Wrapup" Section, *Business Week*, 3 October 1977, p. 129.

[40] "SEC May Require More Data on Auditors," *Los Angeles Times*, 14 June 1977, p. 9.

[41] Michael C. Jensen, "Senate Unit Softens Auditor-SEC View," *New York Times*, 14 June 1977, pp. 49, 60.

[42] Denzil Y. Causey, Jr., *Duties and Liabilities of the CPA*, Studies in Accounting 5, Bureau of Business Research, University of Texas, Austin, 1973.

[43] Henry R. Jaenicke, *The Effect of Litigation on the Independent Auditor*, Research Study 1, Commission on Auditors' Responsibilities, New York, November 1977.

[44] R. James Gormley, "Accountants' Professional Liability—A Ten-Year Review," *Business Lawyer*, July 1974, pp. 1205-1224.

[45] Carl D. Liggio, "The Accountant's Legal Environment for the Next Decade," in Sterling, ed., *Institutional Issues in Public Accounting*, pp. 99-121.

[46] Carl D. Liggio, "The Expectation Gap: The Accountant's Legal Waterloo?" *CPA Journal*, July 1975, pp. 23-29; reprinted from *Journal of Contemporary Business*, Summer 1974, pp. 27-44.

[47] Ted J. Fiflis, "The Meaning and Implications of *U.S.* v. *Simon* as to the Legal Role of Accountants," in Sterling, ed., *Institutional Issues in Public Accounting*, pp. 122-136.

[48] Melvin A. Eisenberg, *The Structure of the Corporation: A Legal Analysis* (Boston: Little, Brown & Company, 1976).

[49] A.A. Sommer, Jr., "What Are the Courts Saying to Auditors?" in D.R. Carmichael and John J. Willingham, *Perspectives in Auditing*, 2d ed. (New York: McGraw-Hill Book Company, 1975), ch. 4, pp. 147-162.

[50] Denzil Causey, Jr., "Newly Emerging Standards of Auditor Responsibility," *Accounting Review*, January 1976, pp. 19-30.

[51] U.S. House, Committee on Interstate and Foreign Commerce, Subcommittee on Oversight and Investigations, *Federal Regulation and Regulatory Reform*, 94th Cong., 2d sess., October 1976.

[52] *Ernst & Ernst* v. *Hochfelder et al.,* No. 74-1042, 30 March 1976 (1976, CCH Fed. Sec. L. Rep. §95,479).

[53] Wayne E. Green, "Supreme Court Softens Liability of Audit Firms," *Wall Street Journal,* 31 March 1976, p. 4.

[54] Jeff A. Schnepper, "The Accountant's Liability under Rule 10b-5 and Section 10(b) of the Securities Exchange Act of 1934: The Hole in Hochfelder," *Accounting Review,* July 1977, pp. 653-657.

[55] John S. Stoppleman, "Accountants and Rule 10b-5: After *Hochfelder,*" *Journal of Accountancy,* August 1977, pp. 49-54.

[56] Henry B. Reiling and Russell A. Taussig, "Recent Liability Cases—Implications for Accountants," in Carmichael and Willingham, *Perspectives in Auditing,* ch. 4, pp. 162-190; reprinted from *Journal of Accountancy,* September 1970, pp. 39-53.

[57] Peat, Marwick, Mitchell & Co., *Research Opportunities in Auditing* (New York, 1976).

[58] "Legal Treasure Hunts," editorial in *Business Week,* 6 June 1977, p. 112.

[59] Saul Levy, "Legal Responsibility and Civil Liability," *CPA Handbook,* ch. 6, (New York: American Institute of Certified Public Accountants, 1952), p. 39; quoted in ref. 42, p. 26.

[60] Carleton H. Griffin, "The Beleaguered Accountants: A Defendant's Viewpoint," *American Bar Association Journal,* June 1976, pp. 759-763; reprinted in *National Public Accountant,* October 1976, pp. 30-34.

[61] Carl D. Liggio, "Expanding Concepts of Accountants' Liability," *California CPA Quarterly,* September 1974, pp. 18-19.

[62] "Record Settlement of Equity Funding Suits Is Approved," *Wall Street Journal,* 12 May 1977, p. 11.

[63] "Settlement of Mattel, Arthur Andersen Suits Is Approved by Court," *Wall Street Journal,* 27 May 1977, p. 28.

[64] "Accountants to Pay $3,250,000 into Fund in Clinton Oil Suit," *Wall Street Journal,* 12 May 1977, p. 21.

[65] "The Chilling Impact of Litigation," *Business Week,* 6 June 1977, pp. 58-64.

[66] California Citizens' Commission on Tort Reform, "Professional Liability," Staff Background Paper, Los Angeles, Ca., September 1977.

[67] "The Law Closes In on Managers," *Business Week,* 10 May 1976, pp. 110-116.

[68] "How Companies Fight Soaring Legal Costs," *Business Week,* 16 November 1974, pp. 104, 106, 108.

[69] Commission on Auditors' Responsibilities, *Report of Tentative Conclusions* (New York, May 1977).

[70] "Thumb on the Scales," editorial in *Business Week,* 31 October 1977, p. 122.

[71] "Accounting Straitjacket," editorial in *Business Week,* 8 November 1976, p. 112.

[72] Frederick Andrews, "Accounting Board Assails Criticism of Its Rule-Making," *New York Times,* 21 October 1976, p. 55.

[73] U.S. Senate, Committee on Government Operations, Subcommittee on Reports, Accounting, and Management, "The Accounting Establishment," A Staff Study, 94th Cong., 2d sess., December 1976.

[74] "Internal Reforms by Accountants Urged as Senate Hearings Open; Bill Not Likely," *Wall Street Journal,* 20 April 1977, p. 16.

[75] Robert D. Hershey, Jr., "Percy Chides Big 8 Accountants about Reports As Hearings Begin," *New York Times,* 20 April 1977, p. 51.

[76] Deborah Rankin, "Hard Senate Inquiry on Auditing Practice Ends on Softer Note," *New York Times,* 14 November 1977, pp. 53, 55.

[77] Leonard Stone, "Hurdman's Battle with Foster Wheeler," *New York Times,* 3 May 1977, pp. 59, 71.

[78] "Accountant, Heal Thyself," editorial in the *New York Times,* 19 May 1977, p. 22.

[79] Frederick Andrews, "Pressures on the Independent Auditors," *New York Times,* 5 April 1977, p. 57.

[80] Harold M. Williams, "Audit Committees—The Public Sector's View," *Journal of Accountancy,* September 1977, pp. 71-74.

[81] Russell E. Palmer, "Audit Committees—Are They Effective? An Auditor's View," *Journal of Accountancy,* September 1977, pp. 76-79.

[82] Richard J. Farrell, "The Audit Committee—A Lawyer's View," *Business Lawyer,* July 1973, pp. 1089-1095.

[83] Harry Anderson, "Bigger Audit Committee Role Urged," *Los Angeles Times,* 23 March 1977, p. 14.

[84] M.L. Lovdal, "Making the Audit Committee Work," *Harvard Business Review,* March-April 1977, pp. 108-114.

[85] "SEC Backs Big Board's Audit Committees Rule," *Wall Street Journal,* 10 March 1977, p. 13.

[86] *The Public Accounting Profession and Its Critics,* proceedings of a conference sponsored by the Wharton School, University of Pennsylvania, 25 May 1976 (Philadelphia, 1976).

[87] "Big Board See Tightening Rules to Curb Bribes," *Wall Street Journal,* 21 April 1976, p. 3.

[88] Abraham J. Briloff, *More Debits than Credits,* (New York: Harper & Row, 1976).

[89] "Should CPAs Be Management Consultants?" *Business Week,* 18 April 1977, pp. 70, 73.

[90] ASR 173, "In the Matter of Peat, Marwick, Mitchell & Co.," 2 July 1975, footnote 92.

[91] "Why Everybody's Jumping on the Accountants These Days," *Forbes,* 15 March 1977, pp. 37-43.

[92] Homer Kripke, "A Search for a Meaningful Securities Disclosure Policy," *Business Lawyer,* November 1975, pp. 293-317.

[93] Attributed to a Price Waterhouse position paper, "Common-sense Accounting in an Era of Persistent Inflation," as reported in "Notable and Quotable," *Wall Street Journal,* 16 May 1977, p. 18.

[94] Thomas W. McRae, "Inflation Accounting—Report of the Inflation Accounting Committee (U.K.)," *Journal of Accountancy,* February 1976, pp. 99-100.

[95] Frederick Andrews, "Replacing-Cost Accounting Plan Adopted by SEC," *Wall Street Journal,* 25 March 1976, p. 6.

[96] "Too Many Figures," editorial in *Business Week,* 12 April 1976, p. 110.

[97] "Replacement Costs: Clarification or Confusion?" *Business Week,* 9 August 1976, pp. 54-56.

[98] "Accounting in Erewhon," editorial in *Business Week,* 9 August 1976, p. 80.

[99] L. Todd Johnson and Philip W. Bell, "Current Replacement Costs: A Qualified Opinion," *Journal of Accountancy,* November 1976, pp. 63-70.

[100] Stephen F. Black and Albert A. Koch, "Replacement Cost—Charting the Uncharted Sea," *Journal of Accountancy,* November 1976, pp. 72-76.

[101] Robert N. Anthony, "A Case for Historical Costs," *Harvard Business Review,* November-December 1976, pp. 69-79.

[102] James H. Sadowski and Mark E. Nadolny, "Inflation Accounting, A Survey of Current Opinion," paper presented at the Southeastern Regional Conference of Beta Alpha Psi, 2 April 1976; reprinted in *Arthur Andersen Chronicle,* January 1977, pp. 8-18.

[103] "Inflation? Account for It," *Forbes,* 1 March 1977, pp. 64-65.

[104] Charles N. Stabler, "How Recently Issued Accounting Rules Are Affecting Corporate Annual Reports," *Wall Street Journal,* 30 March 1977.

[105] Terry P. Brown, "Auto Makers Say Depreciation Expenses Differ 49% to 120% in Two Cost Methods," *Wall Street Journal,* 6 April 1977, p. 9.

[106] Vasil Pappas, "Inflation Accounting, in SEC-Ordered Test, Irks Many Companies," *Wall Street Journal,* 23 May 1977, pp. 1, 25.

[107] "The Newest Numbers Game," *Business Week,* 20 June 1977, pp. 85, 88.

[108] "How Current-Value Data Affect the Balance Sheet," *Business Week,* 27 June 1977, p. 48.

[109] Robert D. Hershey, Jr., "Standards for Inflation Accounting Sought in Britain," *New York Times,* 6 September 1977, pp. 22-23.

[110] Thomas D. Flynn, "Why We Should Account for Inflation," *Harvard Business Review,* September-October 1977, pp. 145-157.

[111] "Accounting Rules May Discourage Investment," *Business Week,* 17 October 1977, pp. 68-69.

[112] Harvey Kapnick, "Let's Abandon 'Generally Accepted,' " in Sterling, ed., *Institutional Issues in Public Accounting,* ch. 11, pp. 375-393.

[113] Deborah Rankin, "Ways to Report Earnings Stirs Debate," *New York Times,* 9 August 1977, p. 43.

[114] Philip L. Defliese, "The Search for a New Conceptual Framework of Accounting—A Critique of the FASB's Discussion Memorandum and the AICPA's Experimental Program," *Journal of Accountancy,* July 1977, pp. 59-67.

[115] "Framing a Constitution for the Accountants," *Business Week,* 20 December 1976, pp. 58-59.

[116] Lawrence Revsine, "The Preferability Dilemma," *Journal of Accountancy,* September, 1977, pp. 80-89.

[117] Richard E. Cohen, "Calling the Accountants to Account," *National Journal,* 28 May 1977, p. 832.

[118] Eli Mason, "A Proposal for Restructuring Our Profession," *CPA Journal,* July 1975, pp. 19-22.

[119] Frederick Andrews, "Mason's Plan for Revamping Profession," *New York Times,* 26 April 1977, p. 56.

15 The Profession Responds: Self-Examination and Steps toward Reform Since 1975

The immense expansion of American industry in this century, coupled with increasingly complex income tax laws requiring the advice of professionals, caused the real growth of the public accounting profession [1, p. 54]. The movement toward conglomerates in the 1960s and the corresponding increase in the number of large publicly held companies practicing before the SEC simply accelerated that growth. Yet most Americans hardly noted the rise of the profession, probably because of accountants' penchant for anonymity and their "rather aloof public posture" [2, p. 56]. The picture has changed. Auditors, auditing firms, and the accounting profession in general now operate in the glare of the public spotlight, bombarded with criticism and threats to their autonomy. This chapter examines the responses of the profession on matters of formulating accounting principles, improving auditors' independence, and adapting its organization to new environmental demands placed on it.

Formulating Accounting Principles

Given the conclusions of the Moss and Metcalf reports, it must have been a comfort to the FASB that most witnesses who testified at the Metcalf committee hearings pledged full support to the FASB and urged that accounting rulemaking remain in the private sector.[a] An independent survey done in 1977 also found that its respondents clearly preferred "financial accounting reporting standards [to] be set within the private sector, by a body similar in its mode of operations to the current FASB" [4, p. 14; 5]. Those reassurances aside, standard setting for the accounting profession is "at best ... a joint public-private undertaking" [6, p. 91; 7, 8]. The FASB operates at the pleasure of and sometimes in the wake of SEC initiatives.

The FASB replaced the APB in 1973, when the recommendations of the Wheat study group were implemented [9]. Confidence in a rulemaking institution was low. There was considerable pressure to act quickly. The APB had left untouched a sizable agenda, and it was widely thought that the FASB was the profession's last chance to show that the private sector was capable of setting standards. Much apprehension and hope attended its birth.

[a]Supportive witnesses included representatives of the AICPA, the SEC, the AAA, FEI, and CASB, and the Financial Accounting Foundation; see ref. 3.

In its first four years, the FASB has issued twelve accounting standards and fielded numerous exposure drafts and discussion memoranda for comments, and has many projects on its agenda. Whether that output fits criteria of adequacy or sufficient speed is moot; output cannot be judged solely in terms of quantity. From the beginning, observers differed over which questions the FASB should address. The APB had been accused of taking on the simpler issues to build a good track record, after discovering the difficulty of resolving the more consequential ones. Some have similarly accused the FASB. True, in 1975, the board's emphasis seemed to shift to solving practice problems [6, p. 91], probably in response to pressure from practitioners with short-term concerns. The Moss report concluded that the FASB "had accomplished virtually nothing toward resolving fundamental accounting problems" [10]. However, the board's current agenda is replete with weighty issues, the most significant of which is its landmark study on the conceptual framework of financial accounting [11].[b]

What makes the work of the FASB so difficult and vulnerable to criticism is that despite the technical excellence and rigor it brings to bear on issues, it must produce a solution that is generally accepted by accountants and by issuers and users of financial statements. Its work, therefore, is highly political; some observers have described it as setting policy rather than standards or rules.[c] Even

---

[b]Part I of the study defines the basic elements of financial statements (assets, liabilities, capital, earnings, revenue, expenses, gains, losses); part II sets forth the qualitative characteristics of financial information; and part III treats measurement issues, exploring such alternatives as historical cost accounting and five types of current-value accounting. See also refs. 12 and 13.

Marshall S. Armstrong, chairman of the FASB, expressed the complexity of developing a conceptual basis for accounting in an address before the Third Annual Securities Regulation Institute in San Diego, January 16, 1976:

In my view, ... accounting, like law, is an art whose rules are not susceptible to pragmatic tests of validity, such as those available to the physical sciences. Accounting is, rather, a convention supported only by general acceptance, consensus, and verifiable against no immutable standard or natural law. Absent such validating tests, there must be many views of equal authority, for perceptions among individuals vary widely; so broad, in fact, is this diversity in perception that, in my view, true consensus is impossible.

Let me point this up for you. In our first discussion memorandum on the conceptual framework of accounting, we sought an expression of opinion from respondents on the following as a basic objective of financial statements; it is taken directly from the Trueblood report: "The basic objective of financial statements is to provide information useful for making economic decisions." Could there be disagreement with a statement such as this? I am sure you will be astounded to learn that only 37 percent of our respondents were able to recommend the adoption of this objective. Twenty-two percent recommended that it be rejected out of hand; and 10 percent insisted that it needed further study. It is difficult to believe that only 37 percent can agree that the basic objective of financial statements is to provide information useful for making economic decisions. I think this suggests the problem quite clearly [6, p. 96].

Horngren also points up the confusion surrounding even the premises of such a study [6, p. 96]: "What is a basic framework? Do you believe accounting's fundamental purpose is to measure economic income and wealth? to report on stewardship? to abide by laws? to help facilitate fiscal policy? to facilitate decisions?"

[c]As Horngren has said: "Whether we like it or not, accounting policymaking is in the political arena. ... My hypothesis is that the setting of accounting standards is as much a product of political action as of flawless logic or empirical findings. Why? Because the setting of standards is a social decision. Standards place restrictions on behavior; therefore,

within the profession, the board must satisfy several factions, such as the small and large firms, which involves complex trade-offs.[d]

Its most difficult decisions may involve unpleasant trade-offs among vested corporate interests, most clearly illustrated by its recent pronouncement on accounting for the extractive industries [17].[e] Any change in an accounting

they must be accepted by the affected parties. Acceptance may be forced or voluntary or some of both. In a democratic society, getting acceptance is an exceedingly complicated process that requires skillful marketing in a political arena" [6, pp. 92-95]. Dale Gerboth has said: "When a decision-making process depends for its success on public confidence, the critical issues are not technical: they are political.... In the face of conflict between competing interests, rationality as well as prudence lies not in seeking final answers but, rather, in compromise—essentially a political process" [14, p. 479].

[d]In a testimony before the Metcalf subcommittee, William R. Mette, Jr., of Alexander Grant & Co., criticized the FASB for a "total lack of understanding" of the problems of small and medium-sized companies, in subjecting them "to the same record-keeping and disclosure requirements as the huge conglomerates and multinational corporations" [15]. Marshall S. Armstrong responded by pointing out the complex trade-off involved. Imposing such burdens on the smaller companies and their accountants had to be weighed against introducing future problems (such as litigation) and loss of credibility by drafting variable standards. He cited compelling reasons to support the FASB's choice of the former alternative [16].

[e]This pronouncement is a good example of how politicized rulemaking for accounting has become. The FASB has been joined by the SEC and the Congress in annoying the oil and gas producers, especially the independent ones opposed to "successful-efforts" accounting. As part of its 1975 Energy Policy and Conservation Act, Congress asked the SEC to establish accounting procedures for oil and gas producers by 22 December 1977. The SEC delegated the task to the FASB. The FASB quickly produced an exposure draft of the proposed statement. In response, about one hundred of the affected companies joined to complain to the Senate that the FASB decision would hurt them badly and to urge a strict interpretation of energy reporting as required by the act. The Senate, in a unanimous voice vote, approved an amendment to the act directing that the SEC's rules for energy reports not "be construed to establish or affect the establishment of generally accepted accounting principles for financial reporting purposes." Thus the FASB's standard would be required only for reports to the Department of Energy and not to shareholders in company financial statements. The implied challenge to the FASB's stature as the accounting profession's rulemaking body was moderated some days later, when the SEC said that even if such language survived in the final legislation, public companies would still be required to use the proposed standard in financial statements to be filed with the commission.

While the SEC is within its authority to make such a ruling (and approve the FASB's action), it has been accused of failing to consider the anticompetition effects of those rulings on the oil and gas industry [18]. Many of the smaller independents striving for growth and necessary capital may be forced out of business.

The threat to the FASB's authority has brought it fully into the political arena. In an effort to block passage of the amendment, it enlisted the support of two of its severest critics, Senator Lee Metcalf and Representative John E. Moss, both of whom contend that uniform accounting rules for oil producers are vital for investors, who until now have been hampered in comparing results of different oil companies because of alternative accounting methods permitted. The board's lobbying efforts have also been stepped up. The experience of setting that standard may have taught it a painful lesson—never to tackle a controversial issue without marshaling its political as well as technical forces [19].

In a separate action based on a University of Texas study, the SEC has required oil and gas producers to estimate the dollar value of their proven reserves (hitherto they had been required only to estimate the quantities of proven reserves). The SEC had wanted disclosure of the replacement-cost values of those reserves, but calculation of such figures was found to be infeasible. The ruling blithely goes beyond the FASB's proposed standard, and it has aroused strong opposition from the oil and gas producers. Such an action does not ease the FASB's tasks or its relations with those companies [20-22].

principle, or an elimination of alternatives, invariably harms some class of corporation by causing an adverse restatement of its financial position. The board was asked to choose between the two methods of accounting for the oil and gas industries: full-cost accounting, where all exploration attempts are capitalized and slowly expensed as revenues materialize, and successful-efforts accounting, where only the costs associated with the relatively few successful attempts are capitalized (the costs for unsuccessful attempts or dry holes must be expensed in that year). A decision for either one would hurt some group. A *Forbes* article proposed allowing both methods as a solution to the dilemma [23]. But the board finally chose the successful-efforts method, continuing its drive to narrow and possibly eliminate the choices available in applying accounting principles [24-27].

Other standards have been controversial, but the board has nevertheless taken positions it could defend, such as on accounting for R&D [28], for pension liabilities [30], and for foreign subsidiaries' financial reports [36]. It has also commissioned Robert N. Anthony, a professor at Harvard's business school, to study the feasibility of developing uniform accounting standards and reporting concepts for nonprofit organizations, the largest of which seem to be state and local governments [37, 38].f

---

fThe FASB ruling on accounting for R&D calls for charging off all R&D expenses in the year in which they occur and outlawing the practice of capitalizing them, deferring their recognition as costs until the research pays off. In criticizing it, Sidney Davidson, a professor in the University of Chicago's business school, shows that such a decision is heavily dependent on an underlying conceptual framework of accounting principles: "[Expensing all these expenditures for research and development] is conservative, . . . uniform, and . . . *wrong*. It does not help the public understand today's world. If assets are indeed future benefits, and I hope the FASB's conceptual statement will come out soon to say so, then what we accountants are saying is that American industry is spending billions of dollars annually without getting any assets—that is, any future benefits—in return. Of course, estimates of the amount of future benefits are subjective, are probabilistic, but so is this world. Somewhat arbitrary assumptions would have to be made if we were to capitalize R&D and amortize it, but anyone who thinks that zero is a nonarbitrary evaluation is kidding himself. In the aggregate, I would suggest to you that zero is the least likely valuation to ascribe to the future benefits of R&D expenditures made by industry. Keynes once remarked that it is much better to be vaguely right than precisely wrong" [29, p. 12].

The proposed ruling for pensions covers the annual financial statements of defined benefit-pension plans and not what information about the plans ought to be disclosed in a company's annual financial statements [31]. The purpose is to help participants assess the security behind the promise to pay benefits. The assets available for benefit payments would also have to be expressed at their current values [32]. A *Business Week* editorial warned that "unless the FASB moves into high gear and settles the major questions in pension fund accounting, it will be inviting heavy-handed intervention by Congress. . . . The problem of adequate funding for pensions is dangerous enough without the added complications of ignorance and confusing accounting practices. The FASB should get a move on" [33]. The board was going to decide the standard by December 1977, but has postponed the deadline to analyze some seven hundred letters it has received on the subject, most of which oppose the guidelines [33; see also 34, 35].

Not only must all gains and losses from foreign operations be included as income in the quarter in which they occur, eliminating reserves, but also "all overseas subsidiaries' nonmonetary assets and liabilities—primarily fixed assets and inventories—are translated at the rate of exchange in effect the day they were acquired; all monetary items collectable or

In another effort, equal in importance to developing a conceptual framework of accounting, the board is studying what the objectives of financial reporting should be. It has not acted on recommendations made earlier [39], most likely because too much disagreement persists within the profession [40-50]. The board has, however, issued preliminary conclusions [51]. Responding to the fears often expressed by businessmen that a change in the accounting rules (including, presumably, reporting requirements) would adversely affect the economy, the FASB is studying such questions as whether accounting changes would lead businesses to make decisions differently, and to what extent stock prices might be affected by accounting changes [52].

Critics of the FASB's lack of progress have attributed it variously to an inadequate research staff, the complexity of the issues before it and a bylaw requiring five of its seven votes to approve any standard. Those criticisms were recently addressed. In December 1976 the Financial Accounting Foundation's structure committee, headed by Russell E. Palmer, managing partner of Touche Ross & Co., undertook a major review of the board. Its recommendations, issued four months later, included opening FASB meetings to the public, letting constituencies know which way the board is leaning while deliberating on an issue, developing more formal procedures for assessing the economic impact of proposed standards, enhancing the job of research director and providing adequate staff, delegating more work to task forces and other professional groups, and allowing approval of standards by a simple four-to-three majority. The most startling recommendation, directed toward curtailing the influence of the accounting profession over the board, was to revoke the AICPA's power to appoint the eleven trustees of the foundation and to abandon the rule that four of the board's seven members be drawn from accountants in public practice [53, 54]. Those recommendations were soon adopted and scheduled for implementation by the end of 1977. The trustees also followed the Palmer report, as it came to be known, in decreeing that representatives from each of the six sponsoring organizations (AAA, FAF, FEI, NAA, SIA, and AICPA) jointly choose new trustees as the terms of present ones expire. Not only have FASB meetings been opened to the public; but so also have meetings of the group's advisory council, task forces, and screening committee on emerging problems [55, 56].

As a result, the AICPA has become one of five equal constituencies of the FASB, from its previous exalted position as founder and overseer.[g] The AICPA's

payable in cash are translated at the current rate." The ruling eliminates a variety of accounting alternatives that companies have hitherto been free to choose from and gives foreign currency exchange rates a crucial role in the accounting process.

The profession has strong incentives to develop standards for nonprofit organizations. Participants at the recent hearings on defining a conceptual framework for accounting suggested that the FASB develop a similar framework for nonprofit organizations, and Professor Anthony predicted that state and local governments would face strong pressure from underwriters and bondholders to go along with such rules.

[g]The relationship of the AICPA with the FASB did not change either in anticipation or as a result of the assertions in the Metcalf report that the FASB is controlled by the Big Eight

Accounting Standards Division continues to support the FASB by suggesting emerging problems and by commenting on discussion memoranda and exposure drafts. The division's AcSEC also issues statements of the AICPA's position on a variety of issues. While not binding on the profession, as FASB statements are, they nevertheless influence practitioners and clients in the absence of (or during deliberations of) FASB pronouncements. The division also communicates the institute's position on various issues to the SEC, Congress, and other external professional associations. It even comments on auditing standards proposed by its sister committee AudSEC, as they bear on accounting standards. Most committee work, like that of AcSEC and AudSEC, is accomplished by special task forces, and it occasionally results in a major research study [57, 58]. The AICPA's Federal Taxation Executive Committee performs much the same role in tax matters.

International accounting standards are promulgated by the International Accounting Standards Committee (IASC). Accountants from Australia, Canada, France, Germany, Japan, Mexico, the Netherlands, Britain and Ireland, and the United States formed the committee to unify accounting standards, practices, and procedures throughout the world. It now counts about forty countries as associate members. Auditors practicing before the SEC are not, however, bound by IASC standards but only by FASB statements and SEC pronouncements.[h]

Finally, cost accounting standards for corporations under contract to the federal government and its agencies are issued by the CASB, an independent rulemaking agency established in 1970 by Congress. Accountants having such corporations as clients must adhere to those standards and often interact with CASB members in formulating them.

Improving Auditing Practice

Auditing is a very complex and continually evolving activity. At its core are standards and procedures that enable auditors to check on every material aspect

---

CPA firms through the AICPA. Rather, the change was intended to make the FASB more responsive to its constituencies in recognition that its role had become increasingly political though not less technical. Notwithstanding, the trustees approved the Palmer report's recommendation that no single sponsor be allowed to contribute more than $50,000 or 1 percent of the board's budget, whichever was less. Each Big Eight firm had been contributing $200,000, which together comprised over 40 percent of the FASB's 1976 budget.

[h]The IASC is the largest and most prominent international accounting body, but by no means the only one. Among the others are the Accounting International Study Group composed of representatives from Canada, Britain, and the United States, which has published eighteen studies since its formation in 1967; the International Coordination Committee for the Accounting Profession, which has been framing the constitution and organization of the then proposed International Federation of Accountants; the Inter-American Accounting Association, with headquarters in Mexico City; and the Confederation of Asian and Pacific Accountants, also working toward uniform practices and procedures. In October 1977, the International Congress of Accountants in Munich voted into being a new International Federation of Accountants, to be headquartered in New York City but registered under Swiss law.

of a company's operations and, more recently, on management actions and decisions directly insofar as they may materially affect the financial statements. Rendering an opinion on financial statements rests heavily on the accounting principles used to construct them; but the practice of auditing also involves auditing standards and the ways that firms obtain and retain clients, conduct the audit, and communicate their results.

Auditing standards are currently set by the AICPA's AudSEC, whose part-time twenty-one members are augmented by a research staff of six and by about thirty subcommittees or task forces of volunteers. Besides Statements on Auditing Standards (SAS), the auditing standards division issues audit guides, interpretations that clarify or amplify prior auditing standards or accounting principles, and exposure drafts for comment. With the rise in litigations reflecting auditing failures, AudSEC's work has become more visible and urgent. In the last three years it has issued eighteen SASs. Many of the issues were concurrently being studied by the Commission on Auditors' Responsibilities. By not waiting until the commission completed deliberation to release its SASs, AudSEC asserted its authority for standard setting. The commission acknowledged and enhanced that authority in its tentative conclusions.

The commission recommended that AudSEC continue to operate as part of the AICPA but with full-time members compensated by the AICPA. The proposal for an auditing standards board consisting of five to nine full-time members and a research staff as needed has received modest support. In their testimony before the Metcalf committee, both William S. Kanaga, managing partner of Arthur Young, and John C. Biegler, senior partner of Price Waterhouse, recommended upgrading AudSEC to an auditing standards board. Kanaga also called for outside participation; Biegler wanted to open the meetings but confine participation to AICPA personnel.

The task of setting auditing standards has become increasingly complex. AudSEC faces a perennial dilemma: What must an auditor do to meet his responsibilities while reducing his liability exposure, satisfying the SEC, and persuading the parties involved to adhere to standards? In an uncertain and litigious climate the standards are intended to both guide and regulate the behavior of independent auditors. Therefore the issues are almost always controversial. Moreover, the standards technically apply only to auditors, yet management, its internal auditors and accountants, and its legal counsel also play an important role in an audit engagement. Walter E. Hanson, senior partner of Peat, Marwick, Mitchell & Co., in testimony before the Metcalf subcommittee, advocated federal penalties for corporate officials who falsify books and records or who evade their internal controls. Current state laws, he said, are mere "wrist-slapping" [15, p. 94]. Kanaga in his testimony called for codes of business conduct to be established, without specifying by whom [59].

AudSEC is giving special attention to guidelines by which auditors can advise a client or its audit committee of material weaknesses in its internal accounting controls; AudSEC is presently studying how best that information can be reported to the public [60]. The Commission on Auditors' Responsibilities thought auditors should play a role, a position also supported by Biegler at his Metcalf hearing testimony [15, p. 94]. It is also an area in which CPA firms have traditionally offered management consulting services, and the current deliberations may have to address the advisability of continuing that practice for an audit client. Theodore Barry, retiring president of the Association of Consulting Management Engineers, in testimony before the Metcalf subcommittee urged that CPA firms divest themselves of their consulting practices and refrain from offering consulting services to audit clients [3, p. 8]. Senator Charles Percy (R-Ill.), a member of the Metcalf subcommittee conducting the hearings, advocated publicly disclosing the nature of those activities [61, p. 8]. In perhaps the most radical proposal on the subject, Biegler suggested that the SEC set guidelines for management consulting done by auditing firms for their audit clients [15, p. 94]. The Commission on Auditors' Responsibilities, having found that performing MAS did not usually impair an auditor's independence, took the position that the nature and extent of management consulting activities should be at the discretion of the audit committee and should be determined case by case rather than by a general standard.

The concept and practice of audit committees has gained wide acceptance. Harvey Kapnick, chairman of Arthur Andersen & Co., appearing before the Metcalf subcommittee, went so far as to advocate that an auditor be permitted to accept an engagement only if the client has established an audit committee of independent outside directors [3, p. 8; 15; 62, p. 84].

The Metcalf hearings yielded other proposals for restoring public trust and confidence in the profession. The most radical came from Biegler. He urged that firms auditing publicly held companies be required to register with the SEC, as their clients must, and to disclose their annual financial statements, the pay of their top partners, and their internal quality-control procedures [3, p. 8; 61]. Two of the Big Eight, Arthur Andersen and Price Waterhouse, have voluntarily made such financial disclosures already [63].

Biegler also suggested that firms submit to peer reviews regularly—perhaps every three years—under the aegis of the SEC [3, p. 8; 51; 63]. Firms that did not correct any deficiencies found could be barred from practicing before the SEC. The idea of peer review has generally been well received; disagreements center on who should control the process, who should do the reviewing, and how often it should be done. For example, a countersuggestion to Biegler's came from Norman E. Auerbach, chairman of Coopers & Lybrand. He proposed a new organization within the private sector, separate from the AICPA but governed by an executive board of representatives selected by member firms. All firms practicing before the SEC would have to join this "SEC-chartered" organization, which would direct peer reviews of member firms under SEC oversight. [3; 62, p. 84].

That companies be required to rotate their auditors every few years has occasionally been proposed as a way to make auditors more independent of their clients. The suggestion surfaced most recently in hearings before the Senate Commerce Committee on corporate rights and responsibilities [64] and in the Metcalf report. Opponents cite first the enormous extra start-up costs that would be entailed; familiarity with a company and its industry substantially lowers the cost of an audit. Second, research suggests that many audit failures occur during the first two years of an auditor-client relationship [65, p. 105]. Is it worth exposing firms to greater risk of error to achieve greater independence? Even smaller firms, which would receive more business under such a scheme, oppose it as counterproductive [15, p. 96]. Biegler proposed a more feasible alternative—that audit partners be rotated *within a firm* with respect to their client responsibilities once every five years [63].

The Metcalf report pointed out the concentration of power leading to a lack of competition in the accounting profession. In the subcommittee hearings following the report, witnesses from the Big Eight firms acknowledged the concentration but declared that it was even greater in manufacturing and other industries. (Price Waterhouse studied 450 manufacturing industries and found that in 36 of them the eight-firm concentration ratio was between 90 and 100 percent; each of those industries was much larger than the accounting industry in size and was of basic importance to the economy. Peat, Marwick, Mitchell's study surveyed 18 broader major industry groupings and found that at least half showed more concentration than the auditing profession [15, p. 96].) The witnesses asserted that what seemed to be a concentration of power was in reality a concentration of resources to provide the services demanded by large corporate clients. The size of the client, they insisted, necessitated large auditing staffs, a network of branch offices in this country and abroad, and many specialists [63].

Intense rivalry among the Big Eight firms has stimulated growth not necessarily matched to any client growth. Touche Ross & Co. has openly pursued a policy of growth by merger to improve its competitive edge over other Big Eight firms. It recently completed the largest merger in accounting history, absorbing the domestic practice of J.K. Lasser & Co., to become the third largest accounting firm [66, 67].

Big Eight proponents argue that their very size makes them strong enough to resist client pressures and therefore more independent of their clients [68]. Peat, Marwick, Mitchell and Price Waterhouse each testified that since no client provided more than 1 percent of its total revenues, the firm's dependence on its clients for business was not as great as if one client accounted for, say, 30 or 40 percent of the revenues [15, p. 96; 63]. Others insist, however, that the continued prosperity of the Big Eight firms enables them to maintain a stranglehold on their share of the publicly held corporate audit market. They have the resources to conduct substantial research, perform "overt marketing," mount public relations campaigns, and engage in "symbolic marketing."[i] For those reasons, smaller firms find it nearly impossible to compete with the large firms.[j]

Among the large firms, particularly among the Big Eight, fee competition is fierce.[k] The Commission on Auditors' Responsibilities found that competition excessive. It led to such ills as underbidding for jobs and taking shortcuts (such as skipping a required audit step and not disclosing it, or signing off for work not performed) to complete work on time and within budget [65, pp. 106-113].[l] A system that produces such conduct, according to the commission, violates professional auditing standards.

The profession is taking steps on many different fronts to improve the procedures and standards by which auditing is done. The directions have been set, though there is considerable disagreement over how and how far to move. The Metcalf hearings displayed those disagreements and offered a platform for each firm to try to upstage its rivals and gain public attention. One firm enraged the others by advocating increased SEC regulation of CPA firms, the last thing accountants want.[m] Generally, however, the firms came up with more construc-

[i]In "overt marketing," firm members are assigned to make contacts with companies in certain industries, and they are briefed on current developments in those industries by specialists in the firm. In the large firms, the activity is known as "practice development" and it dominates life there, according to some CPAs who have worked in such firms. Public relations materials include magazines, newsletters, industry accounting guides, guides to computerized accounting systems, tax guides, and guides for doing business abroad. "Symbolic marketing" refers to activities designed to promote the image and name of the firm [69, pp. 580-581].

[j]William R. Mette, Jr., of Alexander Grant & Co., urged in his Metcalf hearing testimony that advertising and open solicitation of clients be sanctioned to allow smaller firms to compete more effectively with the largest firms. The present "ethical" rules are unfair to the smaller CPA firms because the larger firms are able to evade the restraints: "[T]heir size assists them in resisting enforcement and gives them additional opportunities to make contact with potential clients" [15, p. 96]. The Metcalf report's assertions of anticompetitiveness have found a "receptive audience among some smaller accounting firms.... Relations among the Big Eight firms and their much smaller competitors are always sensitive at best, largely because of a problem of 'displacement.' Small firms complain bitterly of losing their most successful audit clients to larger, nationally known accounting firms. Often a banker or underwriter has suggested the company would do better if the name of a more prominent auditor graced its financial statements" [70]. Mette also pleads for the financial community to give the small firms a chance to show what they can do.

[k]Price Waterhouse, in its Metcalf hearings testimony, cited a recent study that examined companies' reasons for switching auditors. Almost half said they changed because "they believed they could get the same service for less money" [15, p. 96].

[l]The commission also learned that many of the hours logged in completing the audit are often not reported in order to bring the job in under budget and to make the audit manager and staff look good to gain advancement. Such distortion of the internal information system in a firm causes subsequent audit bids to be low, perpetuating the pressure in every audit engagement and jeopardizing its quality. The commission was thus very critical of firm supervision of audit engagements. See also [71].

[m]John C. Biegler was the gadfly. Among the objections by leaders of the other Big Eight firms are the following. Russell Palmer of Touche Ross claimed that political considerations would infect the standard-setting process in the public sector. Arthur Andersen's Harvey Kapnick believed that disclosure information the SEC would ultimately collect from firms about clients would enable it to regulate business as closely as the profession; initial

tive suggestions and more new ideas than the AICPA, probably because they had more resources to put into their presentations and because it is easier to speak for a single firm than for an entire profession.

Aside from the proposals that have received widespread support in the profession, many other questions remain unsolved. They include the extent of auditors' responsibility to search for and report management fraud, what MAS may be performed for audit clients, how the audit report should be expanded, and whether companies can pay the full cost of thorough audits. An overriding issue is whether the profession will demand that small firms with small, private clients also be subject to the new standards and procedures, perhaps burdening them unnecessarily, or whether it will draw some distinction among firms.

Adapting the Organization to New Demands

Though at one time the accounting profession may have been more centralized, today it is struggling with its constituency relationships, with maintaining its autonomy, and with staying united. Fundamental questions are being raised about whether the profession's structure and the AICPA's organization are suited to those tasks.

Accountants are regulated by different bodies in different ways, some more direct and some more subtle:

The right to practice is controlled by state boards of accountancy.

The privilege of practicing before the SEC is governed by the SEC; before the U.S. Tax Courts, by the Department of the Treasury and the IRS.

Adherence to the profession's ethical standards is enforced by the AICPA.

Compliance with accounting principles and auditing standards is monitored by accounting firms, the SEC, and the courts (though the courts use different criteria).

The standard a prospective entrant must reach to join the profession is regulated by the AICPA.

Responsibility toward the public interest is monitored by the FASB, the AICPA, the SEC, the courts, firms, the press, and accountants' individual consciences.

If someone set out to design a structure that would enable the profession to discharge its responsibilities in the public service, he might produce something

---

safeguards for the privacy of confidential information would in time be lost. Walter Hanson of Peat, Marwick, Mitchell charged that "by ceding jurisdiction to the SEC's chief accountant over peer review, continuing education requirements, and the scope of management services, Mr. Biegler would create an accounting czar" [62, p. 86].

like the Mason plan [72] ; it is doubtful that he would arrive at the agglomeration of institutional arrangements and intricate relationships that now exist. The changes made in response to ad hoc needs have required the balancing of conflicting interests and have often been the products of compromise. Somehow the system works and things get done. How well they get done, how quickly, and with what effect are matters of contention. Whether the AICPA can maintain its autonomy depends on its relations with its members and constituencies (including the SEC and Congress), on court dispositions, and on the structure of the industry. For example, the degree to which the SEC and the courts preempt the AICPA's leadership in setting auditing standards will depend on its initiative and leadership in that area. Likewise, the quality of accounting education and the role that academic research plays in practice depend on the institute's relations with the AAA and academia and the extent to which they can work together to improve accounting practice. But one of the profession's most sensitive trouble spots is the split in its own industry.

The Metcalf report brought into open debate the controversy over large versus small firms. It drew attention to the concentration of power in the industry and accused the Big Eight firms of influencing accounting rulemaking to support their clients' interests. Not only is the AICPA unable to affect the concentration of power, but it also faces two very different kinds of auditing: one for companies whose shares are publicly traded and who practice before the SEC, and the other for smaller, privately held companies not subject to SEC disclosure laws. The two kinds differ in size and scope, complexity, geographical spread, liability exposure, and in the need to comply with the mass of rules, principles, and standards associated with SEC disclosure laws.

Though the AICPA has tried to respond to the needs of small firms and lone practitioners, the majority of the profession's accounting and auditing pronouncements apply to audits of publicly held companies, which have generated the lion's share of the litigation and SEC actions against auditors. It is thus understandable, though an oversimplification, that small firms have complained about AICPA favoritism toward the large firms, especially since those firms are also the largest underwriters of the AICPA and FASB.

The AICPA has proposed creating two classes of membership, one for firms that audit publicly held companies and one for firms that audit private companies. Under the control of an executive committee, each group would have its own procedures for discipline and peer review of auditing [73, 74, 75]. In September 1977 the proposal was brought before the institute's governing council, which approved a modification creating a new membership division for firms, divided into two sections corresponding to the two divisions of the original proposal [76, 77, 78] . Besides responding to the complaints of the small firms, the new plan gives the AICPA jurisdiction over firms (in the past only individuals could be members). Membership in each section is to be voluntary, and a firm may belong to both simultaneously so long as it adheres to the requirements of each. In the SEC Practice Section members must submit to mandatory peer review, sanctions that include expulsion from the institute, and public reporting of certain information about a firm and its practice. All division activities, especially the effectiveness of the peer reviews, are to be monitored by a public oversight board composed of five prominent individuals.

Critics of the plan have voiced the following objections:

A proposal of such gravity should have been decided by the AICPA general membership and not by its 250-member council, which is believed to favor the positions of the large CPA firms. (CPA Associates, a national organization of accounting firms, has obtained a legal opinion that the AICPA might have violated its own bylaws. CPA Associates may file a lawsuit challenging the plan. AICPA bylaws permit only individual CPAs to be AICPA members, not firms. Admitting firms to membership is thus a change in the bylaws, which requires ratification by the whole membership [74].)

The proposal skirts the issue of representation on the twenty-one-member executive committee of the new division. Because much of its time will inevitably be spent on the business of the SEC Practice Section, the fear is that the Big Eight firms will control enough places on the committee to bias its decisions. A managing partner of a medium-sized firm complains, "The Big Eight don't want to be disciplined by members of smaller firms, and unless larger firms have control, they are not responsive to anything" [78, p. 59].

The separation of firms into two sections will probably lessen competition among accounting firms. The new rules imposed on firms that audit publicly held companies may be so stringent and costly to observe that they will effectively bar many small firms from joining the section. (Those who devised the plan were attempting to avoid just that situaion: "The idea is for firms auditing publicly-held businesses to be held to stricter requirements while relieving firms without any publicly-held clients from meeting those requirements" [74].)

The SEC greeted the plan as a "substantial effort in the direction of reform"; Rep. John Moss (D-Ca.) disagreed: "[D]ividing the institute into separate classes of membership isn't a useful reform"; he added that division would tend to lessen competition among accountants [74].

Even though action was taken hastily and has generated much disagreement, it represents the first concrete step the profession has taken to regulate the activities of the firm directly. It is a firm, not an individual, that a company hires to audit its books, and it is the firm's signature that appears on the auditor's report in financial statements.

But in attempting to regulate firms, the AICPA must distinguish between and deal separately with the destructive and healthy aspects of competition. Much destructive rivalry takes place among the largest firms, where wealth and commercialism predominate over professionalism. If the AICPA were simply a trade association or lobbying group for CPAs, this issue would not concern it. But as guardian of the profession's ethics and image, it must ferret out the unethical behavior inherent in destructive competition without infringing on a firm's legitimate right to compete; in fact, to do so would spur federal antitrust investigations.

In a way that "professionalism" has not been able to do, the firms' competitiveness has provided the necessary incentives to keep their standards and staff competence high, notwithstanding the isolated cases of poor performance that have received wide and damaging publicity. They provide entry-level training and continuing education for their staffs (in fiscal year 1976, Price Waterhouse spent $9 million on continuing professional education alone [15, p. 96]), conduct and sponsor research, define their own auditing control procedures and standards, and make their own decisions about which activities to pursue. Key executives from those firms often confer directly with the SEC, the FASB, university accounting departments, and other constituencies rather than use the AICPA as a communication channel. Thus such firms in a sense duplicate the role of the AICPA and rely less on its services; the small firm, without many resources, seems to have greater need of them.

The AICPA regulates the professional ethics of its members through an executive committee, which revises the Code of Professional Ethics and monitors adherence to it. Some have criticized the AICPA for bringing its disciplinary mechanism into play after the courts, the SEC, or the state boards have initiated their own actions. Even then, they find the performance largely ineffective [79, pp. 350-358].[n]

The institute has developed cooperative programs with forty state CPA societies to enforce ethical standards [80, p. 7]. The Commission on Auditors' Responsibilities recommended that proceedings against an accountant charged with unethical conduct not be deferred until the outcome of any trial unless he can show that the proceedings will jeopardize his case. It also recommended public disclosure of disciplinary actions, including the name of the person penalized. Institute members are now considering a proposal that the Code of Professional Ethics be amended to provide a single set of general standards that would apply equally to engagements in the three major areas of practice—auditing, MAS, and tax advisory services [80, p. 7].

---

[n]Abraham J. Briloff says, "The record [of disciplinary actions] reveals no reference to any expulsion, suspension, or other form of censure of the auditors on the 'A to Y Roll of Dishonor,' from Ampex to Yale Express, including along the way (selected at random) BarChris, Commonwealth United, R. Hoe, Investors Overseas (pre-Vesco and post-Cornfeld), Mill Factors, Penn Central, Performance Systems, Stirling Homex, U.S. Financial, Wall Street's Back Office, Westec. . . ." And "[P]erformance is not required to meet the standard of 'what is right,' but essentially the far lower one of 'what is legal.' " Finally, "[T]he

As the principle spokesman for the profession, the AICPA keeps its finger on the pulse of opinion in its membership and gives advice to various external groups. It supports a lobbying and liaison office in Washington, D.C., to monitor pending legislation and to keep in close touch with key congressmen and staff. Complementarily, it filters news and information to the membership. Executive committees for MAS, federal taxation, and computer services engage in research and publish studies on those topics. *AICPA Annual Reports* give summaries of the activities and accomplishments of the various divisions and executive committees.

The AICPA's efforts in continuing professional education (CPE) are directed toward improving CPE courses and programs [80, p. 17] and persuading state legislators to require CPE as a condition for renewing an accountant's license to practice (twenty-four states now require it).°

Through its board of examiners the AICPA oversees the Uniform CPA examination, recommending changes in its form and grading to the National Association of State Boards of Accountancy. Individual state boards administer the examination every November and May to about 45,000 candidates.

The institute is also developing a voluntary-practice and quality-control program for CPA firms, with the full support of the SEC. In many of its activities, including membership, the institute takes the position that if a practice is adopted voluntarily it is much more likely to achieve lasting acceptance. The AICPA is also developing standards for programs and schools of professional accounting. With the AAA it will establish an Accounting Accreditation Council to administer those standards.

During the past two years the institute has intensified its cooperative and pluralistic efforts, sharing work and information with its constituencies and fellow professional bodies, but nothing fundamental has changed. It responds now to crises as it always has, by making incremental changes—a new committee, another study group, a new division. That strategy has been found effective in the short run without being costly or disruptive to apply, and it will probably characterize the institute's operating style in the foreseeable future. The Commission on Auditors' Responsibilities comes to much the same conclusion: "[T]he current tension and rapid pace of change in the profession, though uncomfortable to many practitioners, are an indication that the present structure is reacting and working. We are not convinced that a complete restructuring of the profession is required, for the present system is adequate" [65, p. 143].

record will show it [the AICPA] is dragged into a judgment by the courts or state agencies, rather than leading its members to the fulfillment of the profession's professed standards."
°The CPE division's EDMAX computer-based library is "the profession's largest cooperative reference library of CPE course materials available to AICPA members." In 1976 "state societies sponsored or cosponsored some 2,400 AICPA course presentations involving the distribution of approximately 68,500 course manuals." Fully 75 percent of the participants in CPE programs are practitioners in small firms.

References

[1] "Certified Public Accountants," *Fortune,* June 1932; reprinted in D.R. Carmichael and John J. Willingham, *Perspectives in Auditing,* 2d ed. (New York: McGraw-Hill, 1975), pp. 51-56.

[2] T.A. Wise, "The Auditors Have Arrived," *Fortune,* November-December 1960, reprinted in Carmichael and Willingham, *Perspectives in Auditing,* pp. 56-78.

[3] "Metcalf Update—Accountants Discount Plan for Greater Control by SEC," *Journal of Accountancy,* July 1977, pp. 4, 8, 12, 14.

[4] Joshua Ronen and Michael Schiff, "The Setting of Financial Accounting Standards—Private or Public?" (New York: Vincent C. Ross Institute of Accounting Research, New York University, July 1977).

[5] "Poll Backs Private Sector for Making Audit Rules," *Wall Street Journal.* 12 May 1977, p. 12.

[6] Charles T. Horngren, "Will the FASB Be Here in the 1980s?", *Journal of Accountancy,* November 1976, pp. 90-96 (paper presented at the Arthur Young Professors' Roundtable, University of Illinois, Urbana, 31 March 1976).

[7] Charles T. Horngren, "Accounting Principles: Private or Public?" *Journal of Accountancy,* May 1972, pp. 37-41.

[8] Charles T. Horngren, "The Marketing of Accounting Standards," in Robert R. Sterling, ed., *Institutional Issues in Public Accounting* (Lawrence, Kan.: Scholars Book Co., 1974), pp. 291-303.

[9] AICPA, *Establishing Accounting Standards* (New York, 1972).

[10] Frederick Andrews, "Accounting Board Assails Criticism of Its Rulemaking," *New York Times,* 21 October 1976, pp. 55, 59.

[11] FASB Discussion Memorandum, *Conceptual Framework for Financial Accounting and Reporting: Elements of Financial Statements and Their Measurement,* (Stamford, Conn., December 1976).

[12] "Framing a Constitution for the Accountants," *Business Week,* 20 December 1976, pp. 58-59.

[13] Hector R. Anton, "Objectives of Financial Accounting: Review and Analysis," *Journal of Accountancy,* January 1976, pp. 40-51.

[14] Dale Gerboth, "Research, Intuition, and Politics in Accounting Inquiry," *Accounting Review,* July 1973, pp. 475-485.

[15] "CPAs Suggest the Watchdogs They Want," *Business Week,* 23 May 1977, pp. 94, 96.

[16] Marshall S. Armstrong, "The Impact of FASB Statements on Small Business," *Journal of Accountancy,* August 1977, pp. 88-90.

[17] FASB Discussion Memorandum, *Financial Accounting and Reporting in the Extractive Industries* (Stamford, Conn., December 1976).

[18] Edward Cowan, "Debate over Oil Company Disclosure," *New York Times,* 17 November 1977, p. 67.

[19] Deborah Rankin, "A Fight for the Accounting Board," *New York Times,* 22 November 1977, p. 55.

[20] Judith Miller, "Accounting Change for Fuel Reserves Proposed by SEC," *New York Times,* 29 October 1977, p. 29.

[21] Charles N. Stabler, "Accounting Standards Board Sees Threat to Its Authority on Oil and Gas Reports," *Wall Street Journal,* 17 October 1977, p. 13.

[22] "SEC Proposes Rule on Reserves of Oil and Gas," *Wall Street Journal,* 31 October 1977, p. 15.

[23] "Can a Dry Hole Be an Asset?" *Forbes,* 15 May 1977, pp. 129-131.

[24] Deborah Rankin, "Accounting Changes May Pare Earnings for Oil-Gas Groups," *New York Times,* 20 July 1977, pp. D1, D10.

[25] Peter B. Roche, "Successful-Efforts Method for Reporting Oil and Gas Search Costs Backed by Panel," *Wall Street Journal,* 20 July 1977, p. 8.

[26] "FASB: A Single Oil Standard," *Business Week,* 1 August 1977, p. 50.

[27] "Draft Calls for 'Successful Efforts' Oil and Gas Accounting," *Journal of Accountancy,* September 1977, pp. 20, 24.

[28] Harry Anderson, "Day of Reckoning Arrives for R&D," *Los Angeles Times,* 4 August 1974, part IX, pp. 1-2.

[29] *The Public Accounting Profession and Its Critics,* proceedings of a conference sponsored by the Wharton School, University of Pennsylvania, 25 May 1976 (Philadelphia, 1976).

[30] "Accounting Board Offers New Rule on Pension Reports," *Wall Street Journal,* 20 April 1977, p. 16.

[31] "Pension-Plan Statements," *Business Week,* 2 May 1977, p. 38.

[32] "Unfunded Pension Liabilities: Growing Worry for Companies," *Business Week,* 18 July 1977, pp. 86-88.

[33] "Accounting for Pensions," editorial in *Business Week,* 18 July 1977, p. 96.

[34] "FASB Postpones Rule on Corporate Pensions," *New York Times,* 4 October 1977, p. 57.

[35] A.F. Ehrbar, "Those Pension Funds Are Even Weaker Than You Think," *Fortune,* November 1977, pp. 104-108, 110, 112, 114.

[36] Linda Snyder, "Have the Accountants Really Hurt the Multinationals?" *Fortune,* February 1977, pp. 85-89.

[37] Deborah Rankin, "Accounting Study Set for Government," *New York Times,* 6 August 1977, p. 25.

[38] "Accounting Board Studies Framework for Municipalities," *Wall Street Journal,* 8 August 1977, p. 12.

[39] AICPA, *Objectives of Financial Statements* (New York, 1973).

[40] James D. Edwards and John B. Barrack, "Objectives of Financial Statements and Inflation Accounting: A comparison of Recent British and American Proposals," *International Journal of Accounting,* Spring 1976, pp. 11-32.

[41] John C. Burton, "The Changing Face of Financial Reporting," *Journal of Accountancy*, February 1976, pp. 60-63.

[42] "More Meat in Annual Reports," *Business Week*, 26 April, 1976, pp. 78-79.

[43] "Focus on Balance Sheet Reform," *Business Week*, 7 June 1976, pp. 52-60.

[44] "Annual Reports That Fail," *Business Week*, 18 October 1976, p. 73.

[45] James H. Sellers and Edward E. Milam, "What's Ahead for Published Financial Statements," *National Public Accountant*, October 1976, pp. 18-23.

[46] N.R. Kleinfield, "An Annual Report Is No Comic Novel, But It Can Be Fun," *Wall Street Journal*, 15 April 1977, pp. 1, 19.

[47] "Some Painful Candor in Annual Reports," *Business Week*, 9 May 1977, pp. 96-98.

[48] "Financial Analysts Cite Areas of Annual Report Deficiencies," *Journal of Accountancy*, July 1977, p. 20.

[49] Wallace E. Olson, "Financial Reporting—Fact or Fiction?" *Journal of Accountancy*, July 1977, pp. 68-71.

[50] Judith Miller, "SEC Survey Shows Investor Reliance on Annual Reports," *New York Times*, 22 August 1977, pp. 39-40.

[51] FASB, *Tentative Conclusions on Objectives of Financial Statements of Business Enterprises* (Stamford, Conn.: December 1976).

[52] Frederick Andrews, "Accounting Board Faces Unhappy Business People," *New York Times*, 22 February 1977, p. 48.

[53] Frederick Andrews, "Rewriting the Standards: Whose Job?" *New York Times*, 12 April 1977, pp. 43-49.

[54] "Accounting Rules Board Should Bolster Ties with Its Constituency, Panel Asserts," *Wall Street Journal*, 12 April 1977, p. 6.

[55] Deborah Rankin, "Accounting Panel's Meetings Public," *New York Times*, 22 June 1977, p. 47.

[56] "Accounting Board Will Admit Public to Its Proceedings," *Wall Street Journal*, 22 June 1977, p. 12.

[57] AICPA, *The Measurement of Corporate Social Performance (Determining the Impact of Business Actions on Areas of Social Concern)* (New York, 1976).

[58] AICPA, *Management Advisory Services by CPAs: A Study of Required Knowledge* (New York, 1976).

[59] "Accounting 'Reform' Urged by Two Firms as Alternative to New Regulation by U.S.," *Wall Street Journal*, 25 May 1977, p. 12.

[60] "New Rules Require Accountants to Report in Internal Auditing," *Wall Street Journal*, 31 August 1977, p. 3.

[61] "Special Report—AICPA Testifies in First Round of Metcalf Hearings," *Journal of Accountancy*, June 1977, pp. 7, 8, 10.

[62] "More CPAs Chime In on Self-Regulation," *Business Week*, 6 June 1977, pp. 84, 86.

[63] Frederic Andrews, "An Upstaged Witness at Metcalf Inquiry," *New York Times*, 24 May 1977, p. 51.

[64] U.S. Senate, Commerce Committee, *Corporate Rights and Responsibilities*, Hearings, June 15-17, 21-23, 1976.

[65] Commission on Auditors' Responsibilities, *Report of Tentative Conclusions* (New York, May 1977).

[66] Deborah Rankin, "Biggest Accounting Merger Joins Touche Ross with J.K. Lasser," *New York Times*, 23 August 1977, pp. 49, 51.

[67] Charles N. Stabler, "Merger of Lasser and Touche Ross Is Announced," *Wall Street Journal*, 23 August 1977, p. 4.

[68] "Bigger Means Better, Say Members of Nation's 8 Largest Accounting Firms," *Los Angeles Times* (reprinted from *Chicago Daily News*), 4 April 1977, part III, p. 13.

[69] C. Richard Baker, "Management Strategy in a Large Accounting Firm," *Accounting Review*, July 1977, pp. 576-586.

[70] Frederick Andrews, "Challenging the Big Eight," *New York Times*, 15 February 1977, p. 45.

[71] "A Sharper Definition of the Auditor's Job," *Business Week*, 28 March 1977, pp. 55-56.

[72] Eli Mason, "A Proposal for Restructuring Our Profession," *CPA Journal*, July 1975, pp. 19-22.

[73] Deborah Rankin, "Quiet Steps toward Self-Regulation," *New York Times*, 16 August 1977, p. 49.

[74] "Big 8 Firms Seeking to Split Accountants into SEC and Non-SEC Practice Classes," *Wall Street Journal*, 16 September 1977, p. 19.

[75] "Price Waterhouse Says It Backs Restructuring of Accounting Group," *Wall Street Journal*, 13 September 1977, p. 29.

[76] Deborah Rankin, "Accountants Adopt Self-Regulation in Revamping Plan," *New York Times*, 19 September 1977, p. 57.

[77] "CPA Panel Clears Plan to Oversee Firms That Audit Publicly Held Companies," *Wall Street Journal*, 19 September 1977, p. 17.

[78] "The CPAs Are Trying to Outrace Congress," *Business Week*, 26 September 1977, pp. 58-59.

[79] Abraham J. Briloff, *More Debits than Credits* (New York: Harper & Row, 1976).

[80] AICPA, *Annual Report, 1976-1977* New York.

16 Synthesis

The most critical problems facing the public accounting profession, as revealed by the two surveys and analysis reported in part I, are (1) inadequate GAAP and the lack of both a consensus and an underlying framework for GAAP, (2) deficient technical standards, ethics, and work performance, (3) the auditor's lack of independence from his client, and (4) uncertainty within the profession about its role in society, which encourages public misunderstanding. In this chapter the survey findings are brought together with events of the last two years to suggest some important steps the profession should take. Because the analyses of survey responses and of subsequent events are merged, the distinction between data-based and observation-based recommendations disappears.

The first survey focused on the profession's fundamental rather than immediate problems, problems that have resisted solution despite considerable efforts and are likely to remain unsolved for the foreseeable future. The four critical problems that emerged from the analysis of the responses to the second survey are now more current than ever. Each is the subject of heated debate, and the first remedial steps are already being taken.

Formulating Accounting Principles and Improving Financial Statements

The survey responses put the FASB's dilemma sharply into focus: the demands placed on it to act quickly directly contradict the inherently slow process of setting standards, which requires the balancing of special interests and the development of empirical research data to throw light on complex issues. The pressure for speedy action stems from the threat of SEC or congressional intervention. Respondents were most concerned about the inadequate state of financial reporting and the profession's indecision about the information that financial reports should contain and the form in which that information should be communicated. Inflation accounting and materiality were especially controversial.

Since the time of the survey, the FASB has conducted a mammoth study on the conceptual framework of accounting, has produced a discussion memorandum on the subject, and has been holding hearings. If consensus can be reached on a conceptual framework, it will go a long way toward resolving related problems stemming from how accounting terms are defined and which accounting model is to be used. Agreement cannot be expected soon; what is being attempted is nothing less than a change in the rules by which accounting measurements are made.[a]

The FASB has made headway toward clarifying the objectives of financial reporting by disseminating its views on the subject. Resolution of that issue should help determine the efficacy of the SEC's idea of differential disclosure and the possibility of simplifying financial reports and making them more intelligible to the "untutored eye of the ordinary investor." It should also shed more light on the feasibility and desirability of financial and earnings forcasts. The profession must convince users of financial statements that the information they contain is neither guaranteed by accountants (to be accurate, complete, or reliable) nor, despite its numerical form, precise. Even the Metcalf report erroneously expected financial reports to be fair, complete, and accurate. The accounting process involves basic uncertainties in measuring, in its assumptions or model used, in reporting, and in checking. In fairness to the public, the profession must spell out those uncertainties in plain English. In fairness to themselves, if imprecise reports expose them to unnecessary liability, practitioners may have to seek limited protection under the SEC's safe-harbor rule. The FASB needs to resolve the financial reporting issue as quickly as possible, both to minimize public confusion and to improve the quality of the financial information reported.

The FASB is now in a position to carry out its work more independently than before. Its special ties with the AICPA have been severed as a result of the Palmer committee report, and its standard-setting process will be more responsive to a broader constituency. We may be on the threshold of an era of accounting *policymaking* such as even the Wheat commission never envisaged. Many of the Palmer committee recommendations answered the Metcalf committee's central criticism, that the Big Eight accounting firms exerted undue influence over the profession's standard-setting process. Any such influence has been sharply curtailed.

There seems little the profession can do in the short run to limit the number of sources from which accounting principles emanate. The SEC will continue to initiate standards on matters it considers important and on which the FASB has not acted; and the courts will continue to delimit auditor responsibility and set the criteria for fairness in financial disclosures. The harshest judgment yet rendered on the quality of accounting principles has been that even if they are

[a]Do accounting methods measure results or do they cause them? Frederick Andrews has leaned toward the latter view: "And in that context [baseball], we could go back last year and rescore every ballgame with just one change in the rules. If you steal home, you win the game. Nothing necessary in the way of additional information. It's just a matter of going back and redoing all the box scores. But would that mean anything? Obviously, if that had been the rule, anybody who had got to third base would be hustling, and you know that the Pete Roses of this world would be much higher paid ball players than they are now. So ... this matter of restating measurements as though something occurred and just simply ignoring the effect of the measuring process itself won't do" [1, p. 28].

followed, the accountant may not be protected from liability if the resulting financial statements mislead those who rely on them. The principles thus offer insufficient guidance to auditors. Will agreement on a conceptual framework raise accounting standards and make them uniform so that an auditor who follows them can reliably produce financial statements that are realistic, fair, and not misleading? If an accountant follows them, will he have a solid defense if he is involved in litigation? It is now unclear that those are FASB objectives.

The FASB has narrowed the choice of accounting principles available to companies. Its recent pronouncement on accounting in the oil and gas industries is a good example. In the short run some companies will suffer, but in the long run financial statements will be comparable and will contain better information. Likewise, the FASB has taken a defensible position in making its rulings applicable to smaller companies. The unnecessary reporting and auditing burden placed on smaller companies appears more tolerable than the confusion and lowered public confidence that would result from a variable standard.

The FASB is under increasing pressure to bring all aspects of financial reporting within its purview. At a recent symposium, eighty members of FASB sponsoring groups "overwhelmingly agreed" that "the FASB . . . cannot confine its deliberations merely to corporate financial statements. Instead . . . the board must take into consideration the whole universe of financial reporting and disclosure" [2]. The board should take care, however, that its standards accord with auditors' responsibilities. If it extends its scope to include disclosure of items other than financial statements, should auditors be required to attest to their validity too? The Commission on Auditors' Responsibilities urged expansion of the audit function, but it did not consider a correspondingly expanded role for the FASB.

Questions remain. How can conflicts between international standards and domestic standards be resolved? Will having a conceptual framework of accounting inhibit the tendency to pronounce "rules" as standards, or will it herald a return to basic "principles"? Will the profession be able to raise its own standards to the level demanded by the courts (a higher lay standard rather than technical standards)? As auditors assume an expanded role, will the FASB broaden its jurisdiction to pronounce standards on disclosure other than in financial statements?

Shoring Up Technical Standards, Ethics, and
Work Performance

Respondents expressed frustration over the profession's vague standards of work and nonexistent criteria of competence. To be sure, such standards and criteria can only be inferred from case dispositions, interactions with the SEC, and the results of peer reviews; nowhere are they listed. The vagueness may owe to the rapid expansion in the scope of auditing, ranging from statistical sampling and auditing of computer-based accounting systems to auditing of governmental organizations and experimentation with social accounting methods. It will be formidable to arrive at consistent standards to cover such disparate tasks. Nevertheless, given the absence of defined criteria, the respondents' exasperation at published accounts of "substandard" or "incompetent" work is understandable. The profession needs to give priority to determining just what constitutes competence in a CPA. Until that is done, it does not make sense to discipline a CPA for incompetent work.[b]

Some critics attribute substandard performance to inadequate training of auditors. Though all states require an accountant to pass the uniform CPA examination to receive a license, state laws differ in other requirements. Some states are doing away with a practice or experience requirement in favor of more education. Yet to perform even the simplest audit functions, CPAs must undergo further training, usually conducted by their firm. In the large firms that training is truly substantial, and further specialized courses and training programs are strongly encouraged. The Commission on Auditors' Responsibilities declared that the large firms enjoy a competitive advantage as a result. The "free," in-depth training they offer makes them more attractive to recruits than the smaller firms with fewer resources [3, p. 87]. Both the expense and competitive advantage might be alleviated if such training were made part of all accountants' preparation.[c] The Commission on Auditors' Responsibilities called for more rigorous initial training and, above all, the inculcation of a sense of professional identity [3, p. 86].

The AICPA and AAA are exploring the possibility of professional schools of accounting, an idea endorsed by the commission. Survey respondents, however, disagreed over the merits of professional schools, particularly the virtues of a broad versus a specialized education. Specialization would give the new graduate

---

[b]The AICPA is not geared to detecting and disciplining incompetent individual work; that is a firm's responsibility. In cases investigated by the SEC, that agency can use (and often has) broad sanctions to remedy individual incompetence. The Commission on Auditors' Responsibilities, though it did not address this issue directly, expressed an awareness of changing levels of competence. The report noted that the uniform CPA examination reflects the educational level of current accounting graduates. If professional schools of accountancy produced more highly skilled graduates, the standard of the examination would have to be raised accordingly [3, p. 89]. Tacitly, therefore, the commission was using the CPA examination as a barometer of beginning CPA competence. But what about the seasoned auditor? Should not his competence also be measured and assessed? And where should the responsibility for that task lie, with the profession or his firm?

[c]An audit internship, similar to that undergone by new physicians, has been proposed as a requirement for graduation from a professional school of accounting or as a condition for receiving a CPA license. In a survey conducted for the Commission on Auditors' Responsibilities, Professor John Grant Rhode found that "over 44 percent of those in public practice believed their college education did not provide sufficient preparation for the auditing work assigned them when they started their careers (the belief was more prevalent among those from local rather than national firms)" [3, p. 86, n. 2].

a readily marketable skill, but it might impair his later ability to make decisions in the face of considerable uncertainty.

The disputes over which type of training is better reveal much about accountants' self-image. So far, the profession has held that only CPAs can be accountants, a CPA being defined fairly narrowly. But accounting has evolved into a multidisciplinary undertaking; today no firm can audit a large client without several kinds of specialists. Given the trend, specialties will probably proliferate in the future.[d] In such an environment, defining an accountant according to what he knows is open to question because that knowledge quickly becomes dated. The profession's difficulty in defining competence and recognizing incompetent performance stems largely from its too-narrow self-image.[e]

Difficulties other than definitional ones have hampered the profession's efforts to police itself. The AICPA lacks the enforcement power of the SEC and the state boards; the profession is uncertain about the auditor's role in society; and there is a dearth of adequate accounting principles, clear guidelines for what a financial statement should contain, and standards for ensuring auditor independence.

Respondents cited the poor quality control of audit engagements by accounting firms. So did the Commission on Auditors' Responsibilities, which extensively documented the pathologies of destructive fee competition, underbidding for audit jobs, inordinate time and budget pressures imposed on audit staffs, low morale, inadequate audit supervision, and underreporting of billable hours to cause firms to submit unreasonably low bids on subsequent audit engagements. Those practices have encouraged substandard work and excessive reliance on client representations without the independent checks expected of auditors [3, pp. 111-118].

Individual firms can tighten their own internal controls and auditing policies and correct many of those deficiencies. Yet corrective action by a few may not cure the malady, which is rooted in the industry and in the norms by which the Big Eight firms conduct their business. Ameliorative action should therefore be taken by all firms practicing before the SEC.

One widely heralded remedy is the review of a firm's auditing standards and quality-control procedures by its peers. Having evolved from an occasionally applied SEC sanction, through voluntary review programs developed by the AICPA,[f] peer reviews are now being advocated on a regular basis for all members

---

[d]The AICPA is deliberating whether to create specialties within the profession; despite specialization in the larger firms, no specialist branch of the profession has been formally recognized that can admit a person qualified in that specialty into professional membership.

[e]An alternative, proposed by Professor John W. Buckley of UCLA's Graduate School of Management, is to define an accountant by his role, not his knowledge [4]. If a computer scientist is on an audit team, he could be considered a member of the profession. That definition acknowledges accounting as a pluralistic and multidisciplinary profession. The AICPA now recognizes non-CPA audit specialists as "associate members," which rankles many of them.

[f]Practice review program, local firm quality review program, local firm administrative review program, and quality control review program for CPA firms [3, p. 138; 5].

of the AICPA's new SEC Practice Section. Hitherto, the SEC has been satisfied with having another CPA firm (or a special committee drawn from other firms) conduct the reviews. Both the Metcalf subcommittee and SEC chairman Harold Williams have doubted the independence of that arrangement; the former would like the SEC to undertake the reviews itself, and Williams would like a body independent of auditing firms to do it. Recent proposals to form an independent, SEC-chartered reviewing agency in the private sector come closest to meeting both desiderata.

Those who contend that the profession cannot regulate itself also cite the AICPA's Code of Professional Ethics and its poor enforcement of ethics violations. They complain that the AICPA is unwilling to act as prosecutor toward a member it is used to serving and supporting, protects the practitioners rather than the public interest in the code, and does not encourage and protect those who volunteer information about unethical or incompetent behavior.

One solution is for the AICPA and states to increase public participation on their disciplinary boards, as some states have done.[g] Nonprofessional participation would relieve accountants of much of the trauma of passing judgment on their colleagues, perhaps the biggest obstacle all professions experience in policing themselves. And moving swiftly once a disciplinary action has begun, as the Commission on Auditors' Responsibilities urged, can do much to restore lost credibility.

Restoring Confidence in the Independence of Auditors

While critical of accountants for their lack of independence from the client, the survey respondents explained some of the structural defects in the system that has made independence difficult to achieve. For example, an auditor must simultaneously handle pressures to present the client corporation in the most favorable light possible, remain committed to honest, consistent, and fair reporting, and try to retain the corporation as a client. Until the advent of audit committees, management enjoyed so much control over the audit process (selecting accounting principles, determining the length and scope of engagement, and hiring and firing the auditor), and audit firms were under such

---

[g]In twenty-one states bills stipulating lay representation on state boards of accountancy have been proposed [6]. The omnibus bill passed in Connecticut reduces the authority of the various professional boards, including accounting, to advisory status; the Massachusetts Society of CPAs helped defeat a lay-member bill in that state; in Wisconsin, the legislature is considering a recommendation to abolish the professional board of accountancy in favor of a totally lay regulatory board. In California Governor Edmund G. Brown, Jr., has personally led the effort to rid regulatory boards of control by the "special interests they were created to regulate." He has already appointed sixty lay members to serve on thirty-nine regulatory boards. Though the healing arts, law, and accounting were excluded from that action, Governor Brown's dedication to lay control of the professions augurs ill for partisans of an accounting board composed entirely of CPAs [7].

pressure to keep old clients and obtain new ones, that one wonders how accountants could have claimed that their main allegiance was to the public. Instead they have confused rhetoric with reality, the role of serving a client with that of checking on it. If accountants are not free to disagree with clients over accounting principles (or other issues, such as what is material) without being replaced, they cannot be considered independent.

The Metcalf report zeroed in on auditors' "alarming lack of independence," citing their advocacy of client positions in public forums and before legislators,[h] their performance of management advisory services for audit clients, and the close relationship with clients that prevents independent action. SEC chairman Harold Williams views auditor independence as the central issue in the profession. Whatever public accountants themselves may believe, other professionals have found much to criticize. While absolute independence may not be possible with the present structure, surely the degree of auditor independence can be raised.

The existence of audit committees in most publicly held companies has put needed distance between auditors and management. Composed entirely or chiefly of outside directors, audit committees hire auditors (subject to shareholders' approval), negotiate the scope and fee of the engagement, and monitor its progress. If any evidence of suspicious activity is uncovered, the committee can decide to press the inquiry, thus supporting the auditor in his disagreeable and hitherto lonely task of telling management something it may not want to hear. Not only has the traditional auditor-client relationship thus been attenuated, but also the auditor's allegiance has shifted from management to the company's shareholders and potential investors. That audit committees have filled a need is evident from the widespread support given the concept by the SEC, the NYSE, industry, and auditors alike.

However, audit committees have not been around long enough to have established roles; norms are still evolving. The Moss report called on the SEC to insure that the members of audit committees are sufficiently independent and qualified and that they have sufficient authority to discharge their responsibilities, including support from an adequate staff and access to outside experts.

The auditor-audit committee relationship may herald a new era for public accountants. It could be the mechanism by which the profession can act on some of the recommendations of the Commission on Auditors' Responsibilities, in particular the recommendation to extend the attest function to other types of corporate financial information. The day may not be far off when information is needed on a company's calculations of market share, the consumer demand for its products, or the costs to meet an environmental protection law. Authoriza-

[h]In contrast, the Commission on Auditors' Responsibilities took the position that auditors do not compromise their independence if they assume an advocacy stance with respect to their client or its industry, as long as they clearly distinguish between the two roles [3, p. 98].

tion of these tasks by the audit committee will help achieve the appearance as well as the fact of auditor independence.

As for the propriety of a firm's performing MAS for audit clients, an issue the SEC is still debating, the Commission on Auditors' Responsibilities refused to prohibit MAS outright, preferring to have a client's audit committee determine in each case whether the auditor would be compromising his independence. For the sake of appearance, though, it did recommend limiting executive recruiting services to positions below those likely to influence an audit engagement, an activity the SEC would like to ban altogether. Another device increasingly used to enhance the independence of auditors is for a company to disclose to shareholders the nature and extent of nonauditing services it buys from its auditors. The SEC is debating whether to make that disclosure mandatory.

When an auditing firm is fired by a client over a disagreement in the choice of accounting principles, the SEC requires that both the company and the auditor file their versions of the story with the commission.[i] The action does nothing to get the auditor reinstated, but it alerts the succeeding auditing firm to difficulties it might encounter. (A corporation with a history of changing auditors might find it not only hard to hire one, but in danger of losing its privilege to trade its securities publicly.) Audit committees will undoubtedly help free auditors of the fear of being replaced if their judgment differs from the client's.

A firm that depends heavily on one client's audit business for a large part of its revenue is undoubtedly more likely to compromise its independence than a firm whose largest client contributes no more than one or two percent of its revenues. Within firms of the former type there are enormous pressures on audit partners, managers, and staffs to do all they can to retain the business of the big client. The line between ethical and unethical conduct is very fine, as is the line between full and partial independence. The size of an audit firm, therefore, can play a positive role in maintaining its independence; the larger it is and the more clients it audits, the more independent it can be. If that were the reason accounting firms are being compelled to disclose financial and operational data, there would be real value to the disclosures. But the Metcalf report's reason— that the public ought to know something about the firms because their work is of public consequence—is trivial. Moreover, the Metcalf report required such disclosure only for the fifteen largest firms, whereas the smaller firms practicing before the SEC are more likely to jeopardize their independence and thus may need more careful monitoring.[j]

---

[i]In Britain auditors cannot be fired because they disagree with management over accounting principles. The rationale is that attesting to the proper use of accounting principles is the raison d'être of auditors in the first place [8, p. 209, n. 70].

[j]The final version of the Metcalf report (November 1977) called for financial disclosure by all firms practicing before the SEC.

The truly independent auditor is prepared to blow the whistle on management if the evidence warrants such action. That has not been easy in the past. Besides jeopardizing a close working relationship perhaps developed over many years, itself essential for doing a good audit, the requirement poses a serious role conflict: Should the auditor also act as policeman or government agent? Until recently the profession's position was that auditors should not act as policemen; that management must bear the responsibility and liability for illegal or questionable acts; and that auditors cannot, under present system constraints, perform audits thorough enough to detect such acts. In 1977 that position altered considerably. The Commission on Auditors' Responsibilities urged auditors to actively search for fraud and management wrongdoing and to always be skeptical of management and its motives (an attitude it characterized as "due professional care"). When an auditor must report any such discoveries is less clear. Activities or transactions that materially affect the company's financial statements must be reported, but "material" is still ambiguously defined. If the activities seem illegal, they should be reported without regard to materiality, said the commission.

Audit committees are making that task much easier to perform. The auditor can bring to the audit committee's attention any suspicious finding, no matter how inconsequential it may appear. The audit committee can then direct the auditor to follow up leads, can ask information directly of management or its legal counsel, and can monitor such inquiries. But who should make the report to the SEC?

The accountant's code of ethics places him under no obligation to blow the whistle; indeed, he has a clear ethical obligation of confidence to his client [9, rule 301]. Neither is the accountant under any legal obligation to report his client's errors, omissions, or misdeeds to the SEC or other government authority.[k] The Metcalf report attacked the AICPA position on the matter and urged accountants to put their civic duty above narrow professional interest in reporting illegal acts to the government.[l]

What complicates the judgment for accountants is the difficulty of esti-

---

[k]David B. Isbell believes, however, that it might be prudent for the accountant to act on a basis other than his legal obligation. Rather than report the client, he says, it may be best to part company with the client. Or it may be advisable to persuade the client itself to disclose the problem or consent to its disclosure. For leverage, the accountant can tell the client that disclosure may have to be made in the next annual statement [10, pp. 278-279]. Nowhere does Isbell advocate that the accountant directly report the client.

[l]"[T]here are no requirements [in the code of ethics] that the independent auditor do anything at all. Instead, there are several suggestions that an auditor should 'consider' such things as qualifying his opinion or withdrawing from the audit engagement. . . . In the wake of continual revelations of massive illegal activities by major corporations, the AICPA proposal that accountants should rely upon corporate managements to report their own illegal acts is truly extraordinary. It raises serious questions about the self-defined role of auditors for publicly-owned corporations. . . . The AICPA proposals on illegal acts by clients do not establish responsible standards to guide CPAs in serving the public interest" [11, pp. 117-118].

mating the impact that disclosures of improper or illegal payments would have on a company and hence whether the amounts are material or not [11, p. 9]. The Metcalf report assailed accountants for defining materiality as 5 percent, which holds big corporations to a lower absolute standard of accountability than the smaller ones [12, p. 117]. Since the courts have recently ruled that materiality should be judged subjectively as anything that might affect an investor's decision making, the accountant is now without any solid guidelines except his own professional judgment.

Audit committees are too new for the extent of their liability to be known, yet the risk of being held liable could prevent them from blowing the whistle on anybody. However, by its very position with respect to the company, the audit committee can minimize its risk; its authority and power enable it to obtain whatever evidence is necessary, and it need not actually blow the whistle until it has accumulated sufficient evidence.[m] And bringing suspicions of corporate wrongdoing and associated evidence to the attention of the audit committee has two distinct advantages for the person disclosing such information. His identity is kept secret (until a formal complaint is made to the SEC), and he can capitalize on the significant power and authority of the committee.

The audit committee has been perhaps the most significant structural change over the past few years and will undoubtedly assuage fears that audit engagements are not conducted independently. Yet it would be a mistake for auditors to relax their vigilance. Relying on the audit committee's independence from management is insufficient without also preserving their own independence of judgment. In this as in other matters, the profession should take the initiative.

Clarifying the Accountant's Role in Society

Not only did respondents directly cite the accounting profession's uncertainty about its role in society as a critical problem, but they also revealed a number of dilemmas that underscore that uncertainty. First, for accountants to extend present services and perform new ones raises the costs to clients and the firm's liability exposure, but for them to confine themselves to present services leaves them vulnerable to charges of being unresponsive to public demands. Second, accountants fear that yielding to public pressure to search for and report management fraud will threaten their relationship with the client, hinder effective auditing, and possibly result in loss of accounts. Third, efforts to

[m]Contrast this with the relatively powerless company employee—even corporate counsel or internal accountant—who can be intimidated by his superiors and even lose his job if he tries to report wrongdoing. Professor Christopher Stone believes that legislation should be enacted to protect him from "malicious discharge": "[T] he employer would be allowed to fire the employee. But if the employee could show that the discharge was for refusing to compromise professional ethics or to participate in immoral or unlawful activity, the worker would have a suit for damages, perhaps even punitive damages" [13, p. 215; see also 14].

narrow the gap between what is expected of public accountants and what they can reasonably deliver are damned on both sides. On the one hand, if the profession tries to lower public expectations—by claiming that accountants are not guarantors, that financial statements are not accurate, that auditors' certificates are only "opinions," that not all fraud can be detected—it is accused of being defensive and self-serving. On the other hand, accountants' fear of liability and their inability to reach a consensus on important issues have prevented them from moving forcefully to fulfill all reasonable public expectations. The inescapable inference is that the profession lacks effective leadership. In the present factious state, some interests will have to be overridden, whatever the profession decides to do. The trade-off appears to be whether the ultimate benefits of increased prestige and credibility with the public are worth that cost. No one seems willing to make the judgment.

The Commission on Auditors' Responsibilities, for all its deliberations, construed the auditor's role narrowly. It concentrated on correcting the more obvious deficiencies and gave a cautious green light to expanding the attest function to any information produced and verifiable by the accounting system. Nowhere did the report consider alternative role models that might have construed the auditor's role differently. Placing the auditor as intermediary between management and the company's shareholders, creditors, and underwriters—the traditional role—limits his function to certifying financial information of interest to those groups. But conceiving of auditors as master attestors, for example, would expand their traditional role to auditing other types of organization (governments, nonprofit institutions) and attesting to nonfinancial data and processes. The new role becomes a viable alternative only to the extent that the auditor remains independent of whatever he attests, the requests for attestation serve a useful social purpose, and the attestation is performed competently and to the limit of present technical capabilities (such as measurement systems).

The survey respondents disagreed over the future role of the profession. One view urged public accountants to eschew all MAS and concentrate on auditing, in the belief that trying to do too many things would diminish accountants' objectivity as auditors. Thus focused, the profession could increase the scope of auditing and keep its quality high. Another view saw government auditing as inevitable and welcomed an expanded role for accountants in advocacy and consulting, as long as there was no conflict of interest. Activities such as social accounting, cost-benefit analysis, and performance auditing were thought appropriate. An intermediate view envisaged the profession having much the same role that it now has but with greater flexibility and effectiveness. Like the medical and legal professions, it could embrace different specialties and provide means for ensuring specialists' competence, such as certificates and examinations. The profession could thus offer expanded services without much fear of liability, which would in turn foster new specialties.

Specialization has been addressed by the AICPA and the AAA in committee, but the larger issues of alternative roles for public accountants and the place of specialties in them have not been debated in public forums or studied in policy research. The neglect may owe to the profession's unfamiliarity with methods of studying the future [15] and the here-and-now orientation of accountants.[n] Another reason is the natural tendency to resist change because the present is known, the future uncertain. Yet because events have shown that the present is quite unlike the recent past, we can no longer assume that the future will be a simple extrapolation of the present. To prepare itself, the profession should conceive of alternative futures, alternative role models, and alternative ways of serving itself and society, and then make its strategic decisions.

Until those decisions are made, the AICPA's role will remain blurred. Even its constitutency is mixed. While it is acknowledged to have become the principal spokesman for public accountants, it counts only 70 percent of all accountants as members. Only 57 percent of its membership are involved in "public practice" [25, p. 20], and substantially less than one-third of them are public accountants or auditors. Though all members are CPAs, their interests, activities, and needs vary considerably.

The factious and diffuse state of the profession may also account for its inability to adapt itself quickly to changes in its environment. Never short on rhetoric, the AICPA has nevertheless so far failed to actually manage the conflicts between large and small firms, between educators and practitioners, between auditors and nonauditors who offer MAS to audit clients, and between auditors and client financial executives (the latter comprise over one-third of the AICPA's public accountant members). Rather than acting on any consistent and long-range goal, the AICPA seems to be indulging in ad hoc activities in an effort to please everybody. Such a stance will not help the profession through its present troubles. It needs to establish a basic philosophy about public accountants and their role in society, organize accordingly to keep control in the private sector, decide on clear priorities, and methodically act on them.

Although it has been the profession's principal spokesman for many years,

---

[n]Professor Marvin Adelson, of UCLA's school of architecture and urban planning, has pointed out that different futures methods can aid the study of different topics. For studying goals, "Utopian imaging" might be used [16]; for objectives, program budgeting [17]; for needed developments, relevance analysis [18]; for process dynamics, formal modeling (for an application of system dynamics appreciation—a way of modeling world views using feedback loops—to the accounting profession, see ref. 19, vol. 1, pp. 88-107; for a description of cross-impact simulation, see appendix A); for informed judgment, the Delphi method [20]; for relationships among developments, contextual mapping [21; 22, pp. 178-181], gaming [23], and cross-impact analysis (see appendix A); and for synthesis, scenario construction [24, pp. 262-264].

The survey respondents manifested this present orientation. Their concepts of emerging problems without precedent very much resembled those the profession has been struggling with for many years, and responses to the fantasy question revealed an inability to imagine a world free of present institutional arrangements and regulations.

the AICPA has yet to resolve the fundamental role conflict inherent in trying both to serve its members and regulate them in the public interest. Nowhere is that more evident than in its inability to effectively monitor accountants' behavior and discipline ethical infractions. One way to resolve that conflict without inviting greater SEC or congressional intervention is to take visible steps to align the profession's self-interest with the public's. Acknowledging that accounting is now a matter of public interest, the AICPA should appoint public (non-CPA) representatives to its key policy committees. The FASB has been operating successfully in this mode for some time, and public participation in its board has just been expanded. The idea has several distinct advantages. It can give the profession's claim that it serves the public interest the credibility it now lacks; help the profession reduce the expectation gap; inject a broader perspective into policy deliberations, enhancing the value of the resulting decisions; dissuade accountants from hiding behind their technical arguments, thereby tightening the profession's standards, policies, ethics rules, and practices to survive future court and legislative challenges; and help explain the profession's goals and accomplishments to a wider audience. Public members on the institute's ethics enforcement committee will relieve CPAs of much of the trauma of disciplining fellow CPAs and act to improve enforcement measures considerably. The greatest benefit their presence can confer is to stimulate change from within the profession, obviating compulsion by the SEC, Congress, or courts of law.

It is not known to what extent the profession's current organization has stifled consideration of the public accountant's appropriate role. Rather than contemplating alternative forms of organization, it makes more sense to clarify that role and then organize accordingly. Interim organizational changes, such as establishing an independent audit review board for SEC-practice firms or including public representatives on policy committees, seem warranted. But fundamental reorganization (of the order proposed by Eli Mason or as would be demanded by a substantial shift in the accountant's role) must await further study. Respondents to the fantasy question in the second survey were not so unusual, then, in calling for different institutional arrangements (see appendix B); yet how were they to know that such changes might not wait until the year 2000 but could occur well before then?

References

[1] *The Public Accounting Profession and Its Critics,* proceedings of a conference sponsored by the Wharton School, University of Pennsylvania, 25 May 1976 (Philadelphia, 1976).
[2] Robert Mims, "Pressuring the FASB to Broaden Its Reach," *Business Week*, 28 November 1977, p. 96.

[3] Commission on Auditors' Responsibilities, *Report on Tentative Conclusions* (New York, 1977).

[4] John W. Buckley, *In Search of Identity: An Inquiry into Indentity Issues in Accounting,* (Palo Alto, Ca.: California CPA Foundation for Education and Research, 1972).

[5] W.W. Ecton, "The AICPA Quality Review Program—Its Record and Prospects," *Journal of Accountancy,* October 1975, pp. 106-108.

[6] "Lay Representation on State Boards of Accountancy," *Journal of Accountancy,* October 1977, p. 24.

[7] Jon Nordheimer, "Brown Places 60 on California Regulatory Boards As 'Lobbyists for People' Instead of Special Interests," *New York Times,* 7 February 1977, pp. 1, 20.

[8] Melvin A. Eisenberg, *The Structure of the Corporation: A Legal Analysis* (Boston, Ma.: Little, Brown & Company, 1976).

[9] AICPA, *Code of Professional Ethics,* rev. ed. (New York, 1973).

[10] David B. Isbell, "An Overview of Accountants' Duties and Liabilities under the Federal Securities Laws and a Closer Look at Whistle-Blowing," *Ohio State Law Journal,* 35:2 (1974), pp. 261-279.

[11] Harry Anderson, "The Outside Auditors: Are They Policemen?" *Los Angeles Times,* 19 October 1975, part 4, p. 6.

[12] U.S. Senate, Committee on Government Operations, Subcommittee on Reports, Accounting, and Management, *The Accounting Establishment,* 94th Cong. 2nd sess., December 1976.

[13] Christopher D. Stone, *Where the Law Ends: The Social Control of Corporate Behavior,* (New York: Harper & Row, 1975).

[14] David W. Ewing, "Protecting 'Whistle-Blowers,' " *New York Times,* 1 September 1977, p. 31.

[15] Marvin Adelson, *Future Perspective and the Accounting Profession,* Working Paper 76-1, Accounting-Information Systems Research Program, Graduate School of Management, University of California, Los Angeles, Ca., 1976.

[16] W.J.J. Gordon, *Synectics: The Development of Creative Capacity* (New York: Harper & Row, 1961).

[17] U.S. Congress, Joint Economic Committee, Subcommittee on Economy in Government, *The Analysis and Evaluation of Public Expenditures: The PPB System,* 91st Cong., 1st sess., 1969, 3 vols.

[18] J.V. Sigford and R.H. Parvin, "Project PATTERN: A Methodology for Determining Relevance in Complex Decision-Making," *IEEE Transactions on Engineering Management,* EM-12, March 1965, pp. 9-13.

[19] Stanley C. Abraham, "The Public Accounting Profession: An Application of Futures Research Methods to Identifying and Clarifying Its Problems" (Ph.D. diss., University of California, Los Angeles, 1976), 2 vols.

[20] Harold A. Linstone and Murray Turoff, eds., *The Delphi Method: Techniques and Applications* (Reading, Mass.: Addison-Wesley, 1975).

[21] Perry E. Rosove, *The Use of Contextual Mapping to Support Long-Range Educational Policy Making,* System Development Corporation, Paper SP-3026, Santa Monica, Ca., December 1967.

[22] Erich Jantsch, "Time-Independent Contextual Mapping," in E. Jantsch, *Technological Forecasting in Perspective* (Paris: OECD, 1967).

[23] Martin Shubik, *The Uses and Methods of Gaming* (New York: Elsevier North-Holland, 1975).

[24] Herman Kahn, "The Use of Scenarios," in Herman Kahn and Anthony Wiener, *The Year 2000: A Framework for Speculation on the Next Thirty-Three Years* (New York: Macmillan, 1967).

[25] AICPA, *Annual Report 1976-77,* New York.

17 The Next Steps

Despite the remarkable progress the profession has made recently in responding to congressional pressures and general criticism, it has not succeeded in supplying either the quality or range of services its beneficiaries expect of it. If it is to stave off new federal legislation, minimize SEC intervention in its affairs, and raise its credibility in the public's eyes, it should seriously consider taking the following steps. Though some may seem unpalatable, the alternatives—stagnation, confusion, and impotence—seem inestimably worse.

The AICPA should clarify the profession's central role in society. It is ironic that after the Commission on Auditors' Responsibilities reported its findings, there still exists a basic unclarity about the profession's central role. It lies at the core of many AICPA policy dilemmas. Whether CPA firms should be advocates of client positions or independent of them (or both, as at present) has not yet been decided; nor has the AICPA fully investigated the desirability of letting its members attest to anything that lies within their competence instead of limiting attestation to the financial affairs of corporate and nonprofit clients. Reducing the profession's often conflicting roles to one or a few compatible ones would help resolve other related issues—for example, how a public accountant should be defined, who should be AICPA members, and how the AICPA might best be organized.

The profession has grown in response to the growth in corporations' size, complexity, and demand for public accounting services. That growth has been ad hoc, and new functions and roles have been added with little regard for how they fit into existing patterns. A full assessment of the cumulative effect of developments has not been made. Unless the time is soon taken for such an assessment and clarification of its role, the AICPA may not be able to shake off its reputation for primarily reacting to problems rather than managing them, thus unnecessarily inviting increasing control from outside.

The FASB should continue to set accounting standards, subject to strong SEC oversight. The present arrangement gets the job done, even though more slowly than some would like. Most important, the FASB has the support of virtually every constituency, and it has convinced the Metcalf subcommittee of its competence. Independent polls endorse it as the profession's standard-setting body; the consensus is that no government agency could do the job as well, let alone better. Despite some strong complaints and dire predictions expressed in the present survey, the FASB has a clear mandate from Congress, the SEC, and the business, financial, and accounting worlds to formulate accounting principles.

That accounting principles are set in the private sector alone is a myth. The SEC in its oversight role has taken many initiatives and made many forays into the setting of accounting principles. In the future it is likely to be even less hesitant about pushing the FASB in certain directions or declaring its position on a controversial issue. The tension between the two agencies is healthy. It reminds one of government by two parties, one in power, the other opposing, the latter always ready to take over, keeping the former on its toes. As Horngren has often noted, standard setting is a public-private sector partnership. Giving the FASB the chief responsibility insulates the process from hidden political agendas and extends application of the standards to companies that operate outside the SEC's jurisdiction.

The FASB has already made considerable headway in a number of crucial matters, such as delineating a conceptual framework of accounting, deciding on the objectives of financial reporting, and accounting for the effects of inflation. It should press on to complete those projects as quickly as possible, while also giving priority to defining materiality and deciding whether accountants should pass judgment on the "preferability" of accounting principles (as the SEC and the Moss report insist) or whether management should retain that prerogative (as the Commission on Auditors' Responsibilities recommends). Though Arthur Andersen's suit against the SEC complained that each auditor, if required to determine the most preferable principle in a given case, would play the role of standard setter, the responsibility does seem inherent to the auditor's role.

The recent structural changes that have reduced the influence of public accountants among the FASB's constituencies will strengthen its commitment to a broader public and to eliminating alternative accounting principles. With a larger budget and research staff, it will be able to make headway fast without sacrificing deliberative care.

Auditors should increase their independence in appearance as well as in fact. Audit committees composed largely of outside directors can be effective in insulating auditors from management influence and enhancing their independence. CPA firms should be prepared, if audit committees so rule, to perform fewer MAS for audit clients. The Commission on Auditors' Responsibilities acknowledged that performing MAS impaired independence in appearance if not in fact. The real issue may be accountants' unwillingness to weigh the revenue they derive from MAS against the possible damage to their credibility and independence. Other reforms under consideration will also enhance independence—refraining from advocacy positions for clients and limiting executive recruiting and placement activities.

Independence is the sole attribute that distinguishes an auditor from other kinds of accountant, and it should be guarded jealously. Audit committees cannot bear the full responsibility. The profession's code of ethics and auditing standards need to spell out and enforce appropriate conduct for auditors. For example, the profession needs to consider whether to allow one CPA firm to review the work and quality-control procedures of another. No matter how independently that task may in fact be done, it lacks credibility to observers. Perhaps the answer is for auditors engaged in reviewing the work of other audit firms to give up their own corporate clients and specialize in quality-control review work (that role could provide an opportunity for smaller firms to grow without competing for clients with the largest firms). To the extent that the desired degree of independence cannot be attained without uniform principles and a strong code of ethics, correcting those deficiencies should be among the profession's highest priorities.

The concentration of power among accounting firms should be reduced. By the very nature of the auditing function, the size of CPA firms will parallel that of the corporations they audit. Without the global reach and specialized staff of large CPA firms, audits of giant corporations would not be possible. This recommendation does not suggest breaking up or otherwise constraining the eight largest firms. Rather, concentration should be reduced by encouraging the merger of smaller firms to form new large firms. That approach would mitigate the alleged dominance and undue influence of the Big Eight without impairing their effectiveness.

First, the AICPA should develop a means of training and certifying a firm to offer "SEC experience" to a client. That should be done through its new SEC Practice Section. Quality-control procedures in SEC-practice firms should be reviewed and enforced by an independent audit review board set up by the profession under SEC oversight.

Second, companies going public should be prohibited from arbitrarily changing their auditing firm to one of the largest firms. (Exceptions should be made for companies that have not used an independent auditor before and for companies whose present auditor does not have or want SEC experience.) Although the financial community may find it hard to adjust at first, such a scheme would permit smaller firms to grow, would provide better auditing capabilities to clients, and would stimulate healthy competition among firms.

Third, mergers among smaller CPA firms that wish to audit publicly held companies should be encouraged. Likewise, new mergers among the Big Eight should be temporarily prohibited.

The AICPA should appoint non-CPAs to its executive committees. In recognition of the greater public interest in and public effect of accounting policy decisions, responsible non-CPAs should be invited to serve on the institute's council, board of directors, and executive committees, especially those that can speak on behalf of the profession without recourse to the institute's governing council.

Public participation on policy committees will broaden a committee's perspective and enrich its deliberations, reduce the burden borne by the ethics enforcement committee in disciplining negligent or unethical accountants whom the institute has hitherto supported, and ensure that accounting policy is responsive to the public interest. The profession's apparent fear that public participation would dilute or adversely affect its own interests is unfounded. For one thing, the FASB has demonstrated both the fallacy of that belief and its benefits; for another, the fear is tantamount to an admission that the profession's and the public's interests differ.

Public participation on the institute's policy committees will not only guard against the profession's straying from the public interest, but will also promote better policy and help keep policymaking in the private sector.

The AICPA should improve and tighten its self-regulatory mechanisms. The AICPA should immediately revise its professional code of ethics to pledge primary allegiance to the public interest. Any infringement of the code should be handled swiftly and decisively, not postponed to await the outcome of SEC actions, trials, or appeals. Once a case has been set in motion, the process and final outcome should be made public, unless the individual concerned can show that his defense in a pending proceeding or trial would be jeopardized thereby. As a rule, the AICPA should subscribe to higher ethical standards than those required or expected by the SEC, Congress, or the courts.

To regulate the performance of firms, especially those that practice before the SEC, the profession should establish a body independent of it (but subject to SEC oversight) to supervise periodic reviews of firms' quality-control procedures and to enforce adherence to professional standards. Firms doing the reviews should be prohibited from auditing clients, to remove any appearance of self-serving. Further, reviewing firms should be encouraged to report violations of the ethics code to the AICPA's trial board.

To ensure continuing competence among practitioners, the profession should consider holding examinations in various specialties and appropriate levels of position in firms (manager, partner). It should also give serious thought to certifying specialties and at least one grade of paraprofessional.

The AICPA should establish an independent institution to perform long-range planning and policy research. Accounting is no longer the simple bookkeeping function it once used to be; it is a complex, quasi-legal, highly probabilistic, dynamic, and multidisciplinary activity. Academic research now has little relevance to the practice of public accounting, and the profession lacks adequate independent resources to support the needs of the policy committees of the AICPA and FASB. For example, the FASB needs empirical research to assess the impact of past pronouncements and working models to provide credible answers to "what if" questions.

The profession's arsenal of research tools is similarly inadequate to the task. Other methods, such as those used by long-range planners and futurists, and related disciplines, such as law, economics, information and computer sciences, statistics, policy analysis, psychology, and political science, should be brought to bear more heavily on the profession's problems.

To bring disciplines and methods together in the service of the profession, an independent research institution should be established. It should aim to make its research processes and results efficient, highly competent, and useful. Its work should both influence and be sensitive to developments in practice, in contrast to current research in the pluralistic, free-form academic environment. Initial funding should be modest, and financial support should grow with the institution's competence, stature, and acceptance.

Appendixes

Appendix A
The Research Study

The research results reported in parts I and II are derived from a doctoral dissertation done at the Graduate School of Management, University of California, Los Angeles, in 1975 [1]. The dissertation had both methodological and substantive objectives. Methodologically, it sought to identify and apply futures research methods[a] to the study of the public accounting profession and to devise a research strategy incorporating several such methods for studying other professions. Substantively, the study sought to compile an inventory of the accounting profession's most critical problems, to learn how they are interrelated, and to find out which ones underlie the profession's current difficulties and hence deserve priority attention. The study's premise was that the profession, too busy reacting to successive crises, was not taking the time to reassess its priorities or direction. The study's aim was to contribute to that reassessment.

The eight-stage research design consisted of two national surveys, a "method string" of analytical techniques,[b] and several desired products. Figure A-1 presents the design in schematic form. The desired products, keyed to the numbers on the right of the figure, are

1. Views of the profession's constituent groups about its most critical problems, reasons for their persistence, what should be done about them, and what might happen if nothing is done.
2. Analyses revealing the relative importance and solvability of the profession's problems, the appropriateness of remedial actions, obstacles to progress, and the reality and urgency of unwanted consequences.
3. Clarification of the profession's problems and role in society as a conceptual model.
4. Findings and recommendations based on the survey results, the conceptual model, and the research experience.

The rest of this appendix describes the selection of the respondents for the two surveys, the survey instruments, the analytic techniques relevant to the findings presented in the book, and the application of those techniques to the accounting profession's problems.

---

[a]"Futures research is an interdisciplinary activity concerned with the development and application of systematic techniques for obtaining and evaluating judgments on the nature and desirability of alternative futures. The basic mission of futures research is to broaden our time horizons and enable us not only to anticipate long-term change *per se*, but also to see how, by controlling such changes, we can increase the range of our alternatives and select alternatives likely to produce a better society in the near and longer time periods" [2, p. 30].

[b]The concept holds that a number of methods used in sequence or in parallel for a particular purpose constitutes a methodology in its own right [3].

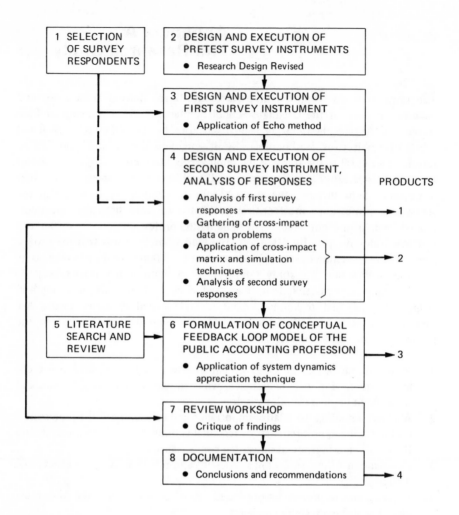

Figure A-1. The Research Design (Product numbers are keyed to the text.)

The Sample

Twelve constituent groups were initially identified. That number was reduced to the following seven after preliminary research and pretesting: (1) auditor-CPAs; (2) nonauditor-CPAs (including staffs of AICPA and state accounting societies); (3) educators, primarily accounting; (4) corporate financial executives; (5) investment company executives/financial press; (6) government personnel, including those in regulatory agencies; (7) lawyers knowledgeable about securities law and accounting. Shareholders were omitted for two reasons. First, it would have been almost impossible to obtain the names of a select list of shareholders who were not also members of at least one other constituent group, which would have biased their responses. Second, the proportion of institutional to private investors has risen sharply during the last decade, so the fifth group was considered an adequate surrogate for the shareholder group; most private investors trade securities through brokers.

Because the study was basically inductive and greater emphasis was placed on the quality of the data than on statistical reults, *who* was chosen to respond was considered far more important than *how many* respondents there were. Moreover, the demands the surveys placed on respondents would have wreaked havoc with any statistical sampling design (adequate sampling rates could have been achieved for each group but only at the expense of response quality). The emphasis on response quality is reflected in the criteria for choosing participants. It was desired that all respondents meet one of the following conditions:

Be an opinion shaper, one whose ideas are at the cutting edge of his field.

Have published articles or books or who has given speeches related to the profession's problems.

Be known for being outspoken in his or her views of the profession's problems.

Be a recognized leader, spokesperson, or authority in the field.

Have been a member of an FASB or AICPA policy committee or have given testimony in its deliberations.

Names were taken from published sources, such as lists of AICPA officers and council members, the AACSB directory for accounting educators, and numerous library sources for leaders of pertinent associations. Letters of inquiry yielded other names. Aiming for at least 10 and perhaps 20 respondents in each group, I invited a total of 647 people, more for the first four groups than the last three, for which enough names were difficult to obtain. (Though the constituent groups were clearly defined, and though invitations to participate were geared to group targets, respondents themselves chose which group they wished to identify with.)

Of the more than half who replied, three-fourths agreed to participate, but just over half of the latter turned in a complete questionnaire for the first survey, a 21.3 percent completion rate. Table A-1 presents the breakdown by group.

Second survey questionnaires were sent to those who completed first survey questionnaires, those who promised to but did not, and new potential respondents. (New respondents were sought especially for groups 5, 6, and 7, to shore

Table A-1
Respondents to First Survey, by Group

				Respondents Completing First Survey		
Group	Invited	Replied	Agreed To Participate	Number	Percent Who Agreed To Participate	Percent of All Respondents
1	234	120	102	44	43.1	31.9
2	46	31	26	18	69.3	13.0
3	112	45	34	23	67.7	16.7
4	91	66	53	27	51.0	19.6
5	45	21	14	9	64.3	6.5
6	36	25	19	10	52.7	7.2
7	83	35	15	7	46.7	5.1
Total	647	343	263	138	52.5	100.0

up low participation rates in the first survey, and for a new corporate activist/public interest group. Because only three respondents from this new group completed the survey, their responses are not analyzed as a group but are included in analyses using all the responses.) Ninety-seven respondents to the second survey also completed the first, and 12 were added from the new invitations sent out. The response rate to the second survey was predictably higher than that of the first survey but still remarkable at nearly 42 percent. Table A-2 shows the breakdown by group.

Table A-2
Respondents to Second Survey, by Group

		Respondents Completing Second Survey					
Group	Invited	Also Completed First Survey	Promised But Did Not Complete First Survey	New	Total	Percent of Number Invited	Percent of All Respondents
1	99	26	10	0	36	36.4	26.9
2	29	13	4	0	17	58.6	12.7
3	36	16	2	4	22	61.1	16.4
4	52	22	4	0	26	50.0	19.4
5	21	6	2	1	9	42.9	6.7
6	30	7	3	1	11	36.7	8.2
7	38	7	0	3	10	26.3	7.5
8	17	–	–	3	3	17.6	2.2
Total	322	97	25	12	134	41.6	100.0

Table A-3
Composition of Respondent Groups 1 and 2: Auditor- and Nonauditor-CPAs

Position in Firm	Big Eight CPA Firm	Second Eight CPA Firm	Other CPA Firm	AICPA and State CPA Society	Retired CPA	Total
Chairman, managing partner	3	2	9	0	1	15
Regional and senior partner, national director	2	1	1	0	0	4
Partner	18	6	21	0	1	46
Manager	5	0	0	0	0	5
Other	0	0	1	4	1	6
Total	28	9	32	4	3	76

The composition of the constituent groups in both surveys is shown below. Table A-3 shows that groups 1 and 2 are heavily weighted (85 percent), as intended, by CPAs with the rank of partner or above. Although about half these respondents represented the sixteen largest CPA firms in the United States, two-thirds of the firms represented were smaller ones (table A-4). Nearly three-fourths of group 3 were accounting educators, as the following breakdown shows:

Business school dean, associate dean	3
Chairman, department of accounting	1
Professor of accounting	19
Professor of law (by choice identifying with group 3, not group 7)	2
Professor of management	1
Professor of sociology	1
Total	27

Group 4, originally intended to represent the broad corporate sector, turned out to be heavy in financial executives (over two-thirds of the group):

Executive vice-president	2
Senior vice-president	3
Vice-president of finance	5
Controller, comptroller, director of finance	10
Assistant controller	5
Other	6
Total	31

Table A-4
Representation of Firms in Respondent Sample

	Big Eight CPA Firms	Second Eight CPA Firms	Other CPA Firms	Total
Number of firms in United States	8	8	14,959[a]	14,975[a]
Number of firms represented by respondent sample	8	8	30	45

[a]As of 1970 [4, p. 28]. Because that figure is 78 percent higher than the corresponding 1960 figure, the 1975 total should be considerably higher.

Group 5, intended to represent "Wall Street," was about equally divided between senior investment company executives and members of the business and financial press:

Investment company executive or partner	5
Portfolio manager	1
Business and financial press editor, department editor, staff writer	5
Other	1
Total	12

Over half of the group 6 respondents worked in regulatory agencies, including the SEC:

Regulatory agency	7
General Accounting Office	1
Cost Accounting Standards Board	1
Other U. S. government agency	2
Other	2
Total	13

Finally, nine of the ten members of group 7 experienced in accounting matters and securities laws were practicing lawyers:

Senior partner of law firm	2
Partner of law firm	6
General counsel of CPA firm	1
Professor of law	1
Total	10

The respondents were experienced and knowledgeable in accounting and financial matters. Their knowledge was roughly guaged by means of questions on accounting policy, current events in the business and financial worlds, and investing. They were also asked to indicate how critical they were, in general, of the public accounting profession's activities or policies, by checking a point on the following continuum:

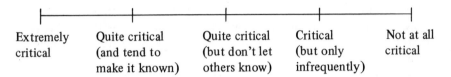

Extremely critical

Quite critical (and tend to make it known)

Quite critical (but don't let others know)

Critical (but only infrequently)

Not at all critical

Numerical values of 9 (extremely critical), 7, 5, 3, and 1 (not at all critical) were later assigned to the five nodes on the scale to evaluate the responses. Group 5 emerged as the group most critical of the profession, followed by group 3; groups 2 and 4 were the least critical. That three of the seven groups had means over the halfway point of the scale, and the remaining four had scores over 4.0, showed that the respondents were not "rubber stamps" but had views and opinions often running against the stream. Table A-5 summarizes the results of the test of informedness and the self-ratings in criticality, as well as average age, by group.

Appendix E presents the names and affiliations of the respondents to the two surveys.

Table A-5
Criticality and Informedness Scores among Respondents

Group	Completed Survey	Average Age (years)	Criticality Self-Rating (1-9)	Informedness (%) Accounting	Investing	Current Events
1	44	48.8	4.7	95	80	69
2	18	55.2	4.0	74	83	74
3	23	49.3	6.0	83	70	83
4	27	47.7[a]	4.1	90	85	67
5	9	46.1[a]	6.3	81	78	63
6	10	58.1	5.1	50	50	63
7	7	44.0	4.6	86	100	81
Total	138	50.3[a]	4.8	85	78	71

[a]One person each in groups 4 and 5 declined to state his age.

The First Survey Instrument

The survey package, sent to those who agreed to participate, consisted of a cover letter, a page of instructions, and the four-part instrument: (1) the questionnaire itself, asking the respondent to identify two continuing, critical problems in the profession and one emerging problem, and probing in depth his views on the problems, (2) an optional fantasy question about the future of the profession,[c] (3) an example of a similar questionnaire about the medical profession, filled in to discuss the problem of the potential nationalization of the health care industry, and (4) a form requesting personal data. The instrument is reproduced in appendix C.

When designing the research, I was concerned that busy executives would not take the time to answer an open-ended questionnaire. The pretest, however, confirmed the feasibility of the instrument's format, proved that it could be completed in a couple of hours (though many respondents took longer), and showed that the instrument could produce detailed information about the profession's strategic problems. The pretest also demonstrated the value of the completed example from the medical profession.

The Second Survey Instrument

The form and content of the second survey instrument derived from the results of the first survey. It comprised six sections: (I) problems, taken singly; (II) problems, interactions between pairs; (III) behavioral descriptors (obstacles to progress); (IV) remedies; (V) opportunities; (VI) consequences. Each section had its own instructions and format (see the reproduction of the instrument in appendix D). In each section the principal findings of the first survey were given. The problems that were the core of the second survey were the twenty-five most frequently mentioned in the first; similarly, the behaviors, actions, opportunities, and outcomes selected for the second were the most frequently mentioned, most provocative (opportunities only), and most clearly stated of the first. The reduction process yielded the following results:

Item	Number in First Survey	Number Incorporated in Second Survey
Continuing and new problems	100	25
Behavioral descriptors	75+	40
Suggested actions, remedies	680	26
Opportunities	50+	33
Consequences	860	25

[c]The fantasy question was made optional because requiring it might have deterred some participants from answering other parts of the questionnaire. Surprisingly, over 44 percent of the respondents completed the fantasy question; I had estimated that only 25 percent would do so.

Because of a lack of time, the second survey instrument was not pretested. Instead, it was reviewed by nine partners of CPA firms and by my colleagues. On the basis of their critiques the instrument was revised and a section on opportunities added.

Both surveys reflect a strong negative tone in the wording of the questions and in some of the lists from which choices were to be made. That bias would have produced questionable results if the purpose of the research had been to explore the values of the profession's members or constituencies. But the deliberate purpose was to focus on the profession's critical problems—in order to aid policymaking and to fill a gap in the literature—and the negative tone was unavoidable. The results are legitimate if the narrow focus is borne in mind.

Analytic Techniques

This section describes three analytic techniques relevant to the findings presented in the book. A fourth technique, system dynamics appreciation (for articulating a world-view of a complex system using feedback loops [5, 6, 7]), was used in the research to synthesize the results of the two surveys [1, vol. 1, pp. 34-36 and 88-107]. That synthesis appears in the comparison of the survey findings with recent developments in chapter 16.

The Echo Method

The Echo Method is a proprietary tool developed by social psychologists at General Research Corporation, Santa Barbara, California [8, 9, 10]. Conceived to study value preferences, it uses a relatively pure form of open-ended questionnaire. In polling techniques, respondents answer only once specific questions that are generally well matched to their culture and population. In contrast, the Echo Method repeats open-ended questions a standard number of times (see the example in figure A-2) to overcome a respondent's resistance to telling the truth and to find out just what is important to him. The repetition exposes opinions that are deeply felt rather than merely conventional or habitual.

To expose such opinions, not to reveal values, the Echo Method was adapted for use in the first survey instrument. Its value in enriching the responses can be appreciated by noting that many respondents showed more original thinking in second and third response attempts than in first attempts (that is, when asked for another action or consequence as opposed to being asked for the first time).

Cross-Impact Matrix Analysis

Cross-impact matrix analysis was developed at the Institute for the Future, Menlo Park, California, in the late 1960s [11-15]. It is part of the broader field

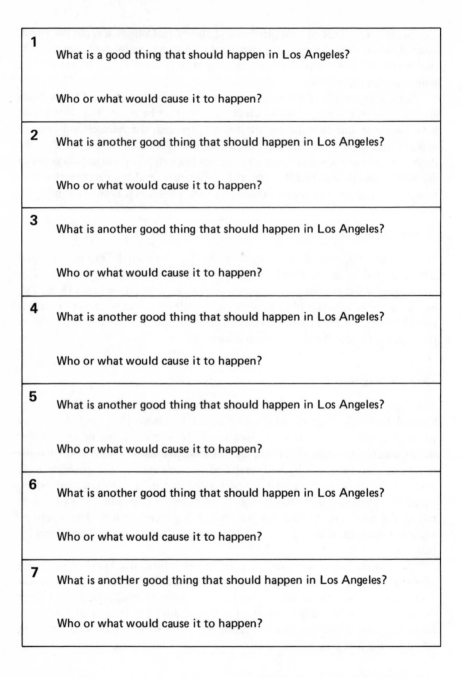

Figure A-2. Typical Echo Political Survey Question Form [10, p. 7]

of cross-impact analysis, which includes methods enabling evaluation of "changes in the likelihood of occurrence among an entire set of possible future events and trends in light of limited changes in probability for some of the items in that set" [2, p. 32].

The cross-impact matrix considers a set of events, their likelihood of occurrence at some point in the future, and subjective estimates of the effects that the occurrence of each event in the set will have on the others. The concept is best illustrated by an example. Consider the matrix in table A-6 (adapted from [2], p. 33), which shows four events, A through D, and probability estimates of their occurrence at some point in the future (say ten years). The values in the matrix denote the revised probability estimates given that the event in each row occurs.

If event A occurs, for instance, the probabilities that events B and C also occur do not change, but the probability that event D occurs increases (from 0.5 to 0.6). Also, event C is "uncoupled" from the others since its occurrence neither affects nor is affected by the occurrence of any of the other events. The technique is limited to interactions between pairs. One can estimate and treat impacts of A on B and B on C, but not A and B simultaneously on C, even though such an impact may exist in reality. While there is no theoretical limit on the size of matrix that can be constructed, the effort of making large numbers of estimates is taxing enough to naturally limit the size of most matrices.

A useful way to analyze a cross-impact matrix once it has been constructed is the following sequential procedure [2, pp. 34-35]:

1. The information contained in the matrix is used to compute the changes in probabilities that would result from the nonoccurrence of each event in the set.
2. The changed probabilities are used to compute cross-impact factors for use in computing revised probabilities.
3. An event is selected at random and its occurrence or nonoccurrence is "decided" on the basis of its assigned probability.

Table A-6
Cross-Impact Matrix

Given Event	Occurrence Probability	Probability of Event Also Occurring			
		A	B	C	D
A	0.4		0.2	0.5	0.6
B	0.2	0.5		0.5	0.5
C	0.5	0.4	0.2		0.5
D	0.5	0.3	0.2	0.5	

4. The probabilities of the remaining events are adjusted in light of the result of step 3, using the cross-impact factors.
5. Another event is selected from among those remaining and is decided (using its new probability) as before.
6. This process is continued until all events in the set have been decided. The outcome—the events deemed to have occurred—is then recorded, and all intermediate computations are purged.
7. The matrix is "played" this way many times, so that new probabilities can be computed on the basis of the percentage of times that an event occurs during these repeated plays.

These seven steps constitute a run of the analysis. The first run (base run) is intended to test the internal consistency of the data in the matrix with no perturbations introduced in the input data. After the matrix has thus been balanced, it is ready for step 8:

8. Steps 1 to 7 are repeated using different initial probabilities provided by the experimenters to test the effects of alternative actions.

The technique is receiving increasing attention by scholars, and attempts are being made to extend its flexibility and capability by treating exogenous trends and developments simultaneously in the model [16-19].[d] The final technique discussed here is an offshoot.

Cross-Impact Simulation Using KSIM

KSIM, a computer-based cross-impact simulation model, was devised by Julius Kane at the University of British Columbia [20]. It has been further developed at the Stanford Research Institute [21]. KSIM is a simulation procedure for structuring and analyzing relationships among broadly defined variables in large socioeconomic systems. It was originally developed to allow decision makers to accommodate a mix of hard data and intuitive judgment and to test alternative planning options efficiently [22]. It was designed to do the latter by exploring

---

[d]Helmer writes, for example [16, pp. 79-80], "Not only does it seem that existing models might thus be improved by the introduction of the cross-impact concept, but this approach may even open the way to modeling in areas where researchers have hitherto shied away altogether from the construction of models. Complex social phenomena, such as require careful examination in the context of contemplated legislation, may lend themselves to at least crude cross-impact modeling, by listing relevant events and trends and estimating their interactions. While in many such cases no adequate, well-confirmed theory may be available that would permit highly reliable forecasts of these developments and their interrelations, the cross-impact technique would compel the researchers to give systematic thought to the pairwise influences among them. And the resultant cross-impact matrix may well represent the next best thing to an as yet nonexistent theory."

how a range of likely futures could shape a plan or be subsequently modified by a plan and examining how various changes, such as in public preference, could affect plans.

The procedure, shown in figure A-3, enables a team of planners to define and structure a set of variables describing a perceived problem and then, using a computer, to calculate and display changes in the variables over time. As with other simulations, the team develops a model of the planning situation by observing the changes and then making modifications and refinements. With a model, planners can test various assumptions and alternatives and improve their understanding of the problem.

The KSIM procedure incorporates five basic assumptions: (1) system variables are bounded. All variables have a maximum value of 1 and a minimum value of 0. (2) A variable increases or decreases in value according to whether the net impact of the other variables on it is positive or negative. (3) The response of a variable to a given net impact goes to zero as that variable approaches either bound-threshhold or saturation. (4) The impact of a variable on the system

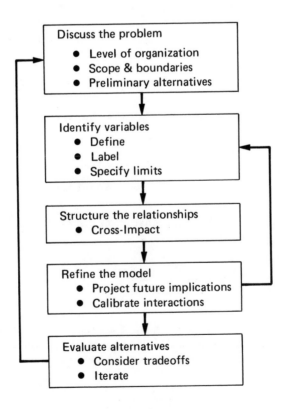

Figure A-3. Steps in a KSIM Procedure [20]

depends on the size of the variable and on the force (magnitude) of the impact. (5) Only binary interactions or cross-impacts are considered.

How does the model work? It calculates the changing probabilities of occurrence of each event or variable in the decision set between now and some future date, say ten or twenty-five years hence. For each intermediate time interval dt revised probabilities of occurrence are calculated from the initial probabilities and cross-impacts estimated. These revised probabilities are used to calculate new estimates for the next time period, and so on. The result is a simulation plot for each event, showing the degree to which the cross-impacts of the other events in the model shape its own probability of occurrence. Often a sufficient number of enhancing cross-impacts will force the probability of occurrence of an event to reach 1.0—or certain occurrence—before the end of the period in question. Thus "pushing" some events to occur before the designated period, contrary to initial expectations or intuition, could reveal either a built-in and unrealistic optimism in the probability estimates or an incomplete and biased initial list of events. (There is a tendency for researchers to include only events that are mutually enhancing unless counteracting steps are taken.)

A variable's changed state (probability) is computed by raising it to an exponent, as follows:

$$x_i(t + dt) = x_i^k \tag{A-1}$$

where $x_i(t)$ is the value of variable i at time t and $0 < x_i(t) < 1$, for all $i = 1, 2, \ldots, N$ and all $t \geq 0$, and k is given by

$$k_i(t) = \frac{1 + dt \,|\text{sum of the negative impacts on } x_i\,|}{1 + dt \,|\text{sum of the positive impacts on } x_i\,|} \tag{A-2}$$

where $k_i(t)$ is the value of the exponent at time t that modifies variable i.

Another way of writing (A-2) is

$$k_i(t) = \frac{1 + \Sigma\,(\alpha_- x(t))}{1 + \Sigma\,(\alpha_+ x(t))} \tag{A-3}$$

where α_- is a negative impact value, α_+ is a positive impact value, $x(t)$ is the value of a variable at time t, and $k_i(t)$ is the net impact on variable i at time t.

The scaling factor $C\alpha$ (alpha multiplier) is estimated as follows:

$$C\alpha = \frac{\ln\,(1 + r)}{-(\alpha B\,dt \ln A)} \tag{A-4}$$

where *r* is the growth rate (say 3 percent), *dt* is the simulation interval (say one year), α is the maximum cross-impact value (for example, +3) between two variables *A* and *B, B* is the value of one variable (say 0.6), and *A* is the value of the other variable (say 0.5).

Typically only $C\alpha$ is computed, and $C\beta$, the beta multiplier, is set at ten times its value. Also, values for *dt* are generally set at one-tenth or one-twentieth the period of the entire simulation. If the simulation is to run from 1975 to the year 2000, *dt* would be one year; for a 1975 to 1985 simulation, 1/2 year.

The following are typical input requirements for the model:

A set of variables relevant to the given problem.

An initial estimate of the size of the variable scaled to a value between 0 and 1. For example, if acreage of grassland is a variable that can vary between 0 and 100 square miles but is now about 35 square miles, an initial estimate for "acreage of grassland" would be 0.35.

A set of cross-impact values between pairs of variables in the set. This is usually done in a matrix, with the variables in the set appearing as both rows and columns. Cross-impact values are generally strong, medium, or mild and range in value from −3 to +3. This fixes the direction and the magnitude of one variable's impact on another. Two cross-impact matrices are completed: an alpha matrix for long-term relationships, and a beta matrix for short-term relationships.

Estimated values, from historical time-series data if available, for an alpha multiplier and a beta multiplier. The purpose of these two multipliers is to tie the cross-impact estimates, through the estimates of the initial sizes of the variables, to real-world data.

A beginning and ending date for the simulation, together with a prescribed value of *dt* for the simulation interval.

Application of the Cross-Impact Matrix and Simulation Techniques

This section describes how the cross-impact matrix and KSIM simulation techniques were used to analyze the responses to the second survey. The products desired were respondents' estimates, by constituent group, of (1) how the solution of one of a pair of problems would affect the solution of the other and (2) how the cross-impacts of the solution of other problems on the solution of each problem would vary over time.

Constructing Mean Likelihood Ratio Matrices

The respondents were asked to assume that a priority problem is solved by 1985 and to consider how the probability of solving another problem would be affected as a result. Would the probability be enhanced, inhibited, or unaffected? Respondents checked a point on a scale to indicate their estimate.

To obtain the likelihood ratios needed for constructing cross-impact matrices, it was then necessary to translate the marks on the scale into percentages, or conditional probabilities—estimates that one event will occur at a point in time given that another event surely occurs. The ends of the scale were made to represent 0 and 100 percent, respectively, while the midpoint was designated "no change" (its value in each case was set equal to the estimated initial probability of solution. Thus, in one case it could be 40 percent; in another, 85 percent. Even 100 percent was not uncommon among the more optimistic estimates). The percentage represented by the mark on the scale was read as follows. A piece of elastic the length of the scale was calibrated into 10 divisions. By stretching it appropriately, interpolations could be made between zero and the initial probability if the cross-impact was inhibiting, and between the initial probability and 100 percent if the cross-impact was enhancing.[e]

Next the conditional probability estimates were translated into likelihood ratios. If P_i is the initial probability of occurrence of an event by some future date, and P_c its revised or conditional probability given the occurrence of another event, then the likelihood ratio LR is given by:

$$LR = \frac{P_c/(1-P_c)}{P_i/(1-P_i)} \qquad \text{(A-5)}$$

For every response, then, a value for LR was calculated with the help of a simple computer program that replaced every elastic-measured conditional probability estimate (there were 134 respondents and up to 72 conditional probability estimates per respondent). Certain precautions were taken: If a respondent had not made an estimate for P_i or P_c, a zero was recorded when the cards were punched. If either estimate was a zero, 001 was entered to distinguish it from "no estimate." The error introduced was considered acceptably small. If $P_c = P_i$, or $P_i = 100$, LR was automatically set at 1.

Finally, cross-impact matrices were generated for each constituent group by collapsing the individual (incomplete) matrices of each respondent in that group. Thus each cell in the composite matrix is the mean of the LRs of those who had an estimate in that cell. The group composite matrices were calculated using a computer program written for the purpose. A composite matrix was also produced for the respondents as a whole. Figure A-4 shows the matrix produced for auditor CPAs.

---

[e]The procedure introduced an error in assuming that the scale was linear instead of curved. The maximum error is quite small, however, and well within the precision of the data.

	1	2	3	4	5	6	7	8	9	10	11	12	13	14	15	16	17	18	19	20	21	22	23	24	25
1	99.0	8.9	9.6	10.1	16.4	2.2	31.9	16.1	9.6	16.2	1.5	26.6	10.0	9.2	8.5	10.5	8.7	16.3	17.1	23.5	18.0	2.5	85.4	16.3	31.3
2	0.0	99.0	*	81.0	1.0	11.0	99.0	21.7	74.7	99.0	49.0	10.8	0.0	32.3	1.0	1.3	1.6	3.8	0.5	0.1	16.0	36.0	0.6	1.6	0.1
3	2.7	20.3	99.0	3.8	18.0	1.6	19.4	12.8	12.2	3.0	1.4	1.5	17.7	19.4	1.2	17.9	4.0	3.1	17.6	17.6	2.3	1.5	21.7	3.3	17.8
4	2.7	1.0	16.7	99.0	37.5	1.5	34.3	2.5	2.6	33.3	0.8	33.7	1.4	33.8	1.0	33.3	1.0	2.4	3.4	1.9	33.2	0.9	5.0	34.2	34.3
5	0.0	0.0	0.0	0.0	0.0	0.0	0.0	0.0	0.0	0.0	0.0	0.0	0.0	0.0	0.0	0.0	0.0	0.0	0.0	0.0	0.0	0.0	0.0	0.0	0.0
6	2.0	11.4	11.1	12.8	12.8	99.0	12.1	21.3	14.9	11.1	1.6	2.8	1.4	3.4	20.5	10.6	2.6	4.5	10.8	20.7	11.7	1.5	5.1	12.0	21.4
7	2.9	1.6	2.9	3.1	0.8	0.4	99.0	3.7	3.7	1.7	1.5	30.6	1.0	1.5	3.1	0.9	1.6	2.1	0.8	1.0	1.1	1.0	4.2	2.7	21.2
8	1.4	1.0	1.0	0.8	1.2	1.7	0.7	19.0	1.4	1.4	1.0	1.2	0.9	20.0	0.9	0.9	1.5	2.0	0.7	0.7	0.9	1.1	1.4	0.8	1.1
9	2.3	1.2	2.0	1.6	2.9	3.5	1.6	11.1	99.0	1.4	1.2	2.1	1.1	7.0	1.0	1.0	1.6	1.6	1.5	1.1	1.3	1.0	2.9	2.5	1.5
10	1.2	3.0	6.1	1.0	1.0	1.2	34.2	1.4	1.6	99.0	3.4	35.8	1.6	34.2	33.4	42.0	1.0	1.4	2.1	2.0	33.8	9.4	1.0	33.7	33.9
11	2.7	2.4	1.8	1.5	1.2	1.5	2.3	2.3	1.7	25.8	99.0	132.0	13.7	15.5	13.8	4.9	12.2	13.5	13.3	13.7	13.1	7.6	12.5	12.4	13.5
12	4.3	10.9	11.5	11.2	20.5	11.0	11.3	13.1	2.9	2.0	1.6	99.0	2.0	1.6	0.8	0.8	10.8	21.3	1.9	11.4	10.9	1.4	11.1	1.1	10.7
13	6.3	40.6	21.2	21.3	40.0	0.8	40.3	20.4	0.8	20.5	9.9	5.9	99.0	20.4	20.4	40.0	0.9	25.4	40.4	59.6	0.6	1.6	1.1	1.4	59.6
14	2.1	2.1	1.0	1.0	1.9	1.8	1.2	8.2	6.4	2.1	2.8	2.0	1.1	99.0	20.5	1.0	22.0	1.6	1.2	20.5	21.4	2.5	2.2	2.1	20.6
15	6.8	99.0	99.0	1.0	99.0	6.0	1.0	1.0	1.0	21.0	27.0	2.3	3.9	5.7	99.0	1.0	1.0	1.0	99.0	16.0	99.0	99.0	1.0	15.6	1.0
16	2.1	27.4	2.1	1.9	2.6	1.2	1.4	2.8	1.6	28.0	7.1	3.3	26.8	27.1	6.9	99.0	3.7	25.7	25.4	32.3	2.8	6.7	26.2	27.1	1.4
17	1.5	1.0	1.0	1.8	2.6	1.4	1.4	1.5	1.4	1.8	1.8	1.5	1.8	3.5	50.0	1.0	99.0	1.6	6.1	50.0	50.0	2.5	3.2	3.6	50.0
18	0.0	0.0	0.0	0.0	0.0	0.0	0.0	0.0	0.0	0.0	0.0	0.0	0.0	0.0	0.0	0.0	0.0	0.0	0.0	0.0	0.0	0.0	0.0	0.0	0.0
19	4.3	1.0	6.0	7.4	1.8	1.0	1.0	3.7	6.0	1.0	1.0	1.0	2.7	1.3	1.0	1.0	1.0	1.4	99.0	1.0	0.8	1.0	2.7	1.0	1.5
20	1.6	0.4	0.4	2.1	1.0	1.3	1.1	1.1	0.4	0.4	0.4	0.2	1.0	0.6	1.0	0.8	1.0	0.1	1.9	99.0	1.2	0.5	1.1	1.0	1.3
21	1.4	1.1	1.3	1.4	2.0	2.2	1.0	1.8	2.0	1.9	2.4	1.0	2.6	1.5	1.0	2.6	1.0	1.4	2.7	1.0	99.0	1.7	1.3	1.9	1.5
22	2.1	2.1	24.2	2.8	1.0	1.6	2.2	2.4	1.4	9.1	9.4	2.7	1.9	4.1	3.0	15.1	1.3	2.0	1.7	3.9	21.8	99.0	2.5	0.0	3.3
23	0.0	0.0	0.0	0.0	0.0	0.0	0.0	0.0	0.0	0.0	0.0	0.0	0.0	0.0	0.0	0.0	0.0	0.0	0.0	0.0	0.0	0.0	0.0	0.0	0.0
24	12.1	99.0	99.0	3.3	99.0	2.3	8.3	13.5	16.0	1.0	1.0	99.0	99.0	99.0	1.0	1.0	1.0	99.0	99.0	1.0	1.0	1.0	99.0	99.0	1.0
25	2.5	50.3	1.0	3.1	50.0	1.0	50.2	0.5	0.5	2.2	8.6	2.0	50.0	50.3	2.8	50.3	1.0	1.8	50.2	50.8	2.7	1.9	1.0	1.0	99.0
INUM =	13	1	6	3	10	5	6	7	3	9	10	5	6	4	2	0	1	5	2	1	2	5	0	1	2
ISUM =	506	1779	340	448	0	339	197	163	155	418	434	285	599	249	806	393	341	0	151	121	223	0	1152	535	

Note: Cross-impacts are row problems on column problems. At the base of the matrix, INUM lists the number of people who made cross-impact estimates for each problem; ISUM presents the row totals of the likelihood ratios for each problem. Problems 5, 18, and 23 were not chosen as priority problems by any of this group, hence no cross-impacts are calculated for them.
*This mean likelihood ratio is too large for the available field.

Figure A-4. Mean Likelihood Ratio Matrix, Group 1 (Auditor-CPAs)

Constructing Impact Number Matrices for KSIM

After mean likelihood matrices were developed for each constituent group and for the overall sample, an impact number (*IN*) was assigned to each cell of the matrices (again, through a simple computer program) signifying the value of the likelihood ratio in that cell. That was done according to the following calibration rules:

If *LR* > 1:   Those having values in the top third of the range: *IN* = +3
                 Those having values in the middle third of the range: *IN* = +2
                 Those having values in the bottom third of the range: *IN* = +1

If *LR* = 1:   *IN* = 0

If 0 < *LR* < 1: Those having values in the top third of the range: *IN* = −1
                  Those having values in the middle third of the range: *IN* = −2
                  Those having values in the bottom third of the range: *IN* = −3

Figure A-5 shows the impact number matrix produced for auditor-CPAs, corresponding to the likelihood matrix shown in figure A-4. The *IN* matrices constitute the primary input to KSIM.

Adapting KSIM to the Problems of the Public
Accounting Profession

The purpose of using KSIM was not to facilitate decision making, nor to solve the profession's problems, but rather to discover how the probability of solving each problem in the set, given the interactive effects of solving the others, would vary over time. The "events" in the decision set were the solutions of the twenty-five problems given to the respondents in section II of the second survey.[f] Estimating the probability that an event would occur at some time in the future meant estimating to what degree a problem would be solved by 1985. The initial "size" of the variable was the value of the initial probability that the problem would be solved by 1985.

The period of simulation was 1975 to 1985, and the simulation interval *dt* was 0.5 year. In the absence of historical data on the rate at which the profession had solved such problems in the past, there was no way to estimate the growth rate *r*, hence the alpha multiplier, as given by (A-5). Therefore, a value of 0.01 was used for *Cα*. By simulating probabilities over a ten-year period, there was no need to construct or estimate a second beta matrix for short-term

---

[f]The original KSIM program could accommodate only nine variables. Pamela Kruzic, Stanford Research Institute, modified it to accommodate twenty-five variables.

	1	2	3	4	5	6	7	8	9	10	11	12	13	14	15	16	17	18	19	20	21	22	23	24	25
1	1	1	1	1	1	1	1	1	1	1	1	1	1	1	1	1	1	1	1	1	1	1	1	1	1
2	-3	1	3	1	0	1	1	1	1	1	1	1	1	-3	1	0	1	1	-2	-3	1	1	-2	0	-3
3	1	1	1	1	1	1	1	1	1	1	1	1	1	1	1	1	1	1	1	1	1	1	1	1	1
4	1	1	1	1	1	1	1	1	1	1	-1	1	1	1	0	1	1	1	1	1	1	-1	1	1	1
5	0	0	0	0	0	0	0	0	0	0	0	0	0	0	0	0	0	0	0	0	0	0	0	0	0
6	1	1	1	1	1	1	1	1	1	1	1	1	1	1	1	1	1	1	1	1	1	1	1	1	1
7	1	1	1	1	-1	1	1	1	1	1	1	1	0	1	1	-1	1	1	-1	0	1	1	1	1	1
8	1	-1	-1	-1	1	1	-1	1	1	1	1	1	-1	1	-1	-1	1	1	-1	-1	-1	1	1	-1	1
9	1	1	1	1	1	1	1	1	1	1	1	1	1	1	1	1	1	1	1	1	1	1	1	1	1
10	1	1	1	0	0	1	1	1	1	1	1	1	1	1	1	1	0	1	1	1	1	1	0	1	1
11	1	1	1	1	1	1	1	1	1	1	1	1	1	1	1	1	1	1	1	1	1	1	1	1	1
12	1	1	1	1	1	1	1	1	1	1	1	1	1	1	-1	-1	1	1	1	1	1	1	1	1	1
13	1	1	1	1	1	-1	1	1	-1	1	1	1	1	1	1	1	-1	1	1	1	-2	1	1	1	1
14	1	1	0	1	1	1	1	1	1	1	1	1	1	1	1	0	1	1	1	1	1	1	1	1	1
15	1	1	1	0	1	1	0	0	0	1	1	1	1	1	1	0	0	0	1	1	1	1	0	1	0
16	1	1	1	1	1	1	1	1	1	1	1	1	1	1	1	1	1	1	1	1	1	1	1	1	1
17	1	0	0	1	1	1	1	1	1	1	1	1	1	1	1	0	1	1	1	1	1	1	1	1	1
18	0	0	0	0	0	0	0	0	0	0	0	0	0	0	0	0	0	0	0	0	0	0	0	0	0
19	1	0	1	1	1	0	0	1	1	0	0	0	1	1	0	0	0	1	1	0	-1	0	1	0	1
20	1	-2	-2	1	0	1	1	1	0	-2	-2	-3	0	-2	0	-1	0	-3	1	1	1	-2	1	0	1
21	1	1	1	1	1	1	0	1	1	1	1	0	1	1	0	1	0	1	1	0	1	1	1	1	1
22	1	1	1	0	1	1	1	1	1	1	1	1	1	1	1	1	1	1	1	1	1	1	1	1	1
23	0	0	0	0	0	0	0	0	0	0	0	0	0	0	0	0	0	0	0	0	0	0	0	0	0
24	1	1	1	1	1	1	1	1	1	0	0	1	1	1	0	0	1	1	1	0	0	0	1	1	0
25	1	1	0	1	1	0	1	-2	-2	1	1	1	1	1	1	1	0	1	1	1	1	1	0	0	1

Figure A-5. Impact Number Matrix, Group 1 (Auditor-CPAs)

effects. For the program, therefore, a matrix of 1's was entered for the beta matrix.

The quality of the cross-impact estimates may be questioned. Each respondent was asked to make 25 initial probability estimates and then 72 cross-impact estimates. The quantity of data sought could easily have fatigued the respondent so as to produce mere guesses instead of reasoned judgments. In the analysis, however, we were alert to signs of lowered data quality. For example, if a respondent checked the same point on the scale all the way down the column, estimating identical cross-impacts for one problem solution on all other problems, those entries were disregarded.

The variables chosen for the KSIM program were biased in favor of mutually enhancing cross-impacts. The reason is that the variables are all problems, thus giving respondents a strong intuitive tendency to "solve" them. In typical KSIM applications, as in the real world, the variables in a decision set are not all of one class; therefore a full range of cross-impacts would probably be estimated for such a set. Given the preexisting bias, it is interesting that some constituent groups thought that some problems would be negatively affected by the net cross-impacts on them.

In section II of the survey, the respondent estimated for each of twenty-five problems the probability that it would be solved by 1985 and estimated, for three problems he had designated top-priority, cross-impacts of each on all the others. Thus three rows of the matrix were completed by each respondent. The idea was that as respondents chose different top-priority problems, more rows of the matrix would be completed.

The cross-impact matrices that resulted for each group were incomplete; that is, the sample size for each group was not large enough for every problem to be given at least one set of estimates. When all group estimates were collapsed to yield the matrix for the entire sample, a complete matrix did result. However, even here, estimates for many of the problems were made by only one person, while other problem cross-impacts were estimated by over thirty people. In view of the sample sizes, and considering that each respondent was required to complete only three rows of the matrix, it was fortunate that even one full matrix was obtained. The results would have been more substantive had more respondents participated. However, care was taken to discount the cross-impact estimates that were made by only one or two people. The results quoted contain estimates by at least six people, an acceptable number given the small sample sizes.

Finally, the output from the KSIM computer program was produced both in tabular and graphical form. Figure A-6 shows the tabular output for group 5, investment company executives and financial writers. Problem numbers correspond to those in the instrument. Figure A-7 shows the same data in graphical form. Immediately apparent are the traces of two problems, one whose probability of solution remains unaffected if all other problems in the set are solved (No. 24: "GAAP are becoming rules that straitjacket practitioners, thus increasingly preempting the exercise of judgment"), and one whose probability of solution is inhibited (No. 15: "The growing dominance and influence of a few large firms within the CPA profession"). With help from the tabular output in figure A-6, we see that the problem whose probability of solution is most enhanced is problem 14, "The increasing likelihood that the government, especially the SEC, will define accounting standards." Solving that problem means diminishing the chances of the SEC defining accounting standards.

Similar outputs were derived for the other constituent groups. The results are summarized in chapter 13.

References

[1] Stanley C. Abraham, "The Public Accounting Profession: An Application of Futures Research Methods to Identifying and Clarifying Its Problems," (Ph.D. diss., Graduate School of Management, University of California, Los Angeles, 1976), 2 vols.

I TIME = 1975.0, F TIME = 1985.0, D TIME = .50.
ALPHA M = .01, BETA M = 1.00.

P R O B L E M S

YEAR	1	2	3	4	5	6	7	8	9	10	11	12	13	14	15	16	17	18	19	20	21	22	23	24	25
1975.0	.49	.50	.57	.56	.42	.58	.64	.56	.44	.49	.42	.51	.57	.44	.31	.48	.41	.59	.26	.41	.57	.36	.41	.24	.47
1975.5	.50	.51	.58	.57	.42	.59	.65	.57	.45	.50	.43	.52	.58	.45	.30	.49	.42	.60	.26	.42	.58	.37	.41	.24	.47
1976.0	.51	.52	.59	.58	.43	.60	.65	.57	.45	.51	.44	.52	.59	.46	.29	.50	.42	.60	.25	.42	.58	.38	.42	.24	.47
1976.5	.53	.53	.60	.59	.43	.61	.66	.58	.46	.51	.45	.53	.60	.47	.29	.51	.43	.61	.25	.43	.59	.39	.42	.24	.48
1977.0	.54	.54	.60	.60	.43	.61	.66	.59	.47	.52	.46	.54	.61	.49	.28	.52	.43	.62	.24	.44	.60	.39	.42	.24	.48
1977.5	.55	.55	.61	.61	.44	.62	.67	.60	.48	.53	.47	.54	.61	.50	.27	.52	.44	.63	.24	.45	.60	.40	.43	.24	.48
1978.0	.56	.56	.62	.62	.44	.63	.67	.60	.48	.54	.49	.55	.62	.51	.26	.53	.44	.63	.23	.46	.61	.41	.43	.24	.49
1978.5	.57	.57	.63	.63	.44	.64	.68	.61	.49	.55	.50	.56	.63	.52	.26	.54	.45	.64	.23	.46	.62	.42	.43	.24	.49
1979.0	.59	.58	.64	.64	.45	.65	.69	.62	.50	.56	.51	.56	.64	.53	.25	.55	.46	.65	.22	.47	.62	.43	.44	.24	.49
1979.5	.60	.59	.65	.65	.45	.66	.69	.63	.50	.56	.52	.57	.65	.55	.24	.56	.46	.66	.22	.48	.63	.44	.44	.24	.49
1980.0	.61	.61	.66	.66	.46	.66	.70	.63	.51	.57	.53	.57	.66	.56	.23	.57	.47	.66	.21	.49	.64	.45	.45	.24	.50
1980.5	.62	.62	.67	.67	.46	.67	.70	.64	.52	.58	.54	.58	.67	.57	.22	.58	.47	.67	.21	.50	.64	.46	.45	.24	.50
1981.0	.63	.63	.67	.67	.46	.68	.71	.65	.53	.59	.56	.59	.68	.58	.22	.59	.58	.68	.20	.50	.65	.47	.45	.25	.50
1981.5	.65	.64	.68	.68	.47	.69	.71	.65	.54	.60	.57	.59	.68	.59	.21	.60	.49	.69	.20	.51	.66	.48	.46	.25	.51
1982.0	.66	.65	.69	.69	.47	.69	.72	.66	.54	.61	.58	.60	.69	.61	.20	.61	.49	.69	.19	.52	.66	.49	.46	.25	.51
1982.5	.67	.66	.70	.70	.47	.70	.73	.67	.55	.62	.59	.61	.70	.62	.19	.62	.50	.70	.19	.53	.67	.50	.46	.25	.51
1983.0	.68	.67	.71	.71	.48	.71	.73	.68	.56	.62	.60	.62	.71	.63	.18	.63	.51	.71	.18	.54	.68	.51	.47	.25	.51
1983.5	.69	.68	.72	.72	.48	.72	.74	.68	.57	.63	.61	.62	.72	.64	.18	.64	.51	.71	.18	.55	.69	.52	.47	.25	.52
1984.0	.70	.69	.72	.73	.49	.73	.74	.69	.57	.64	.62	.63	.73	.65	.17	.65	.52	.72	.17	.55	.69	.53	.48	.25	.52
1984.5	.71	.70	.73	.74	.49	.74	.75	.70	.58	.65	.63	.64	.74	.66	.16	.65	.52	.73	.17	.56	.70	.54	.48	.25	.52
1985.0	.72	.71	.74	.75	.49	.75	.75	.70	.59	.66	.65	.64	.74	.68	.15	.66	.53	.74	.16	.57	.71	.55	.48	.25	.53
ΔP (%)	.23	.21	.17	.19	.07	.17	.11	.14	.15	.17	.23	.13	.17	.24	-.16	.18	.12	.15	-.10	.16	.14	.19	.07	.01	.06
Highest ΔP (rank)	2=	4	8=	5=		8=				8=	2=	8=	8=	1		7						5=			
Lowest ΔP (%)					.07										-.16				-.10				.07	.01	.06
Lowest P_f (rank)					5				9						1				2	8		7	4	3	6

Figure A-6. Tabular Output from KSIM, Group 5 (Investment Company Executives/Financial Press)

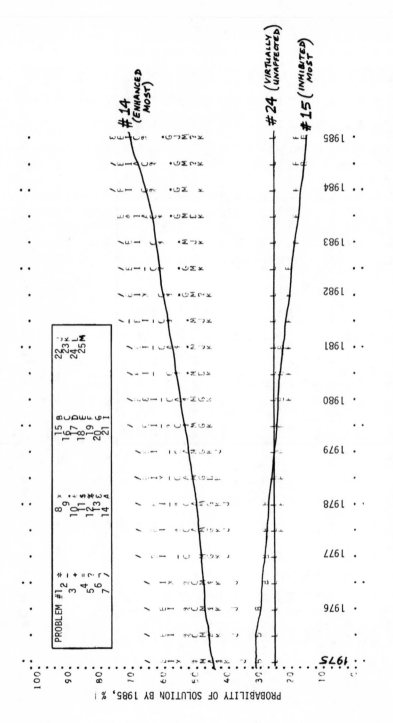

Figure A-7. Graphical Output from KSIM, Group 5 (Investment Company Executives/Financial Press)

[2] Selwyn Enzer, "Cross-Impact Techniques in Technology Assessment," *Futures,* March 1972, pp. 30-51.

[3] Perry F. Rosove, "The Use of Contextual Mapping to Support Long-Range Educational Policy Making," Paper SP-3026, System Development Corporation, Santa Monica, Ca., December 1968.

[4] John W. Buckley and Marlene H. Buckley, *The Accounting Profession* (Los Angeles, Ca.: Melville Publishing Co., 1974).

[5] Stanley C. Abraham, "How to Appreciate Using a Structure of Feedback Loops: A Set of Instructions," Working Paper 13-75, Center for Information Studies, Graduate School of Management, University of California, Los Angeles, February 1975.

[6] Jorgen Randers, "Conceptualizing Dynamic Models of Social Systems: Lessons from A Study in Social Change," (Ph.D. diss., Alfred P. Sloan School of Management, Massachusetts Institute of Technology, Cambridge, Mass., September 1973).

[7] Jay W. Forrester, *Principles of Systems,* 2d preliminary ed. (Cambridge, Mass.: MIT Press, 1968).

[8] R.P. Barthol and R.G. Bridge, "The Echo Multi-Response Method for Surveying Value and Influence Patterns in Groups," *Psychological Reports,* 22 (1968), pp. 1345-1354.

[9] T.W. Milburn, R.P. Barthol, and Richard deMille, "The Echo Method and the Study of Values," Report TM-951, General Research Corporation, Santa Barbara, Ca., 1968.

[10] Richard deMille, "The Echo Method: Technical Description," Report MST-1, General Research Corporation, Santa Barbara, Ca., 1970.

[11] Theodore J. Gordon and H. Haywood, "Initial Experiments with the Cross-Impact Matrix Method of Forecasting," *Futures,* December 1968, pp. 100-116.

[12] Richard Rochberg, Theorore J. Gordon, and Olaf Helmer, "The Use of Cross-Impact Matrices for Forecasting and Planning," Report R-10, Institute for the Future, Menlo Park, Ca., April 1970.

[13] Selwyn Enzer, "Delphi and Cross-Impact Techniques: An Effective Combination for Systematic Futures Analysis," Working Paper WP-8, Institute for the Future, Menlo Park, Ca., June 1970.

[14] Theodore J. Gordon, Richard Rochberg, and Selwyn Enzer, "Research on Cross-Impact Techniques with Applications to Selected Problems in Economics, Political Science, and Technological Assessment," Report R-12, Institute for the Future, Menlo Park, Ca., August 1970.

[15] Richard Rochberg, "Information Theory, Cross-Impact Matrices, and Pivotal Events," *Technological Forecasting and Social Change,* (1970), pp. 53-60.

[16] Olaf Helmer, "Interdisciplinary Modeling," in C. West Churchman and Richard O. Mason, eds., *World Modeling: A Dialogue,* North-Holland/

TIMS Studies in the Management Sciences, vol. 2 (New York: American Elsevier, 1976), pp. 73-80.

[17] Olaf Helmer, "Multi-Purpose Planning Games," *Futures,* June 1972, pp. 149-167.

[18] Elwood S. Buffa and James S. Dyer, "Dynamic Structural Models," in Buffa and Dyer, *MS/OR: Model Formulation and Solution Methods* (New York: Wiley/Hamilton, 1977), pp. 229-256.

[19] Murray Turoff, "An Alternative Approach to Cross Impact Analysis," *Technological Forecasting and Social Change,* 3 (1972), pp. 309-339.

[20] Julius Kane, I. Vertinsky, and W. Thompson, "KSIM: A Methodology for Interactive Resource Policy Simulation," *Water Resources Research,* 9 (1973), pp. 65-79.

[21] Pamela G. Kruzic, "Cross-Impact Simulation in Water Resource Planning," Report 74-12, Stanford Research Institute, Menlo Park, Ca., November 1974.

[22] Julius Kane, "A Primer for a New Cross-Impact Language (with Examples Drawn from Transportation Planning)," *Technological Forecasting and Social Change* 4 (1972), pp. 129-142.

Appendix B
Summary of Responses
to the Fantasy Question

About 44 percent of the respondents in the first survey completed the fantasy question. Many responses touched on several topics; the topics and their frequency are indicated in table B-1. The first five topics are self-explanatory. Scenarios are well-developed and internally consistent narratives, usually on a single topic; many of them are reproduced verbatim in this appendix. Although some are humorous, they are nevertheless stimulating and make a serious point. Responses on the remaining three topics are not considered further; they were either silly, gave answers that were too "canned" and lacked credibility, or bordered on sarcasm, presenting answers to problems the respondent seemed to know could never be achieved.

As expected, role issues were mentioned more than twice as often as the next topic, financial reporting. These two topics also led in the rest of the survey responses. The reason may be that public accountants, both auditors and nonauditors, offered more than half of all contributions, as table B-2 shows. The relatively high number of contributions from accounting educators probably accounts for most of those in the education and licensing topic. Those who saw the demise of the profession were among the oldest respondents in the sample (as were those who contributed many of the trivial and cynical responses), while those writing about financial reporting were among the youngest—and most critical—in the sample.

Table B-1
Frequency of Topics in Fantasy Question

Topic	Number of Times Mentioned (contributions)
Role issues	81
Financial reporting	36
Education and licensing	25
Opportunities and Innovations	21
Demise of the profession	5
Scenarios	12
Trivia	29
Cynicism	10
Miscellaneous	9
Total	228

233

Table B-2
Contributions to Fantasy Question, by Group

Constituent Group	Number of Contributions
1	76
3	54
2	44
5	16
4	12
7	9
6	8
Total	219[a]

[a]Excludes 9 miscellaneous contributions.

The major topics are summarized, followed by ten of the most provocative scenarios verbatim.

Role Issues

Five principal areas were covered.

Better Self-Regulation. Accounting standards have been developed and adopted that can be uniformly applied to both large and small reporting entities; the profession has developed an accounting language for "truth-in-business dealings" (after "truth-in-lending" laws); standardized its procedures; has instituted mechanisms to police itself, involving constant awareness of new problems and issuing opinions and rulings accordingly; brought agreement among the FASB, SEC, FEI, FAF, AAA, and AICPA on the objectives of accounting and on the content of financial statements across industries; accounting problems are quickly solved by the FASB, which has two divisions: New Matters and Problem Solution; and accounting principles, auditing and reporting standards have become international.

Several respondents expressed ideas on how the profession might be reorganized. It could be organized functionally for administrative purposes, but with highly team-oriented project efforts and restated goals and objectives more in line with new demands. The AICPA (it may have changed its name) has a strong international flavor, and cooperates more fully with the state societies, giving them more authority to act as they see fit, though not independently of the national body. The profession is less isolated and plays a far greater role in national and international affairs. Research and training functions are centrally controlled and performed by regional offices of the AICPA. Yet these ideas bear little resemblance to helping the profession achieve better self-regulation.

Two contributions cited the existence of a federal accounting court which, like U.S. Tax Courts, would review all claims and disputes that resulted from professional activities; its accumulated rulings would form a body of legal bases for future rulings.

Broader Role. The typical financial audit represents only about 50 percent of auditors' work. With less emphasis on the attest function, more time is spent rendering business advice and doing consulting work. The profession breaks out of its prison of "little historical dollars" on archaic balance sheets and income statements and instead shows more concern for social cost-benefit analysis. Performance auditing is a principal objective. The attest function expands to cover matters of significant social importance. By contributing greater sums to support progress in education, the profession has become eager to "harness its destiny to emerging technologies."

One respondent gave life to his contribution by placing it within a scenario:

The profession has changed its name to Certified Public Attestors and has broadened its scope of operation giving up some of its consulting, but expanding greatly the level of corporate and noncorporate activities it examines. It has formed several boards—the Attest Criteria Board that develops the principles that are applied to a possible attest engagement to see if it is "auditable" and, if so, how; the Criteria Conformance Board that develops standards to govern attest procedures; and the Quality Review Board that audits the auditors.

Several contributions contradicted this broadened role for accountants, believing instead that the profession would prefer to limit itself to auditing. Management services are performed by separate organizations, in line with professional edicts that eschew all consulting activities, all computer bureau work, and all social responsibility opinions; the profession realized that to try to do too many things could only weaken their objectivity as auditors. Besides not selling management services, they have stopped being investment experts ("by and large, they're lousy at it now").

Related to their broader role, accountants are seen to have acquired management science capabilities for client engagements as well as firm improvement. Tax returns are also accepted as "filed" when signed by a CPA.

Changes in Practice. Auditors are now more independent from the clients they audit. The profession promotes independence not in a minute legalistic rule-making way but as an underlying philosophy. Auditors from one firm serve a client for three years and are then replaced by another firm; while specialists may have a long relationship with a client, no firm can serve a client in more than one specialist category. The auditor is more formally segregated from management, perhaps through structural safeguards imposed by the SEC. One respondent saw auditors assigned to clients by the AICPA, which bills clients for services rendered and allocates fees to the performing accounting firms. Most of all, the profession's independence shows in its overriding responsibility to the public.

Another respondent saw the profession as having severed all direct financial links between the audited company and the auditor. Auditing engagements were to be handled by a national panel, supported by "moderate charges to audited companies and a transactions tax on every purchase of securities (collected by the Treasury and turned over to the panel)." (This contribution is the seventh scenario presented in its entirety later in this appendix.)

Several contributions saw the coming of specialties; all CPAs specialize. The AICPA is composed of a number of sections; there are examinations in and certificates for tax, accounting, auditing, and financial systems design. No firm is involved in marketing, production management, executive recruiting, or actuarial work. One contribution listed specialties in MAS and SEC work, while another saw all specialities tied together by the attest function, with eligibility confined to those with master's or doctoral degrees.

Several opinions about the number and size of practice units surfaced: The largest single firm has less than one hundred partners, most other large firms having split into a number of regional firms; "eight or more large accounting firms continue to exist. The profession has not reached the state where in fact or appearance it is vulnerable to the charge of being an oligopoly"; only one large public accounting firm exists, and that is a publicly held corporation.

Finally, more as an economic necessity than anything else, the profession employs many paraprofessionals; they provide a resource that enables the professional to deal more effectively with client problems and do a better job.

Becoming More Involved in Government. The profession has influenced and helped government by, for example, reducing unneeded and overlapping governmental agencies; speaking up on matters affecting the national interest; helping all businesses maintain "economic order," which in turn fosters social order; and helping to keep the country's international monetary system under control.

Enhancing Its Image. The term *accountant* is, by definition, now understood to designate one who by training, education, experience, and demonstrated performance is accountable, that is, responsible in its work with financial and other management matters in business and government. The profession has enabled the public to understand and trust how "big things" are managed—it has gained respect based on its accomplishments and not on public relations. Accountants no longer hide behind verbiage such as "accounting is an art."

The profession attracts and challenges creative and imaginative minds; people are entering the accounting profession without apologizing for being

CPAs. "Americans in general have some understanding of it—what it is, how it works, and how they can use it. They are no longer intimidated by financial statements, and accountants talk to nonaccountants without hedging everything they say."

Another respondent offers these images: "As a professional, the CPA is accorded the same recognition given to doctors and lawyers. The accountant's integrity is his basic characteristic, followed by his ability to assist his client in surviving in a world entangled with government regulations. No major, and many minor, business decisions are made without the CPA.s participation. Civic and charitable groups seek his services as a board member (not as treasurer) because his logical analysis of problems is invaluable. A satisfying career is open to young people who have a far better grasp of what a CPA does than his father did in 1975."

Like the responses to the main parts of the first survey, these images address many of the same problems and exhibit the same divergence of opinion. Soaking in the luxury of the fantasy situation created for them, the respondents almost without exception saw the profession's problems solved, without finding it necessary to explain how or by whom the solutions came about. These characteristics run through the remaining contributions, too.

Financial Reporting

Inasmuch as financial reporting activities help define the accountant's role, some of the contributions clearly overlap those just given. Despite this minor technical problem, the contributions fell into three principal areas: financial reporting standards and their control; what is reported; and how it should be reported.

Financial Reporting Standards and Their Control. The accounting profession has developed a logical and consistent set of GAAP, with the general objective of presenting financial information useful for making economic decisions. Assets, liabilities, and income are defined rigorously in economic terms. It has also developed principles for making social decisions, taking into account the constraints of relevance, objectivity, and cost-feasibility. Overall, the profession's aim is to ensure that financial statements and major supplements reflect current economic reality. The investor must have a picture of the earnings a corporation is likely to generate in the near future, as well as some grasp of its immediate health (liquidity).

The profession has eliminated alternative accounting principles and provides investors with financial statements that are comparable across industries. Also, accountants now use report language that accurately describes their financial reporting responsibilities. The short-form report is now comprehensible by the public.

One respondent envisioned the profession (probably the AICPA) as a quasi-public agency, where audits are carried out under standards established by the Federal Accounting Standards Board (a combination of the old FASB and CASB). Another saw unified tax and accounting standards, eliminating all differences between tax and financial accounting. (This respondent adds, "But widespread adoption of the VAT made this less of an issue.") International accounting standards have also been formulated and adopted.

Because of the expertise the profession has built up, it now gives Congress and the IRS respected advice on what types and levels of taxes will produce specified results for both individuals and corporations. Better accounting methods have been devised to help government units and the public make better decisions, and the profession is now able to measure the financial impact of corporations on society.

What Is Reported. Financial reports might contain financial projections for both short (one year) and long (ten years) periods, specifying their underlying assumptions, ranges of variation, and past statistical errors (all without legal liability barring fraud or attempts to mislead). Projections would include not only financial data but also economic analyses and other socially significant data; the auditor's assessment of the quality and reliability of a company's internal control system and, on a regular basis, operational or management audits. The accounting profession is actively participating in reporting financial information to investors throughout the year.

How Information Could Be Reported. The profession has shifted from its old historical cost model to a price-level adjusted current-value model in an effort to make the resulting financial information more indicative of the economic situation of companies. After suitable experimentation with methods of determining current values for balance sheet purposes, it is now standard practice for businesses to produce sets of financial statements that show both historical cost and reasonable approximations of current values. (The statements reveal historical cost figures parenthetically or as footnotes, another respondent says, but the major figures are estimates of current values and are so indicated.) All figures are comparable over time because they are first price-level adjusted, thus revealing new information such as real holding gains, gain on monetary debt, and real operating profit (current selling prices less current costs of operations).

Readers are educated to understand that even if the information were as perfect as is humanly possible, the answers to financial questions involve estimates of the future, which neither management nor accountants can predict with accuracy, so their own judgment and estimates must supplement the statements. Another contribution adds that new forms of financial statement no longer require extensive footnotes, thus preventing them from being misleading.

Some contributions emphasized that accounting is not precise, and that greater precision should not be read into financial reports than they contain. For example, total assets, and net income are clearly labeled as estimates. Items that cannot be measured objectively, such as developed goodwill or nonmarket assets, are measured and reported at X or ? dollars (likewise for indeterminate liabilities such as lawsuit contingencies, nonspecific leases, and even past-service costs of pensions), but they are *not* omitted as they were in 1975.

One contribution saw the profession as having developed a logical and defensible structure for the collection, classification, and interpretation of quantitative data about economic operations. Such data were not confined to dollars but extended to units such as barrels, pounds, and cubic feet. Another saw the profession presenting information in disaggregated form, allowing the reader to interpret it. Two or more columns with key alternative interpretations would be produced for convenience, with disaggregated material permitting corrections by the reader.

Finally, financial statements lay out for investors the possible risks and rewards of staying with their investment. For example, cash flows available on a discretionary basis for future investment or distribution are distinguished from that which has already been committed to working capital or fixed assets to maintain existing or planned levels of operation.

Education and Licensing

Three principal areas were covered:

Educating the CPA. The profession has achieved uniformity in the CPA examination, administers it impartially, and has maintained rigor in its content; educational standards for CPAs are uniform throughout the country and require graduate work; undergraduate courses have made the transition from a technician approach to a business one; that is, it includes more management courses with an emphasis on running a business instead of measuring its historical performance. Graduate students can thus cope more effectively with accounting and business problems during the course of an audit. One contribution noted how difficult it used to be for CPAs to be subordinate to lawyers: "The typical CPA now has a law degree as well!" Another noted the management science capabilities possessed by CPAs.

The profession has developed a comprehensive professional development program; though voluntary, it is well attended. The profession's concern for quality will make continuing education mandatory (several contributions noted the existence of continuing education programs that were playing a major role in eliminating substandard performance and had been made exciting and challenging by the profession).

Kinds of Accounting Schools and the Profession's Relationship with Them. One image brimming with confidence proclaims: "CPAs have finally matured and are considered—and consider themselves—the peers of the elite professions: medicine, law, divinity. There are one hundred schools of professional accountancy graduating about 25,000 students each year. There are three or four applicants for each place, and the quality of the entering and graduating students is excellent." (Another contribution saw fifty such schools.)

Another image was more evolutionary: "Beginning in about 1980 it becomes popular for state societies of CPAs to endow schools of accountancy at major institutions. By 2000, these schools are widespread, working well with their sister schools of business and public administration, and producing well-educated, well-motivated professionals." Yet another contribution saw the AICPA, through its committee to study and accredit programs and schools, bringing about the change to professional schools of accountancy.

With oblique reference to the current situation in educational institutions, one contribution noted that the training of CPAs had become problem oriented, with "theory and methodology slaves to purpose and not vice versa." Also, through lables provided by the profession to indicate specialties and levels of competence, CPAs' training is directed more closely to clients' expectations of precisely what they are buying.

The profession is working more cooperatively with educational institutions that prepare entry-level people. Diverse educational approaches exist; the profession has not insisted on a rigid mold for entrants (in contrast to others earlier who imagined more uniform and rigid entry standards). It also provides a greater direct subsidy to promote excellence in teaching and research than it did twenty-five years ago. The attitude that such contributions should be enough only to "buy" graduates has vanished. In its place is a broader view of the profession's social responsibility.

Licensing Issues. A single, highly qualified licensed class performs all accounting services. Uniformity in accountancy legislation has been achieved, and licensing by the states automatically includes a national license. All states have adopted this approach while at the same time retaining the right to set rules of practice that still vary somewhat depending on local conditions.

One contribution seemed to sum it up well. The profession "is serving the public better because of (1) higher standards of continuing education, (2) tighter controls on professional conduct code and ethics, and (3) improved education in college and graduate schools, and in professional schools of accounting." Another said that the "supply of accountants (good ones, not rejects from engineering school) has begun to satisfy demand more adequately."

Opportunities and Innovations

Contributions under this heading were grouped into two parts with extensive overlaps: opportunities, which are primarily extensions of current functions, and innovations, which have virtually no precedent.

Opportunities. The profession has become the "integrity core" of society by extending its attest function to numerous sociological applications where independent verification is essential, such as arms-limitation inspections and independent estimates of needed expenditures (auto repairs, medical and dental services, governmental and public utility costs). The typical financial audit represents only about 50 percent of its work. Certifications of the economy, effectiveness, and efficiency of government programs, election results, and environmental impacts are common. Exotic engagements are undertaken routinely.

The typical CPA firm is multidisciplinary; in addition to one or more financial and management generalists, it has specialists in the attest function, taxes, quantitative analysis and econometrics, and systems and data processing. Audit specialists regularly use the computer. Forecasting, regression analysis, and statistical sampling are used as a matter of course. Interactive and concurrent auditing are commonplace. Modeling is being used in many instances.

The public accounting profession has a very effective central organization in the form of the AICPA which has become, in part, a clearinghouse for ideas, problems, and programs. The profession has also staffed a research bureau to estimate the economic costs and benefits of major proposed legislation intended to regulate business activity.

Innovations. The profession has developed a system of recording business transactions numerically to evaluate and differentiate business success and failure by degree. Business and government have advanced to a high degree of fiscal efficiency largely because of the contributions made by the profession.

The U.S. Department of Commerce-United Nations economic data bank provides information on current purchasing power of the world's monetary systems, and computer capability permits preparation of all historical and forecast financial statements and other information in units of that current purchasing power. That achievement was hastened by the multidisciplinary communication and understanding that has taken place in CPA firms since 1975.

Continuous auditing is common. Quarterly results are put on the "broad tape" on an on-line basis and audited two days after the end of each quarter. The decline in paper documentation of transactions, caused largely by the explosive growth of EFTS, has made it possible for auditors to verify most transactions through computer audit techniques. In fact, detail audit procedures are a thing of the past; the cashless society has arrived, and embezzlements are passé. The laborious, time-consuming jobs have largely been replaced by equipment (computer) capabilities and mechanization at the local firm level. Every accountant's desk is equipped with a terminal on-line to a computer utility.

The seasonal nature of accountants' work has been overcome by staggering deadlines throughout the year rather than bunching up in one part of the year; many companies now use year-ends other than December 31; certain industries are allowed to choose their closing dates.

One final intriguing idea, humorously put: "The public accounting profession (father or mother) and the legal profession (mother or father, whichever the accounting profession is not) proudly announce the birth of a new profession, the Tax Practice Profession, combining the best of the parent professions."

Demise of the Profession

Since there were only five contributions on this theme, they are presented in their entirety.

1. It is difficult to find anything that pleases me with the trends I see developing. I expect that by the year 2000 there will be no public accounting as we know it. All audit work will be done by the federal government through an agency like GAO. This is due partly to our ever-increasing trend toward socialism and partly due to our failure as a profession to display the integrity needed to maintain public confidence in us.

2. Not too much. I still visualize multistate regulation; [g]overnment restrictions; [c]lient selfishness; [p]rohibitive tax structure; [t]ax loopholes; (and) [i]nconsistent reporting methods.

3. Excerpts from the *Wall Street Journal,* year 2000: Bauldy Burton has just announced an agreement, finally accepted by the last of the "Big 3", Priceless Watereddown, concerning the degree to which the audit programs will be monitored by the Financial Information Commission. Field standards, audit checklists, and all audit instructions will now be filed with the Commission 60 days prior to the beginning of the audit instead of only 15 days. The Czar of the Commission stated that this would allow sufficient time for review before the audit commenced and would be in the public interest. Elsewhere in the same edition: [T]he Senate Finance Committee approved a budget increase for the FIC of [$]150 billion . . . for the coming year to finance the increased workload of the commission.

M.Y. Opia, President of the AICPA, speaking at the graduation ceremonies of the College of Information in UCLA, urged those present to enter the maturing profession of accounting. Although admitting that the current membership of the Institute [was] 25,000, . . . down from the earlier high of 125,000, he stated that this was indicative of the development of the profession and stated that their independence was recognized worldwide. Later, over coffee with the ten students who were seeking positions in the public accounting profession, Opia conceded that there were now twenty-five times as many accountants in government as in the practicing profession, and admitted that the Union for the Advancement of Accountants was making serious inroads into the profits of the remaining practice units.

E. Theria, Professor of Information at the Graduate School of Decisions, Harvard, spoke recently at the annual meeting of the American Accounting Association, stating that the major problem facing accounting today was the large variety of generally accepted accounting procedures, and urged a task force be formed to study ways of effecting a reduction.

From the above, you may conclude that there has been little which really pleases me. However, to close on a note of optimism, I should indicate my pleasure that the accounting profession, through the AICPA, has taken positive steps to influence the educational preparation of accountants through its committee to study and accredit programs and schools, and its approval of professional schools of accounting.

4. In my opinion, the trends toward government dominance, the destruction of freedom of choice in the name of consumerism, the "liberal" establishment will all lead to a drastic change in our profit system and private sector. I cannot see the CPA, FASB, and other private institutions surviving present trends. Under these conditions I can't see the CPA doing anything that "really pleased" me. I would hope that before my dire predictions come true, the profession will come to its senses and realize it is building itself up at the expense of other institutions. It really should realize collaboration is the only approach that might work in the long run.

5. In the perspective of seeing all and hearing all, I can't find the public accounting profession even visible. Their work (except lawsuits that hit some newspapers) is not household gossip nor cocktail conversation any more now (in the year 2000) than it was in 1975. The profession is still a bit obscure and not well-understood, and I can think of nothing that would please me more . . . than to see it carve a more recognized place for itself in our economic system and in society and to be recognized as a force for good performance in business, in government, and elsewhere.

Scenarios

Excerpts of many of these scenarios have appeared in the other categories, but here the scenario is preserved in full. The ten most provocative are presented verbatim.

1. The AICPA is now composed of a number of sections. All CPAs specialize. There are examinations in and certificates for tax, accounting, auditing, and financial systems design. None of the firms are involved in marketing, production management, executive recruiting, or actuarial work.

Audit specialists regularly use the computer. Forecasting, regression analysis, and stat[istical] sampling are used as a matter of course. Interactive and concurrent auditing are commonplace. Modeling is being used in many instances. Auditors from one firm serve a client for three years and are then replaced by another firm.

Specialists in other areas may have a long-term relationship with their clients, but no firm can serve the same client in more than one specialist category.

Most of the large firms have split into a number of regional firms. The largest single firm has less than one hundred partners. Functions such as research and training are performed by regional offices of the AICPA. It is generally accepted that auditors look for and are responsible for detecting fraud of a material nature. Government regulations have eased the auditors' exposure in this area. Ownership of corporations is publicly recorded, and stocks may not be placed in the name of a nominee. If a firm is more than 50 percent owned by another firm, both firms must employ the same auditor. The decline in paper documentation of transactions, caused largely by the explosive growth of EFTS, has made it possible for auditors to verify most transactions by the use of computer auditing techniques.

Auditors are now involved in reviewing and expressing an opinion on a wide variety of activities. The typical financial statement audit represents only about 50 percent of their work. Certifications of the economy, effectiveness, and efficiency of government programs, election results, and environmental impacts are common.

2. I am most delighted that the integrity and independence of public accounting has been enhanced by the evolution of its broadened role in business since 1975. *Accountant* . . . is now understood to designate one who by training, education, experience, and demonstrated performance is "accountable", i.e., responsible, regarding financial and other management matters in business and government. The few CPAs practicing alone are primarily tax specialists and their number is waning. The typical CPA firm is multidisciplinary; . . . in addition to one or more financial and management generalists, [they have] specialists in the attest function, taxes, quantitative analysis and econometrics, and systems and data processing. I am impressed that no one seems encumbered by the details of his or her specialty, since every desk is equipped with a terminal on-line to a computer utility. The attest function has been extended over the years, as predicted, to include financial forecasts and various other summaries, extrapolations, and other analyses of economic and socially significant data. The U.S. Department of Commerce–United Nations economic data bank intertie

provides information on current purchasing power of the world's monetary systems, and computer capability permits preparation of all historical and forecast financial statements and other information in units of that current purchasing power. That achievement was hastened by the multidisciplinary communication and understanding which has taken place in CPA firms since 1975.

3. News Release October 1, 2000: The [c]hairman of the SEC addressed the annual meeting of the American Institute of Certified Public Accountants at a luncheon today in the Mayflower Hotel in Washington, D.C. He stated that the [c]ommission had worked closely with the profession during the eight years he had been a member and, while there had been some differences of view, it was his opinion, shared unanimously by the other members of the [c]ommission, that the profession had made great strides in achieving accounting and auditing standards of which it could be justly proud. He stated that, while the [c]ommission was required by law in the public interest to continue its overview in these areas, the profession's record justified the confidence of the public in the profession's continued position that self-regulation was highly desirable and commendable. His remarks were greeted by a standing ovation.

4. CPAs have finally matured and are considered, and consider themselves, the peers of the elite professions—medicine, law, divinity. There are one hundred [s]chools of [p]rofessional [a]ccountancy graduating about 25,000 students each year. There are three or four applicants for each place, and the quality of the entering and graduating students is excellent. Of course, the eastern schools consider themselves the best, but this claim is hotly disputed throughout the country, particularly in California.

As a result of the intervention of the Justice Department in 1984, audits of companies listed on the National Computerized Interconnected Deregionalized Multifaceted Stock Exchange are handled by about one hundred CPA firms. Switching is frequent, although not required.

There is a national CPA certificate and uniform qualifying requirements. All of the states adopted this approach, while at the same time retaining the right to set rules of practice that still vary somewhat depending upon local conditions. In all states, however, there is only a single class of professionals, [CPAs] authorized to practice public accounting. . . . The dying classes finally did.

CPAs have assumed many responsibilities that they dreaded back in 1975, and [they have] learned to cope with them. Of course, they are subject to lawsuits, but the procedures specified in the Professional Malpractice Act of 1980 seem to be working out.

And, of course, just about all CPAs do very competent work, and most of the public agrees.

5. The profession has taken the change to a semipublic agency in stride. Audits are carried out under the standards established by the Federal Accounting Standards Board which combined the functions of FASB and CASB. The

Federal Accounting Court has established a procedure for hearing cases brought before it, and a set of legal rulings have provided legal bases for future cases.

It was difficult for CPAs to accept a position of subordination to lawyers, but the typical CPA now has a law degree as well. Management services are now performed by separate organizations, and many accountants chose to remain in the private sector in these firms.

Tax and accounting standards have been unified so there is no difference between tax accounting and financial accounting, but widespread adoption of the VAT made this less of an issue.

6. After years of insidious, creeping governmental takeover of the profession, due to the abdication of responsibility by its membership, a new breed of accountants emerged. These thinking individuals recognized there was a need for a private accounting profession that could provide reports to owners of companies about the financial aspects of their companies. Working with managements and owners, they drew up broad, overall guidelines of accounting and reporting principles for all companies. They then formed subgroups of representatives from accounting firms of specialists by industry lines. These subgroups worked with the applicable industry accounting managements and owners to develop more detailed guidelines for each industry. The "accountants in charge"—both from the accounting firm and the individual company—developed the accounting and reporting principles in more detail as applicable to the operations of each individual company. Industry accounting review boards—composed of representatives from accounting firms, management and owners within each industry—reviewed published reports for adequacy, completeness, conciseness, [and] readability. From these reviews good accounting and reporting gradually began to reemerge. The profession gradually began to regain the stature it started to lose in midcentury. Mutual respect of, and by, all three parts—outside accountants, managements, owners—developed and became recognized by the general public and government. As the end of the century approached, the extremely voluminous reports and accounting systems previously mandated by government were exposed for what they were—completely useless and nonunderstandable. In the year 2000 the new accounting and reporting was placed fully in effect as accountants and management worked closely together in mutual trust and understanding. The task had not been easy, but the accounting profession had finally reasserted itself and taken back its responsibility to provide accounting expertise that would assist management in presenting complete financial data in a form and manner that owners could understand.

7. The profession has severed all direct financial links between the audited company and the auditor. This was done after the great scandal in 1990 in which it was revealed that the vaults of First-National-Chase-Yourself Investment Fund were full of rancid salad oil and the president was really Tino De Angelis in disguise.

Auditing is now handled by a National Panel, with the members elected for life by a self-perpetuating executive committee. Great prestige attaches to membership in the panel, and an absolute dedication to totally honest, accurate reporting is expected of all members. At formal dinner parties, members go in ahead of district court federal judges but after appellate judges.

The panel hires a suitable staff of seniors, juniors, and assistants to do the work. It also supports an extensive research operation to identify problems and recommend solutions. The panel itself, sitting *en banc,* determines what shall be considered "generally accepted accounting principles."

All this is financed by moderate charges to audited companies and by a transactions tax on every purchase of securities (collected by the Treasury and turned over to the panel). The theory, of course, is that the principal beneficiary of the audit is the investor who relies on it when he makes a purchase.

Traditional accounting has been combined with probability theory, and the information is delivered in the form of answers to questions. For example, What earning power did this company demonstrate last year? Answer, It demonstrated the power to earn x-million to x plus y million. The probability is 8 out of 10 that it will fall within this range under similar conditions next year. . . .

The old-line independent accounting firms survive, supplying advisory service, tax help, and internal information systems to clients. Their income is greatly reduced because they no longer attest statements. Only members of the panel can do that.

Panel members are paid salaries designed to give them a life-style equivalent to that of a senior corporate officer. They make no investments for themselves; anything they save goes into a blind trust. In the old days of the 1970s, such an arrangement might not have been sufficient to get the best men for the panel. But with the growing emphasis on public service and the stigma attached to excessive consumption in the final quarter of the [twentieth] century, election to the panel is the dream of all ambitious accountants.

8. The profession has changed its name to Certified Public Attestors and has broadened its scope of operation giving up some of its consulting, but expanding greatly the level of corporate and noncorporate activities it examines. It has formed several boards: [t]he Attest Criteria Board that develops the principles that are applied to a possible attest engagement to see if it is "auditable" and, if so, how; [t]he Criteria Conformance Board that develops standards to govern attest procedures; and the Quality Review Board that audits the auditors.

The profession has developed a number of specialists, tied together by the attest function, and recruits into its ranks only [m]aster's and [d]octoral graduates.

The auditor-attestor, left over from the old CPAccountant days, attests to management's report in all three parts: [t]he policies and plans, [t]he past results, and [t]he future forecasts.

The number of large firms has increased both due to [the] growth of middle-sized firms and [to the] splitting of the largest ones [as a result of] government and client pressure.

9. Corporate accounting is not monolithic, but the investor is able to compare easily companies within the same industry. [O]verall, he has confidence that the basic financial statements (or major supplements) reflect *current* economic reality—he has a picture of what the corporation is likely to generate in the way of earnings in the near future as a going concern—and has a little grasp on its health (liquidity) on an immediate cash basis. Better accounting has been devised in order to help public and government units make better decisions—and measures of corporate financial impact on society have been devised. Thanks to leadership by CPAs and financial executives, there is less concern on putting the best face on things, but an emphasis on getting the best measure of economic reality, painful as it may be. [B]etter accounting has led to more sophisticated public planning through continued and strengthened competition in the marketplace rather than through a centrally directed and inflexible government process.

10. A profession peopled only by holders of graduate degrees, understood by the public to be *not* infallible, and to function only on a test basis when conducting audits. The profession is also understood, and understands itself, to value independence above all else. Each of its clients expects outside auditors to be totally dispassionate when examining and reporting upon the company's financial statements. The clients also know that it is a serious *crime* (felony) to *lie* to the auditors. As a result, the level of management integrity is at an all-time high.

Contributing also to the new integrity is the requirement that management may *not* own any securities of the company. Each company has an audit committee made up of outside directors.

The SEC and the profession work closely together. The auditors are permitted, notwithstanding their ordinary, ethical restraints, to report evidence of fraud to the SEC.

Each public company is audited on a quarterly basis; nonpublic companies are audited annually. Forecasts are reviewed by the auditors for the reasonableness of their assumptions.

The accountants' liability is limited (but not eliminated); the scope of his risk is reasonably foreseeable, and the period of open exposure is fixed and uniform.

The language of accounting is essentially the same worldwide.

Appendix C
The First Survey
Instrument

Instructions

This questionnaire is divided into FOUR parts.

THE FIRST PART presents an illustration of a completed questionnaire drawn from another context, the medical profession. Although the main questionnaire asks for up to three critical problems or issues to be identified, only one problem is worked through in the illustration. Because the respondents of our pre-test exercise found it generally helpful to them in their efforts to complete their questionnaires, we are including it in your package. We hope you will find it as helpful.

THE SECOND PART solicits some specific information about yourself. We are asking for your telephone number only in the event that any of your responses require clarification or interpretation. Neither your name nor that of your institution will be connected to any of your responses. This assures their confidentiality. We would, however, appreciate permission to use your name in a list of participants when the study is finally published. There is a place in Part II (at the bottom of the page) where you may give or withhold such permission.

THE THIRD PART comprises the main questionnaire, of which Part I is an illustration. What we want here is for you to give us your personal perceptions in your responses. We do not want you to tell us what "other people" or even accountants themselves think or believe about the issues you raise. What we are expecting is your unique viewpoint, and one which is more or less consonant with the constituent group with which you identified yourself in Part II.

Please read carefully through all the questions in Part III before starting. It will soon become apparent to you that all the questions in it revolve around specific problem statements that you are asked to supply. Try to choose a problem statement, therefore, that enables you to answer these other questions. You may find it helpful to jot down your ideas on some scratch paper before you begin. Also, trying to state the problem you select as precisely as possible will help you to clarify your thinking.

Part III itself is subdivided into three 'sections'. The first and second sections are basically the same. They merely provide space for you to supply and answer questions about two continuing problems or issues. (You are not obliged to supply more than one problem, though two-thirds of our pre-test sample did and we want to be sure to capture the extra data. For those of you who want to take the extra time to supply us with three or more problems, we ask that you use the same format on additional sheets of paper and staple them to these sheets.) The third section requires you to suggest and answer questions about an impending problem, i.e., one for which there is no historical precedent. Again, please choose one that enables you to answer the remaining questions. Here also, if you are able and willing to provide more than one impending problem statement, use additional sheets of paper and a similar format.

THE FOURTH PART consists of a "fantasy" questionnaire, and is optional. We are hoping that you will be sufficiently intrigued with the idea to want to complete it. If you do, please be as specific and as comprehensive as you can, and use additional sheets of paper if necessary.

The only parts of this questionnaire we want you to complete and return to us are the second, third, and fourth parts. For this reason, you will find these three parts stapled together. After completing these three parts, please check that your name and initials are on each part and that any additional sheets of paper used are stapled next to the question concerned (and so referenced). A stamped self-addressed envelope is provided for your convenience in mailing the responses back to us.

Thank you, and good luck.

Part I: Illustration

1.0 What is a very critical issue or problem that <u>you</u> think has been troubling, or should have been troubling, the medical profession? Please choose one that has been in evidence <u>for some time now</u> and which is likely to be so at least into the foreseeable future.

The threat of government control or nationalization of the health care industry.

What made you suggest this particular problem?

The existence of bills currently in congress, articles in the press, and a feeling that the government bureaucracy is incapable of managing the delivery of such services on such a scale.

1.1 Has the medical profession, to your knowledge, taken any action to solve, settle, or ameliorate this issue or problem?

[✓] Yes   [ ] No   If 'NO', could you put forward a reason for this inaction?

1.2 If 'YES', what is an action the profession has taken to solve, settle, or ameliorate this issue or problem?

The AMA has introduced its own version of a health insurance plan 3-4 years ago. This includes provisions for tax reductions for people who subscribe to private health insurance plans, and a scheme for indigents to have their contributions met by the government.

What are some reasons for this action not succeeding, or not being effective?

- *It may not be as intentionally cost-limiting as some legislators would demand.*
- *Legislators may not support a proposal that 'mixes' public and private sector remedies, to such an extent: this would limit government control.*
- *The implications of the proposal have not been thought through.*

1.3 If 'YES', what is <u>another</u> action the profession has taken to solve, settle, or ameliorate this issue or problem?

The profession has vigorously opposed, through its lobbying efforts, the Social Security mechanism of compensating the <u>providers</u> of health care services.

What are some reasons for this action not succeeding, or not being effective?

- *An inability to change an entrenched government mechanism, especially one where billions of dollars are involved.*
- *The 'brainwashing' of the public, who believe the Social Security system is working and will "come through" for them.*
- *The absence of specific, constructive, and feasible alternatives offered by the profession.*

/continued . . . . .

1.4 Imagine yourself at the time when you think this issue or problem first became a reality. Given the gift of hindsight, what would you now suggest the medical profession should have done at that time?

Have organized a series of specific research studies to explore feasible alternatives for providing adequate, "equal", and low cost health care to Americans. Political and social feasibility as well as economic feasibility would be addressed.

How might things be different now as a consequence? (That is, how would things be now were the profession to have acted then the way you are now suggesting?)

- *Public expectations would be different and more realistic.*
- *"Average" family health care costs and premiums might be 20–50% lower.*
- *The current crisis in health care insurance proposals might have been averted.*
- *The profession could not have been blamed for poor or no action.*

1.5 What is an action the medical profession should take now with respect to this problem? (Please be specific):

Continue to fight vigorously any and all legislative attempts, including repeal or modification of existing law (e.g. Public Law 92-603 the Bennett Amendment of Oct. 72 establishing PSROs, significantly increasing government control of the medical profession).

What are some possible problems or obstacles the profession might experience were it to act on your suggestion?

- *The cost of lobbying and generating public support.*
- *Changing the public perception, which holds that costs are high and delivery is poor, a situation that makes government control logical.*
- *How to avoid damage to the AMA image. This action could be construed by many as a blanket defense of its "own" (protecting its members at the expense of the greater good), a matter of some delicacy and concern.*

1.6 What is another specific action the medical profession should take now with respect to this problem?

Develop short- and long-range strategies for visibly improving health care delivery to communities: (a) at reasonable cost, (b) covering a definition of health care broader than physical or somatic distress, (c) with increased eligibility and accessibility to such care.

What are some possible problems or obstacles the profession might experience were it to act on this suggestion?

- *Requires a change in philosophy among the medical community. Its present attitude of tying rewards to personal wealth should give way to tying rewards to role in the community.*
- *Encouraging the generalist, not the specialist, and more use of paramedics.*
- *Develop ways of using the full spectrum of community health resources.*
- *Re-educating public expectations re quality, range, & cost of services.*
- *Doctors not trained in innovating in the socio-economic-political areas of health care delivery.*

1.7 What might be a consequence if the profession would either (a) take no action with respect to this problem, or (b) not act on any of your suggestions?

Too much power given to a few doctors put in the position of passing judgements on the activities, diagnoses, and decisions of their fellow doctors. This "policing" would also destroy the privacy of the doctor-patient relationship, and would open private records to quasi-public scrutiny.

What might be another consequence?

With nationalization and central control of the health care system, doctor loyalty would switch from the patient to the govt. controllers who dictate their functions, assignments, freedoms, and who pay them.

What might be another consequence?

Inequities in the provision of health care services would persist. Any publically financed program would support middle- and upper-income person health care delivery when they are the ones who could most afford it. And because doctors tend to practice in these areas, their accessibility to these groups would be greater.

Part II: Personal Data Sheet

Full Name:	Telephone No: (Please include the area code)	Age:

Title, Organization, and Address: (include zip code):

With respect to the following constituent groups, with which <u>one</u> do you currently identify most? (Even though you may belong to more than one, please nevertheless <u>choose only one</u>):

☐ CPA (Auditing) ☐ Corporate management ☐ Business/financial press

☐ CPA (non-Auditing) ☐ Labor union official ☐ Government regulatory commission or agency

☐ Academia (CPA or teaching accounting) ☐ Corporate legal counsel ☐ Judiciary

☐ Academia (non-accounting) ☐ Investment/securities analyst, dealer, etc.

☐ Other (please specify): _____

Regarding the public accounting profession, please try to state the general extent to which you feel you are critical of its activities or policies. Do this by placing a checkmark ( ) at one point on the continuum below:

Extremely Critical	Quite Critical, (and also tend to make it known)	Quite Critical, (but don't let others know)	Critical, (but only infrequently)	Not At All Critical

Could you please answer the following questions?   YES   NO

1 To keep yourself informed, do you regularly read or watch TV programs about the national economic situation? ☐ ☐

2 Do you have strong opinions and talk often about the social responsibility of corporations? ☐ ☐

3 Do non-fiction economic/business/government books and journals comprise the major part of your reading? ☐ ☐

4 Do you monitor and occasionally read articles in the accounting periodical literature? ☐ ☐

5 Do you receive and read FASB pronouncements, discussion memos, and exposure drafts? ☐ ☐

6 Do you read the Accounting Release Series put out by the SEC? ☐ ☐

7 Are you regularly involved, either personally or professionally, in investment transactions of one sort or another? ☐ ☐

Can we have your permission to include your name, title, and organization among the <u>list of participants</u> to this research project? ☐ Yes ☐ No

Thank you very much.

Part III: Main Questionnaire

NAME _____

1.0 What is a very critical issue or problem that <u>you</u> think has been troubling, or should have been troubling, the public accounting profession? Please choose one that has been in evidence <u>for some time now</u> and which is likely to be so <u>at least into the foreseeable future</u>.

What made you suggest this particular problem?

1.1 Has the public accounting profession, to your knowledge, taken any action to solve, settle, or ameliorate this issue or problem?

☐ Yes ☐ No

If 'NO', could you put forward a reason for this inaction?

1.2 If 'YES', what is an action the profession has taken to solve, settle, or ameliorate this issue or problem?

What are some reasons for this action not succeeding, or not being effective?

1.3 If 'YES', what is <u>another</u> action the profession has taken to solve, settle, or ameliorate this issue or problem?

What are some reasons for this action not succeeding, or not being effective?

/continued   . . .

254

1.4 Imagine yourself at the time when you think this issue or problem first became a reality. Given the gift of hindsight, what would you now suggest the public accounting profession should have done at that time?

How might things be different now as a consequence? (That is, how would things be now were the profession to have acted then the way you are now suggesting?)

1.5 What is an action the public accounting profession should take now with respect to this problem? (Please be specific):

What are some possible problems or obstacles the profession might experience were it to act on your suggestion?

1.6 What is another specific action the public accounting profession should take now with respect to this problem?

What are some possible problems or obstacles the profession might experience were it to act on this suggestion?

1.7 What might be a consequence if the profession would either (a) take no action with respect to this problem, or (b) not act on any of your suggestions?

What might be another consequence?

What might be another consequence?

/continued . . .

2.0 What is <u>another</u> very critical issue or problem that <u>you</u> think has been troubling, or should have been troubling, the public accounting profession? Please again choose one that has been in evidence <u>for some time now</u> and which is likely to be so <u>at least into the foreseeable future</u>.

What made you suggest this particular problem?

2.1 Has the public accounting profession, to your knowledge, taken any action to solve, settle, or ameliorate this problem?

☐ Yes   ☐ No

If 'NO', could you put forward a reason for this inaction?

2.2 If 'YES', what is an action the profession has taken to solve, settle, or ameliorate this issue or problem?

What are some reasons for this action not succeeding, or not being effective?

2.3 If 'YES', what is <u>another</u> action the profession has taken to solve, settle, or ameliorate this issue or problem?

What are some reasons for this action not succeeding, or not being effective?

/continued . . . .

2.4 Imagine yourself at the time when you think this issue or problem first became a reality. Given the gift of hindsight, what would you now suggest the public accounting profession should have done at that time?

How might things be different now as a consequence? (That is, how would things be now were the profession to have acted then the way you are now suggesting?)

2.5 What is an action the public accounting profession should take now with respect to this problem? (Please be specific):

What are some possible problems or obstacles the profession might experience were it to act on your suggestion?

2.6 What is another specific action the public accounting profession should take now with respect to this problem?

What are some possible problems or obstacles the profession might experience were it to act on this suggestion?

2.7 What might be a consequence if the profession would either (a) take no action with respect to this problem, or (b) not act on any of your suggestions?

What might be another consequence?

What might be another consequence?

/continued . . .

3.0 What is a very critical issue or problem that <u>you</u> think will, in time, trouble the public accounting profession. **Please** choose one that the profession <u>has not yet experienced</u> or one that it is <u>only just beginning to experience.</u>

What led you to identify this particular issue or problem?

3.1 Do you think the public accounting profession is aware of this issue or problem? ☐ Yes ☐ No

3.2 What is a specific action the public accounting profession should take with respect to this problem?

What implementation problems or obstacles might the profession encounter if it acted on this suggestion?

3.3 What is <u>another</u> specific action the profession should take with respect to this problem?

What implementation problems or obstacles might the profession encounter if it acted on this suggestion?

3.4 What might be a consequence if the profession would either (a) take <u>no</u> action with respect to this problem, or (b) <u>not</u> act on any of your suggestions?

What might be <u>another</u> consequence?

What might be <u>another</u> consequence?

258

Part IV: (Optional): Fantasy Questionnaire

NAME _____

I want to introduce you to my MAGIC HELICOPTER, a truly amazing flying machine. Anyone who flies in it is immediately bestowed with magical vision, hearing, and perception. And the machine itself is able to travel through time and be in several places at once.

Take a ride in it. Let it take you 25 years into the future. It is now the year 2000 and you can see and hear all that is going on all over America--each document, conversation, thought, and action existing or taking place. Take your time and survey the scene. Go back a year or two, or more, if you like. Play with the helicopter. Feel how it feels to have these magical no-holds-barred qualities. Let your imagination go.

When you are ready, write down everything you can about what the Public Accounting Profession has done and is doing that REALLY PLEASES YOU.

Appendix D
The Second Survey
Instrument

There are SIX sections in this survey. Please complete all
sections. Each section has its own questions and instructions.

When you have finished, please enter your name and initials
on the data sheet portion of each section.

A self-addressed stamped envelope is enclosed for your convenience in mailing the completed survey back to us.

Glossary

The following abbreviations are used in this survey:

AAA   American Accounting Association
AICPA   American Institute of Certified Public Accountants
AccSEC Accounting Standards Executive Committee (of the AICPA)
AudSEC Auditing Standards Executive Committee (of the AICPA)
CASB   Cost Accounting Standards Board
CPA   Certified Public Accountant
EFTS   Electronic Funds Transfer System
FAF   Financial Analysts Federation
FASB   Financial Accounting Standards Board
FEI   Financial Executives Institute
GAAP   Generally accepted accounting principles
GAAS   Generally accepted auditing standards
IASC   International Accounting Standards Committee
IRS   Internal Revenue Service
PLA   Price-level adjusted
PR   Public relations
SEC   Securities and Exchange Commission

Section I

INSTRUCTIONS

1. Read the list carefully: it represents the twenty-five most frequently mentioned problems suggested in the earlier survey.
2. Respond to the questions posed at the head of each column.
3. Place a checkmark (✓) against the selected problem statements in columns (1) and (2).
4. Enter priority numbers from 1 to 5 (1=most important) in column (3).

NAME : _____

P R O B L E M S T A T E M E N T S	(1) TO WHICH FIVE PROBLEMS HAS THE PROFESSION GIVEN ITS GREATEST ATTENTION?	(2) TO WHICH FIVE PROBLEMS HAS THE PROFESSION GIVEN ITS LEAST ATTENTION, OR IGNORED?	(3) WHICH FIVE PROBLEMS SHOULD THE PROFESSION CONSIDER AS TOP PRIORITY? (Please rank order).
1 Public misunderstanding of the role of auditors and the meaning of the auditor's opinion.			
2 Lack of independence in the CPA-client relationship.			
3 The CPA's growing dilemma of who to serve--the client, the public, or who?			
4 The profession's narrow concept of the role and responsibility of CPAs.			
5 Price-level and other attempts to achieve current value financial statements.			
6 Deciding on and applying the objectives of financial statements.			
7 Certification and other problems concerning unaudited and interim financial statements.			
8 The need to define and reach consensus on "generally accepted accounting principles".			
9 The need to develop an underlying theory, framework, or rationale for "generally accepted accounting principles".			
10 Erosion of technical standards and/or ethics in the profession.			
11 The problem of substandard performance by both individuals and firms.			
12 The increasing threat of litigation, auditor liability, and mounting liability insurance premiums.			
13 The auditor's responsibility for detecting management fraud and other improprieties.			
14 The increasing likelihood that the government, especially the S.E.C., will define accounting standards.			
15 The growing dominance and influence of a few large firms within the CPA profession.			
16 Loss of 'professionalism' and a concurrent rise in 'commercialism'; includes unfair competition and bidding.			
17 The FASB's inadequate handling of emergency practice problems & slow reactions to a changing economy & social conditions.			
18 Uncertainty as to the proper scope of the audit and attest function.			
19 Whether accountants should develop and apply methods of social and other non-financial accounting.			
20 Conflicts between audit and M.A.S. and other types of non-audit services.			
21 Problems of recruiting, educating, training accountants at a time of great change in the profession.			
22 Self-discipline and self-regulation problems within the profession.			
23 Financial reports are too technical and contain too much jargon; they are generally not understandable by the public.			
24 GAAP are becoming rules that straitjacket practitioners, thus increasingly pre-empting the exercise of judgment.			
25 The need for specialization and/or sectionalization within the profession.			

Section II

The purpose of this section is to establish interrelationships among the problems and to determine which problems, by their resolution, would have an effect on other problems.

INSTRUCTIONS

1. Read the list given in the table on the next page. It is the same list as the one given in Section I.

2. In column (1), enter a number for each problem statement between 0 and 100, which represents your best assessment of the degree to which the problem will be resolved or substantially ameliorated by the year 1985.

3. Refer to your responses given in Section I and select the problems which you identified as priorities 1, 2, and 3.

    a. Enter the problem statement number for each priority in the column headings (2), (3), and (4).

    b. Using the problem statement at the head of each column as a reference point, and for each problem statement in the list, enter an "X" on the scale (somewhere between the extremes A and B) which represents your best assessment of how the solution to each of the priority problems at the heads of the columns would affect (i.e., improve or worsen) the chances of solution of each of the other problems.

    In other words, if problem statement #18 were selected as the profession's top priority problem, what effect would its solution by 1985 have on all other problems in the list (except #18)? Would their chances of solution by 1985 be worsened or improved? Or would they remain unaffected (no change)? Express the degree of effect on each of these problems by placing an "X" on its scale in column (2). Repeat this procedure for the second and third priority problems in columns (3) and (4).

4. When you have completed this section, check the table you have just completed. Every scale in each column should have an "X" on it except for three (being the one problem statement in each column that matches the priority problem at the head of that column).

Illustration:

Problem Statement	P	# 18 Worse No change Better		
1	65	A X B	A	
2	47	X		
3 . . etc.		X		

PROBLEM STATEMENTS	(1) P (Chances of Solution by 1985)
1 Public misunderstanding of the role of auditors and the meaning of the auditor's opinion.	
2 Lack of independence in the CPA-client relationship.	
3 The CPA's growing dilemma of who to serve--the client, the public, or who?	
4 The profession's narrow concept of the role and responsibility of CPAs.	
5 Price-level and other attempts to achieve current value financial statements.	
6 Deciding on and applying the objectives of financial statements.	
7 Certification and other problems concerning unaudited and interim financial statements.	
8 The need to define and reach consensus on "generally accepted accounting principles".	
9 The need to develop an underlying theory, framework, or rationale for "generally accepted accounting principles".	
10 Erosion of technical standards and/or ethics in the profession.	
11 The problem of substandard performance by both individuals and firms.	
12 The increasing threat of litigation, auditor liability, and mounting liability insurance premiums.	
13 The auditor's responsibility for detecting management fraud and other improprieties.	
14 The increasing likelihood that the government, especially the S.E.C., will define accounting standards.	
15 The growing dominance and influence of a few large firms within the CPA profession.	
16 Loss of 'professionalism' and a concurrent rise in 'commercialism'; includes unfair competition and bidding.	
17 The FASB's inadequate handling of emergency practice problems & slow reactions to a changing economy & social conditions.	
18 Uncertainty as to the proper scope of the audit and attest function.	
19 Whether accountants should develop and apply methods of social and other non-financial accounting.	
20 Conflicts between audit and M.A.S. and other types of non-audit services.	
21 Problems of recruiting, educating, training accountants at a time of great change in the profession.	
22 Self-discipline and self-regulation problems within the profession.	
23 Financial reports are too technical and contain too much jargon; they are generally not understandable by the public.	
24 GAAP are becoming rules that straitjacket practitioners, thus increasingly pre-empting the exercise of judgment.	
25 The need for specialization and/or sectionalization within the profession.	

(2) PRIORITY PROBLEM #1	(3) PRIORITY PROBLEM #2	(4) PRIORITY PROBLEM #3
# ____	# ____	# ____
Worse — No Change — Better →	Worse — No Change — Better →	Worse — No Change — Better →
A B	A B	A B

NAME _____

A = "No Chance of Solution Whatever by 1985".
B = "Will Also be Solved by 1985".

Section III

NAME :

INSTRUCTIONS

A number of behavioral descriptors about the profession were culled from responses to the earlier survey. Please read each one carefully and check (✓) whether you think it is 'TRUE', 'FALSE', or you are unable to make a determination ('DON'T KNOW').

BEHAVIORAL DESCRIPTORS	TRUE	FALSE	DON'T KNOW
THE PROFESSION			
1 ..has not done enough to improve its political position and visibility.			
2 ..is too busy to tackle "really important" matters.			
3 ..has not clarified sufficiently the distinctions between accounting & bookkeeping.			
4 ..is not sufficiently skilled in forestalling public criticism.			
5 ..is reluctant to change except through outside pressure.			
6 ..does not give sufficient support to the AICPA on very fundamental issues.			
7 ..is not structured to deal quickly and effectively with new problems.			
8 ..is politically naive.			
9 ..has not been able to get those who most need it to engage in meaningful continued professional education.			
10 ..supports the FASB on the one hand while undercutting it with the other.			

BEHAVIORAL DESCRIPTORS	TRUE	FALSE	DON'T KNOW
THE PROFESSION			
21 ..finds the causes of its inadequacies and shortcomings frequently within its own ranks.			
22 ..is "run" by the large national CPA firms.			
23 ..has not recognized that many of its problems are interrelated.			
24 ..is unable to confront the S.E.C. on issues which impede its (the profession's) effectiveness or run counter to its objectives.			
25 ..fears the loss of income from clients.			
26 ..does not act quickly enough on a host of controversial issues needing prompt resolution.			
27 ..is reluctant to make its rulings mandatory.			
28 ..prefers the strategy of setting up committees rather than taking direct executive action.			
29 ..is afraid of a confrontation with the government, especially the S.E.C.			
30 ..is hampered in its efforts by the resistance to change embodied in the CPA-client relationship.			

11	..and especially small practitioners fear that computers will 'put them out of business'.	
12	..cannot control its own destiny: it is buffeted by external & internal problems.	
13	..is thwarted in many of its efforts at problem-solving by the attitudes and divergence of views between large and small practice units.	
14	..is intimidated by the vastness of a problem and avoids it rather than electing to chip away at it methodically.	
15	..cannot agree as to what its problems really are.	
16	..compromises and takes non-controversial positions in order to achieve a consensus.	
17	..through the AICPA allows the committees it appoints to reach leisurely conclusions, procrastinate, and delay timely action.	
18	..strives for a unanimity of opinion among its members on issues rather than being content with a simple majority.	
19	..is many-faceted and thus finds increasing difficulty in "speaking with one voice".	
20	..is too preoccupied in finding the perfect or optimal solutions to problems.	

31	..acts objectively.	
32	..has more difficulty interpreting financial statements to users than attesting to them.	
33	..is not aware that the purposes of accounting are still obscure to a great many users.	
34	..has a set of GAAP which has wide acceptance.	
35	..does not possess adequate enforcement machinery.	
36	..avoids actions which are contrary to the special interests of its various constituent groups.	
37	..does not challenge the credentials of persons who are unqualified but nevertheless purport to speak authoritatively on accounting problems and issues.	
38	..does not discipline individual members who violate ethics & standards: they are sheltered by the firms to which they belong.	
39	..reacts to public criticism by gearing up its PR machinery rather than through meaningful internal reform.	
40	..spends too much effort on problems and too little on opportunities.	

Section IV

The list of possible outcomes--virtually all of them undesirable--was synthesized from the responses to the earlier survey. They represent the most recurring themes of what might happen if the profession chose not to act on a variety of problems. Our interest here lies in the possibility of translating some of these outcomes into goals for the profession (i.e. in making sure the undesirable outcomes do NOT occur).

INSTRUCTIONS

2. Respond to the questions posed at the head of each column.
3. Place a checkmark (✓) against the selected outcomes in columns (1), (2), and (3).
4. Refer to the list of problem statements given in Section I. For those outcomes checked in columns (1) and (3) only (they need not all be different, so that the outcomes checked in the two columns should sum to between 3 and 6) enter problem statement numbers for the problems which, if they remained unresolved, might contribute to these outcomes. More than one problem statement may apply per outcome. The problem statement numbers are entered in column (4).
5. For these same 3 to 6 outcomes checked in columns (1) and (3), state the earliest year (e.g., 1985) in which you expect them to occur if their associated problems remain unresolved, in column (5).

NAME : _____

POSSIBLE OUTCOMES	(1) CHECK THE THREE WHICH WOULD MOST ADVERSELY AFFECT THE PROFESSION.	(2) CHECK THE THREE THAT WOULD MOST BENEFIT THE PROFESSION.	(3) CHECK THE THREE THAT WOULD MOST ADVERSELY AFFECT THE LARGER SOCIETY.	(4) WHICH PROBLEMS (1-25) IF UNSOLVED, WOULD CONTRIBUTE TO THE OUTCOMES CHECKED IN COLUMNS 1 & 3?	(5) FOR OUTCOMES CHECKED IN COLS.1 & 3, STATE EARLIEST YEAR OF OCCURRENCE.
1 Financial reports will become so complex that even professional security analysts will have difficulty processing the amount of information disclosed.					
2 Financial statements will no longer be comparable with other companies.					
3 The end of accounting as a useful input to investment decisions.					
4 Lawsuits against CPAs will triple in number.					
5 Insurance coverage for CPA firms & individuals will become prohibitively expensive and uneconomical.					

6 Non-CPA firms & entities, such as banks, will enter traditional fields practiced by CPAs.					
7 Unilateral action by the SEC to require the CPA to acknowledge greater responsibility for the client's financial reports.					
8 Choice of the profession as a career will drop to tenth or greater by graduate students considering it.					
9 Investment activity will center in large institutional investors powerful enough to have their own auditing arms.					
10 Creation of an Accounting Court, like the U.S. Tax Courts, to settle accounting disputes and claims.					
11 Cessation of forecasting & other non-audit functions by CPAs because of peer pressure caused by incr. litigations.					
12 Smaller businesses will turn regularly to practitioners not regulated by the profession as compliance costs rise.					
13 Substandard work by CPAs will become more prevalent as their workloads increase, & will be accepted as the norm.					
14 The role of CPAs would be limited to the "attest" function based on applicability of outmoded GAAP and GAAS.					
15 Withdrawal by U.S. corporations from their financial support of the FASB.					
16 The federal government will require a financial information quality control program for firms practicing before the SEC.					
17 Bankruptcy of many (small) CPA firms and a 25% reduction in the number of those still in practice.					
18 Federal government to underwrite all liability insurance for CPAs because of unavailability elsewhere.					
19 Audit costs to clients will double (due to requirements for greater detail, thoroughness, & insurance costs).					
20 Courts succeed in defining the extent of the auditor's responsibility and liability in detecting fraud.					
21 CPAs will render unqualified opinions only after having performed extensive testing geared to fraud detection & may refuse a client whose internal controls are 'wanting'.					
22 All CPAs work for the government under control of a government bureau.					
23 Accounting principles & auditing standards have become so minutely specified as to require no judgment in interpretation.					
24 Formation of rival groups and accounting "institutes" to solve the profession's problems, esp. setting standards.					
25 Demise of public acceptance of the FASB as an independent body & assumption of the role by a new government agency.					

Section V

The purpose of this section is to determine which opportunities, if any, are worth pursuing by the profession. The statements were drawn from the responses to the 'fantasy' questionnaire portion of the earlier survey.

INSTRUCTIONS

1. Please read the list carefully.
2. Respond to the questions posed at the head of each column.
3. Place a checkmark (✔) against selected opportunities in columns (1), (2), (3), and (5).
4. Enter most likely dates of occurrence in column (4) as instructed.

NAME _____

OPPORTUNITIES	(1) CHECK THE FIVE OPPORTUNITIES WHICH WOULD MOST IMPROVE THE PROFESSION'S PUBLIC IMAGE.	(2) CHECK THE FIVE OPPORTUNITIES THAT WOULD MAKE THE BEST CANDIDATES FOR INTENSIVE RESEARCH PROGRAMS.	(3) CHECK THE FIVE TOP PRIORITY OPPORTUNITIES THE PROFESSION SHOULD CONSIDER (You may include any checked in columns (1) or (2))	(4) FOR THE FIVE CHECKED IN COL.(3), WHAT ARE THE MOST LIKELY DATES WHEN THESE OPPORTUNITIES MIGHT BE REALISED IF VIGOROUSLY PURSUED BY THE PROFESSION?	(5) CHECK THE FIVE OPPORTUNITIES THAT ARE PURE FANTASY, i.e., UNREALISTIC.
1 To make accounting principles, auditing & reporting standards uniform throughout the world.					
2 To attest routinely to forecasts, economic feasibility studies, and social accounting.					
3 To execute management audits regularly for all public companies.					
4 To make 'performance auditing' the profession's principal objective.					
5 To extend the attest function to numerous social applications where verification is important (e.g., arms limitation inspection, independent estimates of needed expenditures such as medical & dental services, auto repairs, public utility costs, etc.)					
6 To develop and apply methods for social cost-benefit analysis.					
7 To recognize the public as its client.					
8 To devise better accounting systems to help government & public units make better decisions, including better measures of the impacts of corporations on society.					
9 To develop a numerical system of recording business transactions so as to evaluate & differentiate business success & failure by degrees.					
10 To have audit specialists regularly use the computer to the point where interactive & concurrent auditing are commonplace, and forecasting, regression analysis, & stat sampling are used as a matter of course.					

11 To be able to audit quarterly results of corporate operations two days after the end of the quarter by putting data on the "broad tape" on an "on-line" basis (continuous auditing).

12 To take advantage of the explosive growth of EFTS and the simultaneous decline in paper documentation of transactions and have regular automatic verification of transactions by auditors.

13 To equip the desk of the typical CPA with a terminal connected on-line to a computer utility.

14 To have the AICPA and state societies assume the primary responsibility for practice research & professional development functions for all accounting firms.

15 To create a research bureau which would estimate the economic costs & benefits of proposed legislation intended to regulate business activity.

16 To organize & support an independent institution to perform long-range planning & futures research for the profession.

17 To increase the effectiveness of the AICPA by having it act as a central clearinghouse of ideas, problems, and programs.

18 To create a new profession--the Tax Practice Profession--combining the best of the CPA and legal professions.

19 To have the AICPA assign auditors to clients, bill the latter for services rendered, & then allocate fees to performing accounting firms.

20 To establish a Federal Accounting Court, procedures for hearing cases brought before it, and a set of rulings as a legal basis for future cases.

21 To establish industry 'accounting review boards', composed of representatives from accounting firms & managers & owners within each industry, to review published financial reports for adequacy, completeness, etc.

22 To create a National Panel which would set GAAP, oversee an extensive research operation that identifies problems and finds solutions, & perform all required audits of publicly-held corporations; to finance the operation of this Panel through moderate charges to audited companies & by a transactions tax on every purchase of securities, the latter to be collected by the Treasury & turned over to the Panel.

23 To create a number of 'Boards' within the profession, namely: The Attest Criteria Board that develops the principles that are applied to a possible attest engagement to see if it is 'auditable' and, if so, how; The Criteria Conformance Board that develops standards to govern the attest procedures; & the Quality Review Board that audits the auditors.

24 To eliminate the seasonal nature of work by establishing reporting deadlines staggered throughout the year rather than bunched in at one time.

25 To replace monotonous, laborious, & time-consuming jobs especially at the local firm level by increased mechanization & more modern equipment.

26 To establish examinations in, & certificates for tax, accounting, auditing, & financial systems design (to recognize specialization within the profession.)

27 To encourage the 'typical' CPA to earn a law degree as well.

28 To unify educational accreditation standards for accounting curricula throughout the country.

29 To require graduate work as a part of the CPA's academic preparation.

30 To use paraprofessionals effectively to allow the professional more time for challenging judgmental & intellectual decisions.

31 To unify tax & accounting standards and eliminate the differences between tax and financial accounting.

32 To encourage greater contributions by the profession to raise the degree of fiscal efficiency achieved in business & government.

33 To gain expertise & information which will enable the profession to give Congress & the IRS advice on what types and levels of taxes will produce specified results for individuals, corporations, and other interest groups.

Section VI

The purpose of this section is to elicit your perceptions as to the relative desirability, feasibility, and relevance of the actions given in the list below. The actions in the list are a summary of the most frequently mentioned ones suggested by respondents to our earlier survey to various problems of their own choosing, and have been made specific.

INSTRUCTIONS

1. Read the list carefully.
2. Respond to the questions posed at the head of each column.
3. Place a checkmark (✓) against the selected action statement in columns (1), (2), (4), (5), and (6).
4. Refer to the problem statement list given in Section I. For the actions checked in column (1) only, enter those problem numbers *in Col.(3)* the actions would help ameliorate. For each action, there may be more than one problem number entered.

NAME _____

P O S S I B L E A C T I O N S	(1) CHECK THE THREE THAT ARE MOST DESIRABLE.	(2) CHECK THE THREE THAT ARE MOST UN-DESIRABLE.	(3) FOR ACTIONS CHECKED IN COL. (1), ENTER PROBLEM NUMBERS (1-25) THEY MIGHT HELP AMELIORATE.	(4) CHECK THE THREE THAT ARE EASI-EST TO IMPLEMENT.	(5) CHECK THE THREE THAT ARE MOST DIFFICULT TO IMPLEMENT.	(6) CHECK ACTIONS APPROPRIATE TO THE TOP FIVE PRIORITY PROBLEMS SELECTED IN SECTION I, COL. (3).
1 Restructure the AudSEC along the lines of the CASB with a small (5-7 man) group of volunteers & a larger more competent staff.						
2 Educate the investing public to give it a better understanding of the limitations of independent audits.						
3 Work closely with the SEC to help improve the quality and relevance of financial disclosures.						
4 Revise its Code of Ethics to prevent use of accounting treat-ments by a new CPA firm which the former CPA firm has rejected.						
5 Establish a more effective mechanism for identifying, evaluating, and taking action with respect to incompetence & unethical behavior.						

6 Require that PLA financial statements be provided in supplemental statements when inflation levels reach predetermined proportions.

7 Emphasize the study of alternative costing methods in accounting curricula and the CPA examination.

8 Separate all tax and management services from audit functions so that the former cannot influence the latter.

9 Invite professional experts in other fields to take key planning and advisory roles in bringing about change in the profession.

10 Shift the burden of "accounting standards" to a public agency & concentrate more attention on lobbying, auditing standards, and technical and professional development.

11 Forbid the independent auditor, if retained to audit a client, from engaging in any other activity for that client.

12 Generate widespread literature and visual presentations for grade and high schools, and place advertisements in widely-read "people" magazines to improve the profession's image and visibility.

13 Create an Accounting Court, similar to the U.S. Tax Court, to hear and promptly dispose of accounting claims, controversies, and appeals.

14 Specify non-conflicting roles for, and clarify the purposes of, the AccSEC and AudSEC of the AICPA, IASC, CASB, & the FASB.

15 Research the requirements and attributes of competent CPA performance & then structure the profession to meet them as quickly as possible.

16 Establish academies within the AICPA which recognize special competence and exceptional service (An "Oscar" in Accounting).

17 Establish a framework for specialization within the profession with appropriate criteria for licensing.

18 Join with other affected and concerned parties (such as MDs) to obtain legislation that would curb the legal profession's practice of accepting cases on the basis of a contingency fee.

19 Limit the number of successive times that an auditing firm can audit the statements of a given client (requires rotation of firms).

20 Take positive and swift disciplinary action against incompetent members of the profession (after having first tested for incompetence) and publicize the actions.

21 Institute a mandatory public practice review program for all firms associated with the AICPA.

22 Stop fighting the public demand to detect and report management fraud, and begin doing it (Gain the required expertise).

23 Testify constructively and lobby intensively in all pending legislation involving the application of accounting principles in the Congress and Federal agencies.

24 Persuade the FASB to operate on a 4-3 majority requirement instead of the current 5-2.

25 Stand up more forcefully against the self-interest of the large firms, in the interests of the profession.

26 Accredit accounting curricula and enforce accreditation through the examination requirement and in hiring practices.

Appendix E
Respondents to the
Two Surveys*

Respondents Completing Both Surveys

Anreder, Steven S., News Editor

Barron's Weekly
22 Cortlandt Street
New York, New York 10007

Baker, C. Richard, Assistant Professor

Graduate School of Business
Columbia University
New York, New York 10027

Barr, Andrew

Blamey, Philip, Comptroller

Union Oil Company of California
P.O. Box 7600
Los Angeles, California 90051

Bland, Duane A., Controller

Getty Oil Company
3810 Wilshire Boulevard
Los Angeles, California 90010

Bowen, Willard G.

Cordle & Associates
1400 Western Federal Savings
    Building
Denver, Colorado 80202

Bowes, Kenyon D., Senior
    Vice-President

G.D. Searle & Company
P.O. Box 1045
Skokie, Illinois 60076

Braverman, Sidney M., Partner

Davie, Schulman, Kaplan &
    Braverman
600 Reynolds Arcade
Rochester, New York 14610

Briloff, Abraham, Professor of
    Accounting

City University of New York
The Bernard M. Baruch College
New York, New York 10010

Brown, Wesley Warren, Assistant
    Comptroller

American Telephone and Telegraph
    Company
195 Broadway
New York, New York 10007

---

*Organizations and addresses current as of Fall 1975.

Buckley, John W., Associate Dean and Professor of Accounting and Information Systems

Graduate School of Management
University of California, Los
   Angeles
Los Angeles, California 90024

Butler, Jay E., Deputy Administrator

Commissioner of Treasury
City of New York
506 Municipal Building
New York, New York 10007

Calvert, George H., Partner

Ehlman & Calvert
3182 Cedar Ravine Drive
Placerville, California 95667

Campbell, John B., Vice-President and Controller

Northrop Corporation
1800 Century Park East
Los Angeles, California 90067

Carmichael, D.R., Director, Auditing Standards

American Institute of Certified
   Public Accountants
1211 Avenue of the Americas
New York, New York 10036

Chetkovich, Michael N., Managing Partner

Haskins & Sells
1114 Avenue of the Americas
New York, New York 10036

Churchill, Neil C., Professor of Business Administration

Graduate School of Business
   Administration
Harvard University
Boston, Massachusetts 02163

Cobbs, John L., Editor

Business Week
1221 Avenue of the Americas
New York, New York 10020

Cohen, Herbert R., Partner

Cohen, Kirkpatrick & Company
1736 East Sunshine
Springfield, Missouri 65804

Corbin, Donald A., Professor of Accounting & Business Economics

College of Business Administration
University of Hawaii
Honolulu, Hawaii 96822

Davidson, H. Justin, Dean

Graduate School of Business and
   Public Administration
Cornell University
303 Malott Hall
Ithaca, New York 14853

Dixon, Arthur J., Managing Partner

Oppenheim, Appel, Dixon & Company
One New York Plaza
New York, New York 10004

Eggert, Nat L., Partner

Eggert & Baughman
P.O. Box 1445
El Cajon, California 92022

Fertig, Paul E., Professor of
   Accounting

Ohio State University
1775 South College Road
Columbus, Ohio 43210

Finnegan, J. Paul, Partner

Coopers & Lybrand
100 Federal Street
Boston, Massachusetts 02108

Fowler, Hubert F., Managing Partner

Fowler, Suttles & Company
2211 East 54th Street
Indianapolis, Indiana 46220

Garner, Paul

1016 Indian Hills Drive
Tuscaloosa, Alabama 35401

Gentilcore, James, Assistant
   Controller

Transamerica Corporation
600 Montgomery Street
San Francisco, California 94111

Gibbons, William J., Administrative
   Law Judge

Office of Hearings
Interstate Commerce Commission
Washington, D.C. 21423

Giffen, Hilliard R., Consultant

Baker, Peterson & Franklin,
1630 East Shaw Avenue, Suite 165
Fresno, California 93710

Gips, William M., Partner

J.K. Lasser & Company
666 Fifth Avenue
New York, New York 10019

Gray, Milton H., Senior Partner

Altheimer & Gray
One IBM Plaza
Chicago, Illinois 60611

Greenwald, Bruce M., Manager, Tax
   Department

Arthur Young & Company
277 Park Avenue
New York, New York 10017

Gridley, F.W., Assistant Comptroller

Chrysler Corporation
P.O. Box 1019
Detroit, Michigan 48231

Grissom, Garth C., Partner	Dawson, Nagel, Sherman & Howard 2900 First of Denver Plaza Denver, Colorado 80202
Guin, Winford H., Director, Internal Auditing	American Telephone & Telegraph Company 195 Broadway, Room C-2777 New York, New York 10007
Hughes, John S., Assistant Professor	Amos Tuck School of Business Dartmouth College Hanover, New Hampshire 03755
Ingram, Glenn, Jr., Partner	Glenn Ingram & Company 150 North Wacker Drive Chicago, Illinois 60606
Jacobsen, Lyle E., Professor of Accounting & Finance	University of Hawaii 2404 Maile Way Honolulu, Hawaii 96822
Jaszi, George, Director	Bureau of Economic Analysis U.S. Department of Commerce 1401 K Street, N.W., Washington, D.C. 20230
Johnson, Charles Edwin, Partner	Main Lafrentz & Company 700 Kennecott Building Salt Lake City, Utah 84133
Kapnick, Harvey, Chairman, Chief Executive	Arthur Andersen & Company 69 West Washington Street Chicago, Illinois 60602
Kipnis, Louis	Law Office 250 Broadway New York, New York 10007
Klein, Joseph Mark, Executive Vice-President	Cyprus Mines Corporation 555 South Flower Street Los Angeles, California 90071
Knox, Robert E., Jr., Executive Vice-President and Treasurer	Lake Ronel Oil Company P.O. Box 179 Tyler, Texas 75701
Kripke, Homer, Professor of Law, Specializing in Securities and Accounting	School of Law New York University Washington Square New York, New York 10012

Lano, C. Jack, Controller

Pacific Lighting Corporation
810 South Flower Street
Los Angeles, California 90017

Lea, Richard B., Manager

Peat, Marwick, Mitchell & Company
345 Park Avenue
New York, New York 10022

Leach, Ronald L., Assistant
Controller, Financial Accounting

Eaton Corporation
100 Erieview Plaza
Cleveland, Ohio 44114

Leslie, Fred E., Director of Finance

The Aerospace Corporation
2350 East El Segundo Boulevard
El Segundo, California 90245

Leventhal, Kenneth, Partner

Kenneth Leventhal & Company
Two Century Plaza
2049 Century Park East
Los Angeles, California 90067

Lewis, Melvin E., Chief Accountant

U.S. Postal Rate Commission
Washington, D.C. 20230

Luton, James P., Jr., Partner

Luton & Company
P.O. Box 20448
Oklahoma City, Oklahoma 73120

Lynn, Edward S., Professor of
Accounting

College of Business and Public
Administration
University of Arizona
Tucson, Arizona 85721

Martin, Kendall D., Senior Vice-
President

Bank of America NT&SA
555 South Flower Street
Los Angeles, California 90071

McDonough, John J., Associate
Professor

Graduate School of Management
University of California
Los Angeles, California 90024

Mims, Robert E., Finance Editor

Business Week
1221 Avenue of the Americas
New York, New York 10020

Minahan, Eugene J., Controller

Atlantic Richfield Company
515 South Flower Street
Los Angeles, California 90071

Minter, Frank C., Director, Accounting Classifications	American Telephone & Telegraph Company 195 Broadway New York, New York 10007
Mitchem, Dennis E., Partner	Arthur Andersen & Company 34 West Monroe Phoenix, Arizona 85003
Mock, Theodore J., Associate Professor of Accounting	School of Business Administration University of Southern California Los Angeles, California 90007
Moonitz, Maurice, Professor	School of Business Administration University of California, Berkeley Berkeley, California 94720
Nail, N. Kenneth, Partner	Nail, McKinney, Tate & Robinson, P.O. Box 196 Tupelo, Mississippi 38801
Neff, Edward J., Partner	Neff & Company 7001 Prospect Place N.E. Albuquerque, New Mexico 87110
Neumann, Russell Harry, Accounting Officer	Manufacturers Hanover Trust Company 350 Park Avenue New York, New York 10015
Norr, David, C.F.A., Partner	First Manhattan Company 30 Wall Street New York, New York 10005
Oliphant, Walter, Professor of Accounting	Amos Tuck School of Business Administration Dartmouth College Hanover, New Hampshire 03755
Richter, Robert F., Partner	Laventhol & Horwath 1845 Walnut Street Philadelphia, Pennsylvania 19103
Romak, Theodore, Partner	Arthur Young & Company 277 Park Avenue New York, New York 10017
Ruffle, J.F., Comptroller	Morgan Guaranty Trust Company 23 Wall Street New York, New York 10015

Ryan, William M., Partner

Fulbright & Jaworski
Bank of the Southwest Building
Houston, Texas 77002

Sargent, Arthur M. (retired)

492 Sand Hill Circle
Menlo Park, California 94025

Schroeder, Donald W., Partner

Coopers & Lybrand
One Bush Street
San Francisco, California 94104

Sergio, George D., SEC Professional
    Accounting Fellow

Securities & Exchange Commission
500 North Capitol Street
Washington, D.C. 20549

Skinner, Robert G., Partner

Ernst & Ernst
1300 Union Commerce Building
Cleveland, Ohio 44115

Stanger, Abraham, M., Senior Partner

Trubin, Sillcocks, Edelman &
    Knapp
375 Park Avenue
New York, New York 10022

Stans, Maurice H. (retired)

Stough, Sellers, Comptroller

Standard Oil Company of California
225 Bush Street
San Francisco, California 94104

Swinarton, Robert W., Vice Chairman

Dean Witter & Company, Inc.
14 Wall Street
New York, New York 10005

Tanzola, Frank J., Senior Vice-
    President and Corporate Controller

U.S. Industries, Inc.
250 Park Avenue
New York, New York 10017

Thorne, Robert D., Controller

United States Gypsum Company
101 South Wacker Drive
Chicago, Illinois 60606

Tonkin, George William, Managing
    Director

Tonkin, Swenson & Johnson
1419 West Bannock Street, Suite B
Boise, Idaho 83706

Wald, Haskell P., Chief

Office of Economics
Federal Power Commission
825 North Capitol Street, N.E.
Washington, D.C. 20426

Warren, Joseph Donald, Jr., Audit
    Manager

Coopers & Lybrand
1010 Jefferson, Suite 1200
Houston, Texas 77002

Werbaneth, Louis A., Jr., Regional
    Partner

Touche Ross & Company
P.O. Box 3220
Pittsburgh, Pennsylvania 15230

Weston, Frank Thomas, Partner

Arthur Young & Company
277 Park Avenue
New York, New York 10017

Wheeler, John T., Professor

School of Business Administration
University of California, Berkeley
Berkeley, California 94720

White, Robert H., Partner, National
    Director of Governmental and
    Institutional Services

Lester Witte & Company
150 South Wacker Drive
Chicago, Illinois 60606

Wilson, James A., Partner

Haskins & Sells
550 Broad Street
Newark, New Jersey 07102

Eight respondents wish to remain anonymous.

Respondents Completing Only First Survey

Barnes, William Truman, Partner

Coopers & Lybrand
1800 M Street, N.W.
Washington, D.C. 20036

Boutell, Wayne Struve, Professor of
    Business Administration

School of Business Administration
University of California, Berkeley
Berkeley, California 94720

Bull, Ivan O., Managing Partner

McGladrey, Hansen, Dunn & Company
908 Davenport Bank Building
Davenport, Iowa 52801

Champion, John E., Professor of
    Accounting

Florida State University
Tallahassee, Florida 32306

Creamer, Daniel, Consultant

The Conference Board
845 Third Avenue
New York, New York 10022

Curtis, Warren E., U.S. Senator	734 Walnut Street Cherokee, Iowa 51012
Dresselhaus, J. Bernard, Managing Partner	Philip G. Johnson & Company 1224 Sharp Building Lincoln, Nebraska 68508
Fisher, Michael M., Audit Manager	Arthur Andersen & Company 34 West Monroe Street Phoenix, Arizona 85003
Flynn, Thomas D., Partner, Vice- Chairman, Management Committee	Arthur Young & Company 277 Park Avenue New York, New York 10017
Galloway, Jay Jones, Managing Partner	Alexander Grant & Company 6842 Van Nuys Boulevard Van Nuys, California 91405
Gregory, William R., Managing Partner	Knight, Vale & Gregory 1500 One Washington Plaza Tacoma, Washington 98402
Hall, Dorothy L.	Harris, Kerr, Forster & Company 425 California Street San Francisco, California 94104
Hershman, Arlene, Senior Editor	Dun's Review 666 Fifth Avenue New York, New York 10020
Higgins, J. Warren, Associate Professor	University of Connecticut Storrs, Connecticut 06268
Huizingh, William, Associate Dean and Professor of Accounting	College of Business Administration Arizona State University Tempe, Arizona 85281
Isler, Robert F., Partner	Isler, Colling & McAdams 2500 First National Bank Tower Portland, Oregon 97201
Kent, Ralph E., Senior Partner	Arthur Young & Company 277 Park Avenue New York, New York 10017
King, Alfred M., Vice-President, Finance	American Appraisal Association, Inc. 525 East Michigan Street Milwaukee, Wisconsin 53201

Koons, Robert L., Manager,
    Accounting Research and Policy

Shell Oil Company
P.O. Box 2463
Houston, Texas 77069

Martin, Richard F., Partner

Battelle & Battelle
1785 Big Hill Road
Dayton, Ohio 45439

McCord, Frank M., Partner,
    Professional Development

Peat, Marwick, Mitchell & Company
810 Seventh Avenue
New York, New York 10019

McGrew, William C., Professor of
    Accounting

College of Business Administration
University of Oklahoma
305 West Brooks
Norman, Oklahoma 73069

Morse, Ellsworth H., Jr., Assistant
    Comptroller General

The U.S. General Accounting Office
441 G Street, N.W.
Washington, D.C. 20548

Nest, Richard A., National Director
    of Accounting and Auditing

J.K. Lasser & Company
10 East 53rd Street
New York, New York 10022

Oates, R. Wayne, Assistant Vice-
    President, Finance

PPG Industries
Pittsburgh, Pennsylvania 15222

Piser, M. Mendel, Managing Partner

Crowe, Chizek & Company
210 North Ironwood Drive
South Bend, Indiana 46615

Rescorla, William C., Managing
    Partner

Alexander Grant & Company
726 McKay Tower
Grand Rapids, Michigan 49502

Seitz, James E., Partner

Touche Ross & Company
One Maritime Plaza
San Francisco, California 94111

Sheldon, David A., Partner

James A. Shanahan
1000 Elm Street
Manchester, New Hampshire 03101

Stevens, Wilbur H., Partner,
    National Director

Elmer Fox & Company
1660 Lincoln Street
Denver, Colorado 80203

Stone, Frances, C.F.A.

Merrill Lynch & Company
165 Broadway
New York, New York 10006

Stone, Williard E., Professor of
   Accounting

University of Florida
Gainesville, Florida 32611

Tidyman, Clayton R., Chairman

Department of Accounting and
   Quantitative Studies
School of Business
Fresno State College
Fresno, California 93726

Watt, George C., Research Partner

Price Waterhouse & Company
1251 Avenue of the Americas
New York, New York 10020

Weinstein, Bert B., Managing Partner

Altschuler, Melvoin & Glasser
69 West Washington Street
Chicago, Illinois 60602

Young, Jeffery, Controller

Products Research & Chemical Corp.
2919 Empire Avenue
Burbank, California 91505

Three respondents wish to remain anonymous.

Respondents Completing Only Second Survey

Anderson, Allison Grey, Acting
   Professor of Law

School of Law
University of California, Los
   Angeles
Los Angeles, California 90024

Anderson, George D., Partner

Anderson Zur Muehlen & Company
Box 1147
Helena, Montana 59601

Asimow, Michael, Professor of Law

School of Law
University of California, Los
   Angeles
Los Angeles, California 90024

Blackstone, George A., Partner

Heller, Ehrman, White & McAuliffe
44 Montgomery Street
San Francisco, California 94104

Bushko, Ruth, Director of
   Publications

Interfaith Center on Corporate
   Responsibility
475 Riverside Drive, Room 566
New York, New York 10027

Carson, Dennis R., Partner

500 National Bank of South Dakota
    Building
Sioux Falls, South Dakota 57102

Cole, John N., Manager of Financial
    Accounting and Reporting

Household Finance Corporation
3200 Prudential Plaza
Chicago, Illinois 60601

Dopuch, Nicholas, Professor of
    Accounting

Graduate School of Business
University of Chicago
Chicago, Illinois 60637

Drennan, Lorin H., Jr., Chief
    Accountant

Office of Accounting & Finance
Federal Power Commission
941 North Capitol Street, N.E.
Washington, D.C. 20426

Fay, Clifford T., Jr., Partner

Harris, Kerr, Forster & Company
122 South Michigan Avenue
Chicago, Illinois 60603

Finch, A. Barden, Partner

Hurdman & Cranstoun
2 Embarcadero Center, Suite 2500
San Francisco, California 94111

Fisher, Edward A., Vice-President,
    Investments

Founders Capital Management Corp.
2400 First National Bank Building
Denver, Colorado 80202

Frazier, Curtis L., President

Texas Society of CPAs
3000 Continental Bank Building
Fort Worth, Texas 76102

Hay, Robert D., Professor of
    Management

University of Arkansas
Fayetteville, Arkansas 72701

Hoy, Edwin Leslie, Partner

Briggs Keyes & Company
9 Congress Street
St. Albans, Vermont 05478

Johnson, Carl A., Partner

Alexander Grant & Company
1515 Bond Court Building
Cleveland, Ohio 44114

Johnston, David C.H., Senior Program
    Analyst

Human Resources Network
2010 Chancellor Street
Philadelphia, Pennsylvania 19119

Keller, John L., Managing Partner

Peat, Marwick, Mitchell & Company
P.O. Box 2327
Santa Fe, New Mexico 87501

Kelley, John B., Co-chairperson

Committee for Corporate Responsibility
Graduate School of Business
Stanford University
Stanford, California 94305

Kruer, George R., Economist

U.S. Department of Commerce/SESA/
  Bureau of Economic Analysis
1401 K Street, N.W.
Washington, D.C. 20230

Lapp, Keith V., President

Keith V. Lapp Accountancy Corp.
106 East Boone Street
Santa Maria, California 93454

Lipton, Martin, Partner

Wachtell, Lipton, Rosen & Katz
299 Park Avenue
New York, New York 10017

Mann, Bruce Alan, Partner

Pillsbury, Madison & Sutro
225 Bush Street
San Francisco, California 94104

McClenon, Paul R., Project Director

U.S. Cost Accounting Standards
  Board
441 G Street, N.W.
Washington, D.C. 20548

Montagna, Paul D., Associate
  Professor

Department of Sociology
Brooklyn College
Brooklyn, New York 11210

Pickholz, Marvin G.

Runser, Robert J., Vice-President,
  Controller

The Signal Companies, Inc.
9665 Wilshire Boulevard
Beverly Hills, California 90212

Schaller, Carol A., Assistant Manager

American Institute of Certified
  Public Accountants
1211 Avenue of the Americas
New York, New York 10036

Zick, John W., Partner

Price Waterhouse & Company
60 Broad Street
New York, New York 10004

Eight respondents wish to remain anonymous.

Index

Index

About the Author

Stanley C. Abraham received the master's and doctoral degrees in management from the Massachusetts Institute of Technology, Sloan School of Management, and University of California at Los Angeles, Graduate School of Management, respectively. Before joining The Rand Corporation as a policy analyst consultant in 1976, he consulted for a number of other organizations, notably the Los Angeles City Attorney's Office and the National Commission on Productivity. He has also worked as an analyst for General Research Corporation in economics, long-range planning, and information systems.

About the Author